A further look at BUSES

A further look at BUSES

G.G. Hilditch

LONDON

IAN ALLAN LTD

Previous page: The frontispiece of *Looking at Buses* depicted the interior of the Swinegate tram shed of Leeds City Transport around 1935. This view shows the inside of the garage portion of the Leicester Abbey Park Road premises some four and a half decades later.

Within those 45 years, the vehicles have altered tremendously but the task of the personnel remains basically the same and that, of course, is to ensure that sufficient public service vehicles are presented to the traffic staff so that the day's mileage can be worked in full.

Not surprisingly, new vehicles and their associated new maintenance techniques bring new problems in their train but if such were not the case then a book of this sort would simply not have been possible.

Front cover: Fifty years separate the entry into service of these two single-deckers – the Red Bus Service AEC Regal I with a Craven body which was purchased by the proprietors Bevan & Bark of Mansfield Woodhouse in 1931 and the prototype Dennis Falcon with Duple body work which was built to the order of Leicester City Transport and was first used in passenger service on the 10 April 1981. It is only when one is fortunate enough to be able to drive two machines such as these successively in the space of, say, 30 minutes that it is possible to truly appreciate how much easier bus driving has become over the years. Easier driving, though, involves more engineering complexities which in turn reflect upon the maintenance procedures involved.

Back cover, top: In prewar days the Halifax based BET subsidiary Hebble Motor Services Ltd only had a relatively few double-deckers contained within its fleet of about eighty buses and coaches. A typical example was this Leyland Titan dating from the mid-1930s that spent most of its life on the mountainous Halifax to Bradford routes. These routes contained no restrictive bridges but the clearance under the Walnut Street Depot roof was not then really sufficient to accommodate high bridge buses so for many years passengers travelling on these busy services were inconvenienced by the 4-seat/off-side dropped gangway configuration found in the upper saloon of JX 2539 and its sister vehicles for years to come.

Back cover, bottom: A scene such as this must have brought a smile to the faces of the members of the AEC bus sales force as well as to c1931 coach drivers and their passengers for in next to no time after being offered for sale, the Rackham inspired Regal I had conquered a great many long distance routes by virtue of the technically advanced (for the time) standards of comfort, speed and reliability offered by this most successful petrol engined model. This view forming as it did an official AEC photograph was probably specially posed but even so the London Terminal Coach Station saw hundreds of Regal arrivals and departures throughout the late 1920s and 1930s.

Contents

First published 1981

ISBN 0 7110 1148 6

Published by Ian Allan Ltd, Shepperton, Surrey, and printed by Ian Allan Printing Ltd at their works at Coombelands in Runnymede, England.

Preface

The production of *Looking at Buses* was a task undertaken with a considerable degree of trepidation for in it, and in the original series of articles, I endeavoured to produce a series of chapters that would consist of a judicious mix of manufacturing history, personal reminiscence, and automobile engineering – as practised in bus garages – in roughly equal portions, with the technicalities the latter must inevitably involve being treated in such a way that any non-engineering reader who had never any direct involvement with the gentle art of bus busting could gain some idea as to what it was all about, and here I must admit to some doubts as to what could result.

In the event I was both pleased and heartened by the many kind letters my writing activities generated, once the book was on sale, and by the invitation that was subsequently extended to me to repeat the exercise.

It was rather difficult to know just what to include in *A Further Look at Buses* so I re-read all my copies of *Buses* for those months when Gortonian was a regular contributor thereto, and in the end selected as a base those pieces that seemingly generated the most interest if the Letters to the editor feature was anything to go by.

It struck me most forcibly as I turned the many pages so involved as to the profound change that has come over the bus industry in the ensuing decade, when large numbers of previously wellknown undertakings have completely disappeared as have a high percentage of their former fleets, but the manufacturing side has also changed, indeed almost beyond recognition. Here though the change is for the better, for who say in 1970 could have forecast that by 1980 the Metro-Cammell Weymann concern would have turned into an established chassis builder, that Dennis would be back in the bus business, that Seddon would be building the only Gardner-powered underfloor engined vehicle, and that a posse of foreign builders would either be currently selling their wares or about to launch individual sales campaigns all directed at the home market.

Those of us who have the happy task of purchasing new buses are as a result almost faced with a surfeit of choice but one nevertheless has the uneasy feeling that all this competition might not last, for public service vehicles are very expensive items to buy, and as the bus grant is now under sentence of death, with execution fixed for 1984/85 and severe restrictions on public expenditure are also threatened it may well be that the industry will not be able to turn its stock over as quickly as it would wish. The bus builders will then be forced to look very closely indeed at their production ranges, but here one must add that all this supposes that fuel oil supplies will continue to be available, and at prices which will remain in the economic category. If the price of derv should in the decade to come go 'through the roof' then my municipal transport career that began with a tramway system involvement might well end in the same way.

This year of 1981 could therefore be one of the utmost significance in the long history of our Road Passenger Transport Industry, with the new Road Traffic Act and its controversial licensing provisions forming another factor in the equation.

I hope in consequence that these nine chapters, eight of which have been rewritten, expanded and updated, the other being brand new will provide the reader with some useful information, a further insight into what is still a very fascinating and rather exclusive world, and not a little quiet amusement.

5

Acknowledgements

It would not be possible to produce a work of this sort without someone, somewhere, undertaking a great deal of essential research into records which are not generally available to members of the bus enthusiast fraternity, and so I must express my sincere thanks to some good friends in the manufacturing side of the industry and in particular to: Dion Houghton of Gardner Engine Sales Ltd; Dennis Foster of Willowbrook Ltd; David Burnicle and Colin Watters of Leyland Vehicles Ltd; John Smith and John Hood of Hestair Dennis Ltd; Robert Crouch formerly of the Daimler Company but now with Hestair Dennis Ltd; Stan Shears and Andrew White who also had previous Daimler Company connection; Arthur Danson of East Lancashire Coachbuilders Ltd; Brian Daley, Norman Ardern and John Bennett of Seddon Atkinson Ltd; Dave Cherry of Northern Counties Motor and Engineering Company Ltd; Messers Meadows and Philips of Fodens Ltd; Peter Windsor Smith now of Maxwell Engineering but who in former days had much to do with the development of the Daimler oil engines. Roland Boschell of C.H. Roe Ltd, and last but by no means least Mr Brian Bancroft of British Leyland who commenced his career with AEC Limited of Southall fame.

On the operating side, my municipal managerial colleagues: Messrs Clarke, Marshall, Chadwick, Hyde, Oak, Groves and Bardsley of the Chester, Burnley and Pendle, Hyndburn, Blackpool, Warrington, Nottingham and Thamesdown undertakings respectively have made many efforts or inquiries on my behalf as has Hayden Williams of the Rhymney Valley Transport Department.

I must also make reference to many other friends who occupy or previously held engineering appointments in the Halifax, West Yorkshire and Leicester transport undertakings who racked their memories at my behest, and here I must make a very special mention of Cyril Hart who joined Leicester City Transport as far back as 1925 and who told me more about the vagaries of early Tilling-Stevens and Guy buses in two hours than I had discovered from other sources over the previous 24 years. His memory is truly phenomenal.

Mr John McCloy of South Yorkshire Road Transport and Messrs Tom Marsden and John Little of the Scottish Bus Group have also furnished much essential material.

Finally, in so far as the illustrations are concerned, I have again endeavoured to include as wide a selection of previously unpublished photographs as is possible, and although many have come from my own collection that has been slowly built up over the last thirty years I have been greatly assisted here by the friends mentioned above, and by Mr Robert Mack who opened his decidedly extensive files to me. Again, I have no knowledge as to who actually took many of the pictures but I would pay due tribute to their anonymous photographic activities.

Geoffrey Hilditch
Leicester 1981

Below: The later Titans could if the customer so desired have the so-called St Helens fibre glass bonnet assembly that was a vast improvement over the full width metal production that had gone before. This MCW-bodied version intended for that very corporation shows off the new design that incorporated a most useful 'dish' in the bonnet lid that rendered the nearside kerb so much more visible to the driver.

1

A Titan
amongst buses

The fact that I have chosen to commence this second volume of *Looking at Buses* with a detailed reference to the life and capabilities of the forward engined Leyland Titan double-deck vehicles is no accident, but rather a deliberate and surely well-merited tribute to a design which in the periods 1927 to 1937 and again from 1948 to 1954 was the best of its type on the market for all round performance, reliability and low first cost. Before, though, we come to consider the breed it is desirable to consider Leyland fortunes in the middle of the 1920s.

The company was even then one of Britain's major commercial vehicle manufacturers and had in 1925 set the passenger transport industry talking by producing a range of machines which were specifically intended to carry people rather than being adaptations of lorry chassis which was invariably the case at the time.

The series was known as the L range and consisted of five separate variants. The largest was the aptly named Leviathan which ungainly in appearance was intended to carry double-deck bodies and could never be regarded as a best seller. The other four were all single-deckers consisting of two normal-control machines, the 26-seat Lioness and the smaller but similar 20-seat Leveret, together with the forward control 38-seat Leopard or its 14ft 6in wheel base brother the PLSC1 Lion which could accommodate 32-seat bodies but, before a year was out, the 16ft 4in wheel base 'Long Lion' became available and the Leopard was then rendered virtually redundant.

The two Lions quickly became exceedingly popular and a very high proportion of those that were produced were equipped with the stylish Leyland composite framed single-deck body that deserves a special word of praise. A complete short Lion cost about £1,420 or if you bought a bare chassis then you parted with just £870 and

for that sum a purchaser obtained a very high class product.

The vehicle was powered by a four-cylinder 5.1litre petrol engine which drove through a four-speed crash gear box and a cone clutch, the final drive being via a worm axle that gave a moving Lion a sound of its own. Pneumatic tyres were fitted which at the time represented a most desirable innovation and the whole assembly made most other single-deckers of the day seem quite antediluvian. It is, therefore, not surprising that most of the undertakings I knew as a small boy had some Lion fleet content but fortunately I don't have to refer to childhood reminiscences to tell you what it is like to be a Lion tamer, Leyland style, for I have a 1926 example in full working order currently caged in the garage and when you take that bus out on the open road you appreciate in the only possible way just what a revolution did take place only a few months after JCP 60F first saw the light of day; but here pay no attention to that identity number for the beast was re-registered in 1967 when for the following three years no test certificate was necessary before it was relicensed for the summer months and a further spell of activity.

To wake up the Lion, one first ensures that there is some petrol in the autovac supply tank which is not as easy as you might suppose if it has evaporated or leaked away as there is no filler cap, so you have to disconnect the inlet pipe before refilling. Then you turn the fluid on. Next remove the bonnet side and if the engine is cold enlist the aid of an assistant whose task is to place three fingers over the carburettor air intake so as to form the choke that this bus does not possess.

The captain then climbs into the cab, takes his place on the non-adjustable seat, switches on the ignition switch in the magneto circuit and carefully adjusts the advance/ retard and throttle levers that are affixed in a horizontal plane beneath the small diameter wooden-rimmed steering wheel making sure you have an adequate degree of spark retardation. At this stage a move to the front end is necessary when the brass starting handle is firmly grasped and a smart crankshaft speed worked up, a speed needless to say that depends upon the compression of those four cylinders, the degree of oil drag and the strength of various muscles. After a breath-extracting minute or two, the Lion comes slowly to life when a gallop to the cab is the order of the day to maintain and promote this first flicker of potential activity before it dies down again. You tread that centre accelerator pedal gently, push the advance lever forwards and hope it doesn't back fire or your human choke will go off you – with three blistered fingers.

As soon as there is some heat in the cylinders, you can dispense with the assistant and then contemplate the rest of the controls not that there are very many. A bulb horn coming close to the righthand side of the wheel, a speedometer (obviously an extra), a lighting switch box, an orthodox handbrake lever, two large clutch and brake pedals issuing through two very large holes cut in the floor, and a gear lever set in a substantial gate that necessitates an even larger floor aperture and at this stage you wonder about the draught aspect but please don't.

Instead, push down the clutch pedal, it is quite light, move the gear lever into second and let the pedal back, when with a modicum of gas one has lift off, but I should add here that one needs to set the throttle lever to give as lower tick over speed as possible otherwise further gear changing is going to be a mite difficult. The vehicle will gently accelerate under the urge of that remarkable 53-year old engine, and then a spot of double declutching

with a gentle pause in the middle will bring third and a repeat performance should produce top when if the road is level the maximum speed of about 25mph is reached.

Now you make a discovery. The exhaust pipe runs down the side of the cab and from the panelling come copious blasts of blasting heat when you wish those floor cut outs were ten times the size. You also find that the Leyland body lacks adequate ventilation and there is no opening light on the bonnet side, only a small guillotine like glass in the cab door that is either all open or all closed, and if you swivel the upper portion of the windscreen you get every known combination of heat and draught, but if you are hot now the first corner will make you hotter still.

The steering can best be described as 'quaint'. You make your approach run perhaps changing down as you do so and then wind on a bit of lock. The bus doesn't notice thanks to a wonderful degree of understeer so you add a few more degrees just to let it know who is the boss and the resulting oversteer runs away with you so what more natural than to brake hard but the footbrake works on the transmission shaft and was designed to 1926 standards and it is a mystery to me how laden Lions ever stayed on the road for the only time I had that one up to full standing capacity I was somewhat worried – a condition that would have been shared by my passengers if they had only known what I did. No wonder there used to be sundry notices all over the place instructing drivers to engage low gear on an approaching steeply-descending gradient, but if the worst comes to the worst, there is always the handbrake which operates shoes located in drums hard by the rear wheels on the semi-floating axle.

Without doubt, driving a 50-year old bus is an experience but remember that this Lion like all its brothers and sisters works and works surprisingly well

Left: The Leyland company is a very old established bus builder that was producing double-deckers in its earliest days. This example was purchased by Todmorden Corporation as far back as 1907 when the council became the second municipal bus operator in the country and it continued in service until the 1920s thus setting a long life precedent for the Titans that were to follow.

Judging from the state of the road, the vehicle and its other sisters must have had a hard time but the life of the crew must have been even harder for there isn't even an extended dashplate to give the driver just a modest protection from the effects of a Pennine winter.

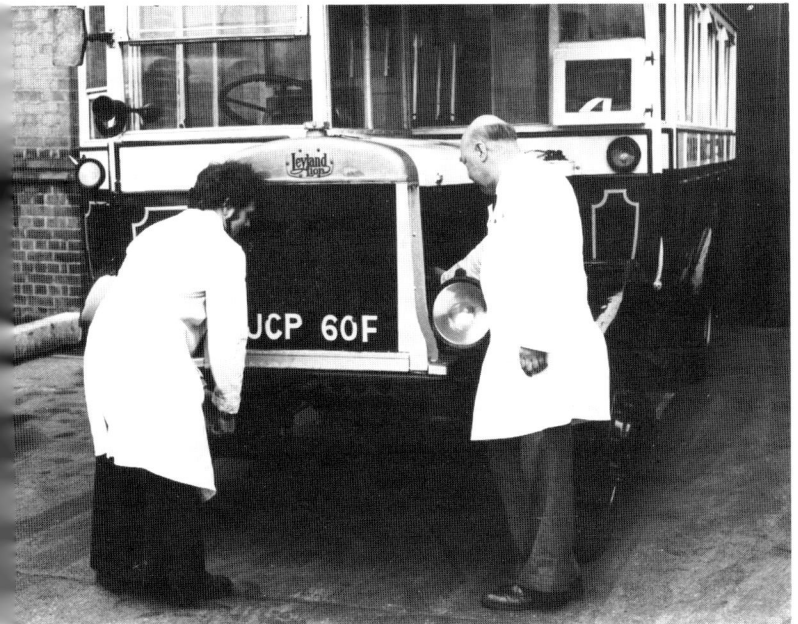

Above: The Lion now in the care of the author that began life in 1926 and spent its working life in the service of Jersey Motor Transport Ltd. Brought back to the main land on withdrawal, it was subsequently repainted in the livery of Edinburgh Corporation prior to appearing in the film *The prime of Miss Jean Brodie*. As mentioned in the text, it is a bus that truly sorts out the men from the boys providing its drivers as it does with a whole range of interesting experiences. Here about to take part in the 1979 Leicester Lord Mayor's Show it is followed by a certain Titan also mentioned in the text.

Left: It really needs three men to prod the Lion to life. Number one works the cab controls, number two provides those essential fingers to fill in for the choke it does not possess, and number three simply has to 'swing her'. This 'action shot' shows just what is necessary, so imagine a winter's morn in some garage with, say, 50 Lions and think of the activity necessary to start them up prior to entering service.

with a two-star petrol consumption of about 7mile/gal and a high degree of service accessibility becomes immediately apparent whenever some repair job becomes necessary, but as I said at the outset, within only a few months of birth it was a virtual 'has been' so what was the reason?

The first signs of the approaching revolution appeared in the personal columns of the trade press of the day, and one little piece in an old volume of mine dated 17 June 1926 reads as follows:

'On the retirement of Mr A. Ferguson after 23 years service, Mr G.J. Rackham has been appointed chief engineer to Leyland Motors Ltd. During the past four years Mr Rackham held the post of chief engineer to the Yellow Coach Company of Chicago of which organisation Mr Green, a former chief engineer to the London General Omnibus Company, is vice-president. Prior to going to Chicago Mr Rackham was with the Associated Equipment Company first as chief designer and later production engineer.'

No further references appear in that journal about the activity that must then have taken place in that Lancashire factory until the issue of 10 November 1927 when in the Olympia Commercial Show section is found the first description of the advanced single-deck Tiger chassis and of its stronger but similar Titan double-deck counterpart. An example of the latter appeared on the manufacturer's show stand as did a long Lion which now had a better clutch and gear-operating mechanism but I doubt if many people spared much thought for that animal not when there was a Titan on view.

The Titan had a brand new six-cylinder 6.79litre engine (414cu in) which with standard road setting produced 105bhp at 2,000rpm and would idle quietly and smoothly at speeds as low as 200rpm. There was an overhead camshaft running in an oil trough, overhead

Below: The Lion's engine. Of 4.25in bore and 5.5in stroke it produces 43.5hp at 1,000rpm. There is a single crankcase with two separate cylinder blocks and two separate cylinder heads each accommodating two bores. This unit actually could be provided with an electric starter as the teeth on the flywheel indicate but at least one Lion wasn't so lucky.

valves and a single cylinder head running the full length of the power unit. The engine was full of modern features and miracle of miracles, a starter motor was fitted as standard so no more cranking. There was also a choke control, a single plate clutch, a unit mounted four speed gear box, still of course of the crash variety, four wheeled vacuum assisted brakes, 3½in wide road springs, front shock absorbers, an underslung worm drive axle, a straight transmission line, and of course that rather special frame that gave a low rear platform which set a pattern for the next four decades as indeed did the whole bus, for the body introduced the lowheight side gangway configuration.

Here I am again lucky for I also have access to a 1931 Titan in full working order which differs from the original version only by having one of the first totally-enclosed bodies whilst the original ones had the open staircase layout, but from a running point of view this should be something of a retrograde feature as extra body work must mean extra weight, so presumably less performance but here is the difference. The Lion trundles whilst the Titan gallops on low throttles and rockets on wider ones.

To take out the Lion and then change to the Titan is a revelation and you wonder how so much development could occur in such a short time. The engine is an absolute honey, the steering is a little on the stiff side but ever so positive, the gear change is just a little difficult at first but once mastered every change gives rise to a sense of satisfaction, the brakes are powerful and sure and the ride anywhere on the bus is quite up to modern leaf spring standards. There are in fact only two problem areas. This vehicle also has a centre accelerator and alas and alack a PUSH on handbrake. Now pushing the lever to the on position is no trouble at all, it's the reverse that brings the problem and tears to the eyes of the unwary.

Above: Two for the price of one. For as long as Todmorden Corporation or the Todmorden JOC purchased double-deckers, the Leyland was the order of the day. This view shows an early Titan but with closed-in bodywork and a contemporary single-decker that came out of the same stable. The latter is one of the relatively few Tigers that bore the head of the animal on the radiator instead of the more usual nameplate.

The bus has a standard circa 1931 Leyland drivers seat of the non-adjustable form and offering a surprising degree of comfort only the rather high seat back has wings where the triming is brought around the wooden frame. Now the righthand edge of that frame is exactly in line with the so called elbow funny bone and if you have put the handbrake on firmly it is necessary to give it an extra push forwards to release the ratchet. The lever will then fly back taking the manipulating arm with it and there is that seat back ready and waiting when the ensuing collision will mean that for the next few minutes the driver will have no feeling at all and when sensations begin to return you truly wish they wouldn't.

Generally speaking, you only suffer once but this inconvenience is a slight price to pay for the joy of driving a Titan. They must have reduced the work load of contemporary drivers to holiday type proportions and, of course, Titans brought smiles to the faces of fleet engineers who had been battling with the vagaries of Karriers and all those other soon to be forgotten makes. Here at last was an all round operator's bus and Leyland sales really took off.

The last three words also came to apply to Mr Rackham in 1928 when he left Leyland to return to his old firm AEC which was by now ensconced in the new works at Southall and not surprisingly AEC soon began to market a range of single and double-deck buses, a range which will be described in greater detail in Chapter 2 of this volume, and which, as both the text and photographs clearly show, was very similar indeed to those original Lancashire productions.

Needless to say, Leyland was not amused by all this but nevertheless in my view continued to maintain a technical lead over its new and now main competitor until Southall with a deal of London Transport assistance produced the very fine RT Regent in the immediate prewar period, hence the gap in the dates quoted in the first paragraph of this chapter, for a 1938 Regent Mark III was a much better city bus than the contemporary Titan.

To some extent, of course, this technical lead was assisted because Leyland had that excellent bodywork department and so, unlike AEC, was able to produce completed vehicles in its own shops quickly turning over to totally enclosed double-deckers as had already been mentioned, and it is perhaps at this point convenient to digress from the main stream of mechanical development to consider the Leyland double-deck body.

The composite models gave very little trouble over the years and what problems were encountered were invariably to be found also on competitive products consisting, for example, of defective seals in the window glazing areas, body bolts working loose and corrosion of the timber underframe and especially so in the vicinity of the wheel arches.

The first six-bay all metal product of 1934/5 with its projecting destination box was, though, a different affair altogether. Now I rather liked the external appearance and interior finish of these bodies which I first met when my local undertaking bought three for trial but the purchase was not repeated, or so the then rolling stock engineer told me, as a result of the framing troubles that were encountered. Leyland was soon on to such faults as there were, however, and the succeeding 1936 version of the metal body with its shapely sloping vee front also set a standard that was to last without becoming dated for the next 20 years.

The various undertakings I knew in the early postwar years had large numbers of these pre-1939 machines running and again we seemed to do little to them apart from replacing damaged panels or badly corroded metal and the same happy state of affairs continued when the first postwar productions had reached the then recertification age of five years. These buses had fairly square window corners and polished wooden finishers internally whilst the last versions had a different form of glazing with metal window pans and a special section rubber and an all metal interior based trim. Certainly the biggest problem on this whole range of Leyland productions that I ever met was caused by the design requirements of one concern that had Leyland vary their standard outline to the one which had been adopted locally and which was of a streamline style that was very much in vogue at the time. This had waist panels which dipped down at every corner when any rain would collect in the depressions and give rise to a rather unfortunate degree of advance corrosion that in the end spelt the demise of what was until the middle fifties a Manchester hallmark.

By that time the Leyland body much to the regret of all who knew them had almost reached the end of the road, all bus body building coming to an end in December 1954 when the space so released was turned over to the commercial vehicle cab production, Trent Motor Traction taking the last complete Leyland registered as FRC 956. AEC conversely had become very involved in the field through its Crossley, Park Royal and Chas. H. Roe subsidiaries of which only the last is currently still with us but again by this time the Titan was nothing like the design that carried this name that existed at the period of it last being mentioned here.

I will due to space reasons only mention two significant prewar developments to the Titan beginning with the

Right: The ancestry of the prewar Leyland bus oil engine is very clearly displayed in this three-quarter view. Like its petrol predecessor it retained the long head, an overhead cam shaft and that front oil cooler. Now, though, a fuel pump and vacuum exhauster were to be found amongst the auxiliaries. This particular engine was later fitted to a vehicle destined for Kingston upon Hull.

arrival of the Leyland diesel engine of 1931/32. Of 8.1litre capacity, $4^3/_8$in bore by 5.5in stroke, with a power output of about 85bhp at 1,900rpm, it represented the first really efficient direct injection design to follow the Gardner; but as those that went into double-deckers were invariably of the improved 93bhp 1933 8.6litre six-cylinder form, the net result was a much more refined performance and it was not too long before AEC were seeking the use of the Leyland combustion chamber patents (pot cavity pistons and single hole injectors) for that company's Acro head or indirect injection offerings were never just as good.

It was generally conceded by all strong Leyland supporters, and they were legion in the 1930s, that the Gardner gave weight-for-weight a better fuel consumption but they claimed with good reason that the Leyland was quieter, much smoother running and much better to work on. You built up the main chunks of, say, a 6LW and then seemed to spend quite a time hanging on sundry pipes whilst the Leyland was so much tidier in this respect. The problem with this vintage of Leyland engine was that the oil engine was very much like its petrol powered predecessor – too much so in some respects – and if only the company had moved off the full length cylinder head which still retained the Rackham style overhead camshaft! Gasket failures were the weak point here, and because the head was so big and heavy it was all too often very difficult to loosen from its holding down studs, and awkward to handle thereafter when it would invariably be found to require surface regrinding to restore the requisite degree of flatness.

The other innovation was the arrival at the 1933 Commercial Show of the so called 'Gearless' bus a fact that was clearly indicated by the appearance of the word in badge form on the lefthand side of the radiator grille, a model that was presumably offered to compete with the AEC or Daimler sales successes with vehicles equipped with preselector Wilson type gearboxes but in many

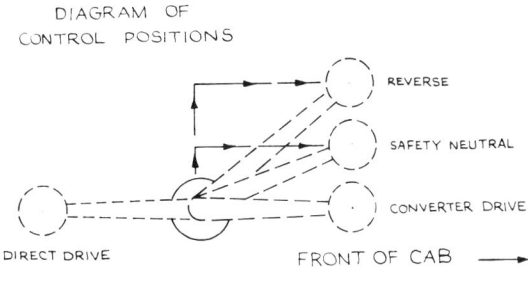

respects Leyland followed a much more adventurous path. Based on Lysholm Smith patents the gearbox housed a torque converter, a lock up top gear, a free wheel device, and some extra cogs to ensure it was possible to make a powered reversal. Additionally, there was in the cab what appeared to be a normal gear lever for we had not yet reached the stage of going fully automatic thank goodness, and this lever could be placed in any one of four distinct positions (as shown in the drawing) one of which was needless to say neutral.

Traction was very easy to obtain. You placed the lever in the first forward position and this brought in the torque converter, which operated on a mixture of 96% paraffin to 4% engine oil, the latter being required to lubricate the various seals. The working fluid was drawn from a large supply tank which had a level sight glass and was housed on the front bulkhead in the place usually occupied by the autovac (there was incidentally a

Below: By 1935 the Leyland oil engine had come to be highly accepted. This line up of brand new Oldham buses was taken in the June of that year and shows the Roe- and Crossley-bodied machines purchased for tramway replacement purposes. Apparently the Leyland-bodied vehicles Nos 102, 103 and 104 had yet to make an appearance.

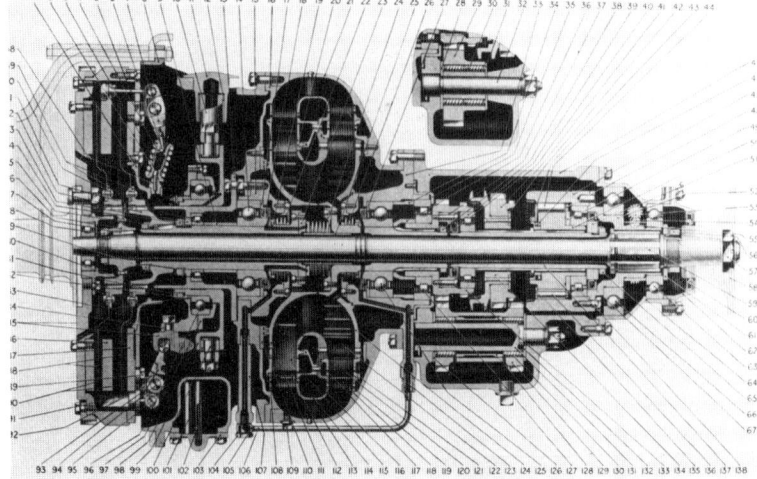

Above: By coincidence the Burnley, Colne and Nelson Joint Committee also took three Leyland buses which had Leyland bodies and the same fleet numbers that same year again for tramway replacement. In this case, however, torque convertors were specified hence the legend 'gearless bus' on the radiators. In later years conventional gearboxes replaced these startling innovations – as, indeed, was invariably the case elsewhere.

Right: Section through the Lysholm-Smith torque convertor fitted in Leyland vehicles.

14

combined reservoir/header tank provided on certain buses), and passed down a supply pipe to the converter where a driving rotor ran inside an outer driven turbine wheel. As speed rose so the driving torque decreased until with continuous acceleration taking place a road speed of around 25mph was attained when the gear lever was pulled right back and straight through drive engaged thanks to the operation of the lock up clutch, and so one had most of the characteristics of a standard Titan of the time but not quite. On encountering a rising gradient, the lever was pushed forwards, and the converter took up the struggle once more, when if the hill was sufficiently steep or the load sufficiently heavy the engine revolutions would continue at a high level whilst those of the road wheels would gently but inexorably decrease. This gave a gearless Titan a sound all of its own and left quite a few characters wondering just what was happening.

The answer could have been that the fluid was becoming over warm but to try to prevent boiling a very large 'vee' type radiator was bolted to the nearside of the frame behind the driver's bulkhead, from whence it was piped back to the supply tank, via sundry flexible pipes. These pipes being flexible could and did leak and despite the existence of the radiator hard worked fluid could and did boil.

The design had some very clever features though. For example, the main seal on the output shaft consisted of a self lapping eccentrically rotating pair of mating surfaces, which were loaded to 26lb one surface being of steel and the other bronze. This seal had an inbuilt oil seepage intended to lubricate the surfaces, when the oil so lost was collected in a special reservoir, piped then to a main collector and then returned by an ingenious injection device to the main supply tank, so no oil loss should have occurred in theory. In fact, it wasn't quite like that as I saw for myself one day in a certain Lancashire town that had both trams and torque converters, plus a rather damp climate. There was a central terminal point on a gradient shared by the trams and gearless Titans, and one rainy afternoon rather too many drops of fluid were no longer contained inside their converters, instead they lubricated the tramway track. Down came a bogie car in something of a rush when the driver on his open front platform endeavoured to make a somewhat over exuberant stop and the sight of his face as his mount literally took off was truly something to behold.

Gearless Titans could though have a braking surprise for the driver as running in a converter meant that no engine braking was available, but if you wanted to convert ex-tram men to buses then here was a decidedly easy drive bus. The fuel consumption though was decidedly on the heavy side, and that sad characteristic worsened if over much fluid was lost. The heat generated could and did carbon up the various connecting fluid pipes but the worst fault was due entirely to the weight of the assembly which was about 6in longer than a conventional gearbox. The unit was hung in the conventional manner from the back end of the engine

when the cantilever effect could disturb the location of the front input shaft bearing with dire results, but there was one corresponding bonus for although my present undertaking ran 33 torque converters over a period of ten years it never in that time ever experienced a failed half shaft, whereas the standard TD5s needed numerous replacements.

The torque-converter Titan coded TDs didn't stay over long although improved transmissions were offered from 1937 onwards, and most places that took any number quietly slipped in normal clutches and gearboxes within a year or two and that wasn't as easy an exercise as the word 'slipped' might convey. Here if I remember rightly only Lytham St Annes where the bus routes were as flat as the proverbial pancake retained its gearless Titans in original form into a ripe old age but by the time this generation of buses was departing from this life there were those who were wishing they had theirs back for in 1946 we met our first PD1 style Titans the first, ordered by the erstwhile City Coach concern which was chassis number PD1 460652 leaving Leylands works on the 19 March, but Bury Corporation Transport had the first to enter passenger service.

My own local concern had never gone gearless but it did acquire 12 PD1s, which like the Bury bus had Roe bodies, in the August of the same year for tramway replacement purposes when 27 old favourites passed into oblivion, one sad Saturday night. The next day I took a ride on one of those brand new buses but didn't appreciate what I saw. We had been spared the rigours of a utility or relaxed utility specification and had in fact benefited in about 1941 when no less than 47 TD5s were put into service after lying unused in the depot from the autumn of 1939, when they had arrived to finish off the aforementioned cars only they, thanks to Mr Hitler obtained a seven-year reprieve. Now these 1939/1941 buses had moquette seating in both saloons, and a full complement of heaters as indeed had every bus built after 1935 which meant the majority in practice, but the new intake had none of these luxury touches. We had leather seats, no warming devices and various other inferior features but I am speaking here from a passenger point of view as the driver obviously was becoming heated because he wasn't changing gear all that well, and as for performance well one of those now redundant 1921 to 1926 tramcars was without doubt a much more competent hill climber.

A little later on my way to work one morning the then deputy traffic superintendent (who was if he will forgive the description a 'hard bitten salt') elected to have a spot of exercise and drive the bus in. He took the wheel at our usual stop, which was on a rising gradient and took off without a fault but when he came to engage third at the top of the hill the rasping noises that came from the gearbox were really quite something, but any grin there might have been on my face was wiped off all too soon.

I was one afternoon at a certain garage when a call came, 'Could I journey instantly across the city and visit an ailing Crossley that was on the point of death?' The connecting bus services though were far from convenient

Right: Until the AEC Regent Mark III came on the scene, there was nothing to beat the Leyland double-deck chassis but connoisseurs always took the view that here the TD5 was rather better in many respects than the later TD7. When one married a TD5 to a Roe body, a very pleasing combination resulted and this mixture found great favour with Oldham Corporation which acquired No 164 in 1937 when again a Titan buried a tram. This offside view shows the 'D' window used to light the Roe patent staircase features that had not appeared before in the Oldham fleet.

so I asked the superintendent if I could borrow a bus for taxi purposes. He replied in the affirmative and sweeping his arm over the flock sitting in the yard said, 'Take your pick'. I mistakenly picked a PD1; I started up and moved smartly out through the gates and then also tried to get third, but again all I got was noise.

I tried every trick I knew from taking it slowly to rushing the thing but that Titan beat me hands down. In the end I cheated, took it to the top of a handy railway bridge in second, which was at least two miles from my starting point, put it into third on the downward side, and stayed in that ratio to the end of the journey when I indicated that the Crossley was much worse than I had been led to believe so I would sit up with the patient if only someone else would return my PD1 whence it came. After that I did some very surreptitious surveillance as to how the more successful drivers handled their charges, followed up the espionage with a spot of quiet practice and only then came to be able to drive a PD1, for these buses had the slowest change I have ever encountered. On going say from second to third one found neutral, let the clutch pedal back, slowly counted one, two, three, four, five and on five moved the clutch pedal and gear lever simultaneously. Later I found a more sophisticated method namely to listen to the whistle of the pneumatic governor, and when it died completely away act fast. There was also a sophisticated mechanism for altering the driver's seat adjustment when a single handle took it diagonally in a straight line from forwards bottom to bulkhead top, which was all very well if your physical features and the diagonal line were compatible only mine sadly were not, but the same seating continued right through the PD1 production and into PD2 days.

As things turned out the PD1 was something of a stop gap but as new buses were then at a premium, it undoubtedly filled a need. The vehicle was new from the radiator with its metal painted or later chrome pressed metal surround to the 7.4litre rigidly mounted engine which now did have both push rods, and separate cylinder heads for the 'T' series arrangement was no more. The engine had a maximum horsepower of 100bhp at 1,800rpm but it really wasn't sufficiently powerful for double-deck use, and when you added that fact to the gear change aspect it was no wonder drivers on hilly routes preferred prewar rolling stock. It was also somewhat noisy.

Mind you, there were some good points. The cab structure was properly designed and was alleged to be draught proof. It really wasn't quite but it was certainly an improvement on what had gone before. The clutch was light, there was a neat instrument panel, the riding was quite acceptable and the triple servo vacuum brakes did stop the vehicle, whilst, thanks to the reduced power output, nothing ever went sadly amiss in the drive line or rear axle, and at the front end you had a steering system that wasn't all that bad either. Then beneath the steering wheel was to be found for the first time since Rackham a PULL on handbrake, only the lever lay at an angle of about 45deg to the floor instead of approaching the vertical position used by every other bus chassis builder. At first this I liked, but the experience of trying to hold a fully laden Titan on a 1 in 7 gradient later in my career made me revise my opinion.

The E181 engine was based on a prewar 6.2litre experimental power unit and had been developed for tank work during the war, but in such situations smoke emissions aren't really a major talking point, now with us they were. To make the buses go at all, you had to give them maximum fuel, but the breathing couldn't have been all that good for if the equipment's condition deteriorated to the slightest extent then from the exhaust pipe came a series of smoke signals that didn't need any Indian to interpret. My boss in this context was a tribe all to himself, but it wasn't always the fault of the injection

16

Left: Again by coincidence a Roe body graced the first postwar Titan to enter service in 1946. Bury Corporation was the purchaser of this historic PD1 No 102 in the series 102 to 116 which also struck yet another new note by being finished in the new green and white livery that replaced the deep maroon used up to this time. The PD1 as the text explains was something of a stopgap and so not everyone's favourite vehicle for gear changing was a highly technical process.

system or fuel pump, for these engines possessed a lengthy timing chain that wove a tortuous path and often stretched when some nimble-fingered fitter had the job of insinuating a replacement.

Apart from the foregoing the PD1 maintenance wise wasn't much of a problem, because one of our fleet in full trim and working order plus a standard 5.4 to 1 rear axle ratio would only reach about 35mph when very flat out, and thanks to that 'interesting' constant mesh gearbox drivers couldn't abuse the bus. Fortunately the 'tushy pegs' therein stood all our uninitiated changing efforts, but here let me add that our company of driving instructors thought these were the best buses for that purpose since the last 'B' type AEC disappeared towards the end of 'Ye good olde days'.

We, however, were in the time of the PD1 with two later variants appearing namely the PD1A which differed only in that it had rubber bonded Metalastik shackle pins, and the PD1/3 that was built to the newly permitted 8ft wide dimension, and so being heavier than ever offered even less in the way of performance, but despite these difficulties, over 1,950 home market PD1 Titans were built up to 1950.

At this stage fortunately for both Leyland and the bus industry there appeared yet another new design which took us all forward with a leap that emulated the Leviathan to Titan movement of 1927, for in July 1947 Rawtenstall Corporation Transport took delivery of the first PD2 based on chassis number 47169 and here was yet another operator's bus.

I met my first PD2 one afternoon a little later in the vicinity of Todmorden where the local joint omnibus committee always a staunch Leyland customer had acquired a first batch which also included the second production PD2. I had gone one Sunday afternoon to visit a friend and as the day was fine, it was suggested that we went for a ride into the country, so we took our places

Above: The succeeding PD2 was yet another outstanding bus that provided the manufacturers with a very steady supply of orders. The O600 engine was another masterpiece and the postwar Leyland body also gave a good account of itself. This is one of a batch of nine acquired by Halifax Corporation Transport for evaluation against the then standard AEC fluid drive Regent III, and was to end its career with Oldham Corporation. In this generation of Leyland bodies, the metal-framed assembly was fitted with window pans having quite squared corners and the interior trim employed polished wooden strips.

in a very long queue of people who had the same intention. Numerous buses of pre- and postwar vintage arrived, filled, and left without us, but as our turn to board came I was disheartened to find what appeared to be a PD1 come onto the stand. There was though, a slightly different engine note apparent, as we took our places on the front nearside lower saloon seat, but then when we had about twenty standing we received the starting signal and a revelation.

That bus which was complete with a Leyland body positively swept up the quite substantial gradients which lay between the town and our destination and I began to realise that this was one of the new O600 engined buses that my chief had mentioned some time earlier in something that approached awed tones, and I by the end of the ride had come to the distinct conclusion that here was a machine that could outpace a Regent Mark III which was then rather dear to our hearts, so the next question was. Where were ours?

They were not as it happened too far away, and so commenced our association with this remarkable bus, starting with the PD2/1 7ft 6in wide version although the 8ft wide PD2/3 did come later.

The first object of attention was the 9.8litre 4.8in bore 5.5in stroke O600 engine that could produce around 125bhp at 1,800rpm with a maximum torque of 410lb/ft at 900rpm and compare this later figure with the corresponding statistic for the 7.4litre unit of the PD1 which was 328lb/ft at 1,150rpm. No wonder the PD2 could step out smartly. Despite the larger size the specific fuel consumption figure of around 0.35 pints per hour of the newcomer was similar to that of the old engine, and this benefit undoubtedly resulted from all the internal design improvements.

The camshaft was now located in a much lower position in the crankcase, and those lengthy timing chains were no more, their place being taken by a train of gears, and contained in the same combined crankcase/cylinder block casting were six removable dry liners so if there was to be a bore wear problem it was not going to be necessary to resort to wholesale removal and dismantling techniques to effect a cure. The crank itself was very much more substantial than anything we had seen before, for we had yet to see a Daimler CD 650 component, and that crank which was hardened was carried in easily fitted thin shell bearings, yet another example of the designers forward thinking. Again two separate cylinder heads were provided and on top of the heads above the rocker covers was a large horizontally mounted air cleaner.

The method of engine suspension was also new, for the power unit and the unit mounted gearbox were carried by four flexible links whose centres were arranged so that a connecting line passed through the centre of gravity of the assembly, and at the rear a pair of rubber snubbers which neatly fitted into two ribs cast into the rear engine cross-member casting restricted oscillations to a suitable extent . . . well almost so.

Behind the engine was a large 16.25in single plate clutch and cored ducts in the centre plate were arranged to allow it to act also as an air cooling fan.

The clutch took the drive into a brand new four speed gearbox that was provided with an inertia lock type synchromesh mechanism on the second, third and top ratios, but bottom gear, to be mentioned later, was of the crash variety.

An inclined pair of propellor shafts of seemingly adequate size led from the gearbox companion flange to the rear axle which had its worm and wheel centres increased from the 7.5in of the PD1 to 8in, so as to cope with the extra torque and to stop the machine, an engine mounted rotary exhauster provided the negative pressure necessary to actuate the triple servo vacuum brakes that had a friction area of 577cu in.

The rest of the chassis consisted of a 0.25in section 3in flanged frame which had a maximum depth of 11in, graded throughout its length to give an almost constant degree of stress intensity, and beneath the frame were some 4in wide road springs that had the metalastik bonded shackles that featured in the PD1/A. There were, however, some echoes of that model as the cab assembly was almost identical, a wing difference letting a knowledgeable person recognise a PD2 at a glance, and the radiator was also of similar appearance to that of the PD1 with a pressed and now chromium plated cowl. The PD2 chassis was though a much improved and strengthened animal as its unladen weight of 4ton 11cwt 1qtr showed for the PD1 had turned the scales at 4ton 5cwt.

Our new toys duly took the road but before very long returned thanks to 'technical difficulties' to the depot and most of these events centred on the gearbox, or 'infamous' gearbox as one of my Leyland friends referred to it. That synchromesh mechanism baulking device on second gear was not all that could be desired, and neither was the layout of some spring plungers and a plate which pressed rearwards against the constant mesh first gear wheel on the main shaft. In fact we reached the stage of having the first seven buses collectively consuming one gearbox a fortnight and that was expensive. The fact that the PD2s were put onto hilly routes didn't help things a bit, and neither did the arrangement of the gears.

If you were driving one and encountered a rising gradient the change from direct drive top to the 1.59 to 1 ratio third was never any problem, once you appreciated that this Leyland box had a long gear lever travel. The next change to the second speed with its 2.63 to 1 gearing was rather more difficult, and quite often a fair amount of pressure had to be applied to the lever to make the teeth engage, and from this characteristic came a spate of snapped off levers that made the parent bus a complete casualty but far, far worse was the problem of getting into bottom for not only did you have the 'crash' problem but that bottom gear had a very low 5 to 1 ratio. Many of our drivers and this scribe had anxious moments for although first was an emergency gear IT WAS IN AN EMERGENCY THAT IT WAS WANTED and such occasions were no times to practise the niceties of bus driving.

Oft times I would emulate that deputy traffic superintendent and drive the bus to work when most days an AEC preselector Mark III would be on the track but now and again a PD2 would appear and as a 1 in 8 gradient lay on the line of route it was a toss up as to whether I then had a drive or saw what the 'professional

Left: Trent number 1256 was the last bus to have a Leyland-built body. Based on chassis number 541780 of the PD2/12 form, it was delivered to Derby on 13 December 1954. After suffering accident damage it was partially rebuilt by Trent and returned as fleet number 745 in 1962 when a different style of windscreen was provided. The bus finally withdrawn on 31 March 1967 when it passed to Whippet Coaches of Huntingdon but fortunately was purchased for preservation when sold by that operator in July 1972.

Now restored to something like original specification, it was repainted in the Trent livery by that concern in 1976 but some refurbishing has yet to be completed. Later Leyland bodies to this design had a metal interior finish and rounded corners to the window pans.

pilot' did, until I did some more surreptitious practising and found the answer. You continued upwards in second until the bus nearly came to a stand then pulled the stick back to neutral, and with the TINIEST of revs shot the stick into the first position when there was no noise and when thanks to that 5 to 1 ratio you could ascend any mountain quite comfortably even with 30 standing passengers.

The cowards way, by the way, was to come to a stand, grab the handbrake, pull it up hard, then engage first and then take away on the hill but here one was back to the angle of the lever I mentioned before.

Taking off though unless on a downwards gradient could be a problem. The buses had a combined pneumatic/mechanical fuel pump governor with the pneumatic part controlling the idling revolutions. If the diaphragm stops were not properly set, the vehicle would take off in a series of leaps and bounds that were quite disconcerting to everyone on board.

All this needless to say didn't do much to help the propellor shafts enjoy a long and healthy life and so new and more substantial assemblies had to be substituted (note here and later how history does repeat itself). Later modified governors, flexible clutch centres and an engine shock absorber killed off the kangaroo.

Those Metalastik bushes too were another good/bad idea for they could be devilish to remove and when they were in situ we had a posse of leaning Leylands, when the unwary could be caught out. It happened to me. One Saturday morning I decided to visit not the office but the library so I repaired with last week's volumes to the bus stop. In rolled a PD2 complete with a worried looking driver who left the cab to tell me there seemed to be a fault on the bus only he couldn't diagnose exactly what it was so please would I? The fact that the gradient was half a mile down the road could have been a primary cause of the request, but I had to rise to the challenge, and so took

his place. We then took the hill in a bound but at the bus stop at the top thereof were standing two girls hockey teams complete with spectators and all of the company who resembled amazons to a man (Can that be right?) just had to go upstairs. Now being a gentleman I had brought that bus to the kerb edge stopping in such a way that the ornate Victorian lamp standard carrying the stop sign was in line with the first nearside saloon pillar to the front of the open platform. When all were on board, the worried one gave me four bells and then a complete peal, for as the girls went aloft so did the bus gently lean to the camber of the road until the upper deck panelling and the gas lamp came into contact above the field of view of my nearside mirror. The said lamp never mentioned the fact until I let the clutch out when there was a considerable crash and one piece of municipal ironmongery arrived hard by the side of the nearside front wing. The affair did not do my image any good as the general manager of the day pointed out that Engineers were supposed to repair buses not bust them and who, by the way, was going to pay for the gas that escaped into the atmosphere? There was no answer to that one, but a return to solid shackles, and the provision of a rear stabiliser on later versions did eliminate the lean.

Leylands also eventually found the answer to the gearbox failings even though for a time the original GB63 assembly we had was augmented by a GB83 version that had a second gear of the constant mesh variety but I never took to this hybrid. We tried a few but they confused the drivers more than ever for the plate that told you what sort of box the bus had would come adrift and then single declutch as you would, you were not going to find second in the expected manner.

Of the remaining faults few could be laid at the engine's door, for that wonderful piece of mechanism went on and on . . . provided that none of the injector pressure or leak offpipes cracked. If they did, the fault could go unnoticed as the injectors were concealed under the rocker box covers, unlike those on the AEC 9.6 engine which were absolutely open. Then the neat fuel oil would drain into the crank case dilute the lubricant and difficulties followed until we began to check the viscosity of a sample at every 6,000-mile oil change and if the oil was undesirably thin further investigation followed. We also had some crankcase casting failures in the vicinity of the water pump but a simple foundry alteration was all that was needed there.

We also tried one or two own account engine modifications, fitting odd examples with delivery valves that were alleged to give high torque at low speeds and low torque at high speeds to obtain very minimal benefits but talking of high speeds, leads me on to an adventure with a fully pneumatic governor, which was duly fitted to a later PD2/3. I drove it on a first test run, and took a rural road, when the leader of the party suggested I might see just what speed the bus could attain before we sealed the control stops. For the first and last time in my life I drove a PD2 at a speed which was somewhere (??) in excess of a mile a minute when the steering felt like rubber but that bus still had some way to go when I decided that enough was enough and no-one behind me disputed the decision.

I do not have the space to deal with the later Titans which by 1968 when production ceased had either concealed or cast sided traditional radiators (the chromium cowls were always cracking) 'power plus' engines, semi automatic gearboxes, first seen on provincial PD2s from 1954, and various other improvements but they still represented good value for money and particularly so if you bought the 30ft long 18ft 6in wheelbase PD3 version that had forsaken its original triple-servo braking system that was very much on the border line for the much more satisfactory air pressure alternative (30ft long buses were legalised from 1 July 1956, when the laden weight limit was lifted from 12 to 14 tons). By the same token the O600 engine had grown into the O680 for the greater weight of these bigger buses had meant more power was desirable, but let me end my Titan saga with a note as to just what a PD3 can do.

Leicester City Transport at the time of my writing this chapter had 44 of the model still in stock, 20 of which possessed the two pedal control semi-automatic, pneumocyclic transmission the other 24 the most recent version of the GB63 synchromesh gearbox. Because we are not fully committed to the one-man bus principle, they are still employed on very busy main line services and below are set out the maintenance records of one of each type of vehicle for the past two years which have been picked out of the files at random:

Bus No 70: synchromesh gearbox. O600 engine. First registered 1 January 1965. Body: East Lancashire.

2 December 1977	Offside front brake relined.
10 March 1978	Nearside rear spring changed.
29 March 1978	Thrust washer replaced.
1 July 1978	Nearside brake relined (rear).
3 August 1978	Offside rear brake relined.
4 August 1978	Offside rear road spring changed.
28 August 1978	Fuel pump changed.
15 January 1979	Alternator defective – replaced.
24 February 1979	Offside rear spring replaced (guarantee work).
6 May 1979	Offside rear brake relined.
16 May 1979	New clutch plate fitted.

Total mileage run between first date and last date 53,000 miles. Average fuel consumption 7.32.

Bus No 20: pneumocyclic gearbox. O680 engine. First registered 1 October 1967. Body: East Lancashire.

27 April 1978	Offside rear spring changed.
4 October 1978	Nearside rear spring changed.
10 February 1979	Offside rear brake reline.
24 April 1979	Alternator defective.
9 June 1979	Starter solenoid failure.

Mileage operated 47,000, average fuel consumption 6.95.

Note how the fluid transmission bus has the higher fuel consumption due to fluid flywheel slip and perhaps the larger engine.

No 70 weighs unladen 8ton 5cwt 3qtr. No 20 8ton 6cwt 0qtr.

It is obvious from these extracts that these old buses coming as they do from a series of highly-developed models, need very little maintenance. I would that some later rear engine machines exhibited such characteristics.

The PD3s like the few remaining PD2s still in service up and down the country may not now be the world's most sophisticated vehicles and no doubt in the eyes of the passengers they are now very outdated but there are those in the garage who look at buses rather differently and who wish that they were still a production model. Incidentally, 8,374 home market PD2s were built as were 3,138 chassis to the PD3 specification. Here, this general manager also gives a wry smile when he thinks that when new in 1964 and 1967, they cost complete £5,761 and £6,504 respectively, and here we come to a matter of pure economics.

It was the Titan and single-deck Tiger that provided the foundation upon which undertaking after undertaking, municipal, combine and private company built and/or developed their services and what finer tribute could you offer to chief engineer Rackham and those who subsequently trod the path he pioneered over fifty years ago than that.

I only hope that when our last Titan comes to the end of its working life, it will be preserved to show future generations of transport enthusiasts just what a good bus looked like and that in the meantime those responsible for the new Titan or its chassis derivative will ensure that in every possible aspect their new product emulates its famous namesake (excepting only the somewhat makeshift PD1 version) and. of course, there is the matter also of those very acceptable prices.

2
A Southall saga

One Friday morning in March 1979, I walked into my local station and booked a ticket to London and here was an event that occurs so frequently as to be commonplace, but this day was one with a difference for the whole process was clouded with nostalgia. The train duly arrived when I boarded not a carriage, but the footplate, and as I did so my mind went back to the days when I used to travel on the front of London trains almost on a daily basis but at the time I did so, one just never imagined that the 'Black Fives', 'Jubilees', compounds, 'Baby Scots' and all those other locomotives that were so familiar in the steam era would in only a few years have been superseded by a very different form of motive power and who by the same token could ever have then foreseen what I should be witnessing at the end of my journey, for I was en route to the AEC Southall works to have a look around on the very last Friday that the production line would be running at something like full capacity for already the final set of frames had been dropped into position and when the last of the chassis that I was to see came out of the works finished, there would be no more AEC vehicles. Sadly, there was no Reliance on the line as I toured those hallowed shops for the final passenger chassis had already been built but there were one or two still on the premises and so I had to have a look over an example for old times sake and, as I did so, I thought back to some of the earlier AEC machines that I had either travelled on or, in a very few cases, had known professionally.

The oldest of these without any doubt is the Regal I single-decker which, with a Craven body, was purchased by Messrs Bevan and Barker (who were the proprietors of the former Red Bus Service of Mansfield Woodhouse) in November 1931. It ran in service until about 1948

when it was withdrawn and fortunately saved for preservation so VO6816, now in my care, forms a very good starting point for this chapter.

AEC as most vehicle enthusiasts will know, was founded by the London General Omnibus Company in 1912 to produce better buses for that concern. Thereafter, there came out of the Walthamstow works (previously owned by the Vanguard Motor Omnibus Company) a whole range of psv and goods vehicles until around 1926 when having outgrown that plant, a move was made to the new works at Southall, the company being almost simultaneously reconstituted and divorced from its operating parent.

By the end of the 1920s, AEC had become a major manufacturer, still with an almost monopoly of London bus sales, and had resumed its solitary state after a two year marketing flirtation with the Daimler Company that lasted from 1926 to 1928 when certain Associated Daimlers had been produced, but future sales prospects were none too good just around this time as a revolution had taken place in the market, a revolution that was described in the previous chapter. Quite obviously, if AEC did not as a minimum produce vehicles that were the equal of the contemporary Leylands, the Southall concern was going to suffer very severely and at this late date one can only contemplate the sort of confidential conversations that must have been carried on behind the scenes for in next to no time Rackham took up a similar post with his old firm and the sales and development war which for years was waged between Leyland and Southall was well and truly on.

The new AEC Regal I single-deck and Regent I double-deck chassis were Southall's answer to the Tiger and Titan and I have included in these pages a series of

illustrations taken from old maintenance manuals which fortunately remain in our possession to show just how many points of similarity there are and particularly so in their respective power units.

That which is to be found in our old Red Bus is the original Southall 6.12litre offering type A130 with six cylinders, 100mm (3.937in) bore x 130mm (5.118in) stroke, an old RAC rating of 37.2hp and a maximum power output of 95bhp obtainable from an engine that can run up to 3,000rpm. The design incorporated the Titan style overhead camshaft contained in a single cylinder head and separate crankcases and cylinder blocks with the main bearing securing bolts coming up through the top of the crankcase to provide the block fixing so as to relieve the crankcase of almost all the combustion forces. Other similarities are to be found in the method of mounting the carburettor and induction manifold, the latter being provided with a hot spot to improve the prospects of earlier petrol vapourisation in colder times of the year but there were certain improvements which had obviously been dictated by experience, not the least of these was the more forward position of the AEC engine which resulted in the radiator being virtually flush with the front of the frame and more room being made available behind the bulkhead for the bodywork with a resulting dimension of 20ft 6in on a Regent and either 21ft 4in or 22ft 6.5in on a Regal depending on whether one chose the 25ft 9in or 27ft long version. All Regal wheelbases though were to 17ft axle centres whilst on the Regent the figure was 15ft 6.5in.

It is pertinent to mention here that like all buses of the period, these machines were equipped as standard with a starting handle, a device that does not now figure in 1979 specifications, but then neither do the ranges of neatly punched holes that could be found until about 1950 in the back panels of very many buses, holes produced when a bus being taken into a parking bay skidded on a damp floor and came finally to rest with its starting handle embedded in the one in front when a very surreptitious reversal was the order of the day. This starting handle was not, though, added for ornament or emergencies, but for a rather sterner purpose for the book of rules indicated that on a cold morning the choke should be pulled and the engine TURNED OVER BY HAND A FEW TIMES before one had recourse to the starter button that reposed on the dash. Here, though, could be a problem.

With a bus petrol engine in fair trim guzzling fuel at the rate of, say, 5.5mile/gal it was obviously uneconomic to proceed further than was absolutely necessary with the richer mixture this device provided so the choke control instead of being as on the Leyland version on the cab side was brought out at the front of the radiator hard by the near side dumb iron where it could simply never be forgotten but, by the same token, it just was not possible for one man to pull the choke out and turn the engine over, and not very easy for two either as the pull rod was in the way of any 'cranker' and quite heavily spring laden into the off position.

Despite all this starting, our Regal which doesn't receive all that much attention, is never difficult. We forget the handle, have an exterior assistant on the choke, set the ignition lever – that is on the cab side – in the appropriate position, switch on the ignition, push the button, wait for three 'whirrs' and off she goes. Then comes the difficult bit. You cannot drive off down the road with a chap racing in front holding the choke so you gingerly tread the accelerator position – yes, it is offside of the brake and clutch pedals, and move slowly away to

sundry misses, backfires and oft times major explosions. At this stage, changing gear can be decidedly difficult, not that it is ever truly easy as the box which has some delightfully simple innards is of the crash variety but eventually that hot spot does its stuff when the driver finds the heat transfers to the cab but cog swopping is a lot less troublesome. All this leads one to suppose that a lot of early morning AEC bus drivers must have had their moments in earlier years for Southall perpetuated the arrangement for some considerable time, but once you become accustomed to all the local hazards, driving a petrol-engined Regal can be quite good fun – as a part-time pastime that is.

Certainly the bus we have is no mean performer. It is quite quiet, will run up to around 50mph and has very smooth brakes of the vacuum-assisted form with a series of rods running to each of the front and rear brake assemblies, and some similar ironmongery connecting up the clutch pedal, and the operating lever. This to modern eyes looks somewhat antedeluvian but then you look under the cab floor from the outside and see that just above the axle beam above the offside spring are three large wing nuts which give instant adjustment for the foot brake, the hand brake and the clutch in marked contrast to later versions that involved a great deal of expensive fitting time.

Our old Regal chassis number 6621015 has 32 seats, weighs around 4ton 19cwt 2qtr and could almost certainly do a day's work on service and keep time, only a conductor would have to be carried, but whether the corresponding Regent would, if we had one, is open to doubt as these were virtually identical except that a lower rear axle ratio of $7\frac{1}{3}$ to 1 could be obtained in lieu of the higher $6\frac{1}{4}$ version that also figured on the Regal as an alternative to the $5\frac{1}{4}$ to 1 gearing that was favoured if an

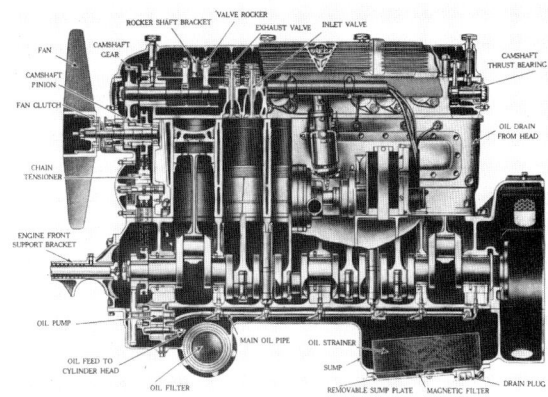

Above: Partial cross sectional view through an AEC petrol engine of the period. The overhead camshaft and the horizontal tube which carries the plug leads across the front of the engine are clearly to be seen. Note how the leads run into the rear end of the magneto and the way in which the housing for the points will prevent any mechanic from having a good view as to what might be happening therein.

operator was involved in coaching or other high speed work, and so the power to weight ratio would not be so advantageous.

AEC though quickly followed up this possible failing as by boring out the cylinders to 110mm, a 7.4litre unit was produced; various double-deckers including the early versions of the three-axle Renowns being so fitted and then in 1932 another version of this 110mm unit was offered with the so called 'higher power head' which as the A162 model could provide 120bhp at 2,400rpm and at this stage petrol engine development for full size buses

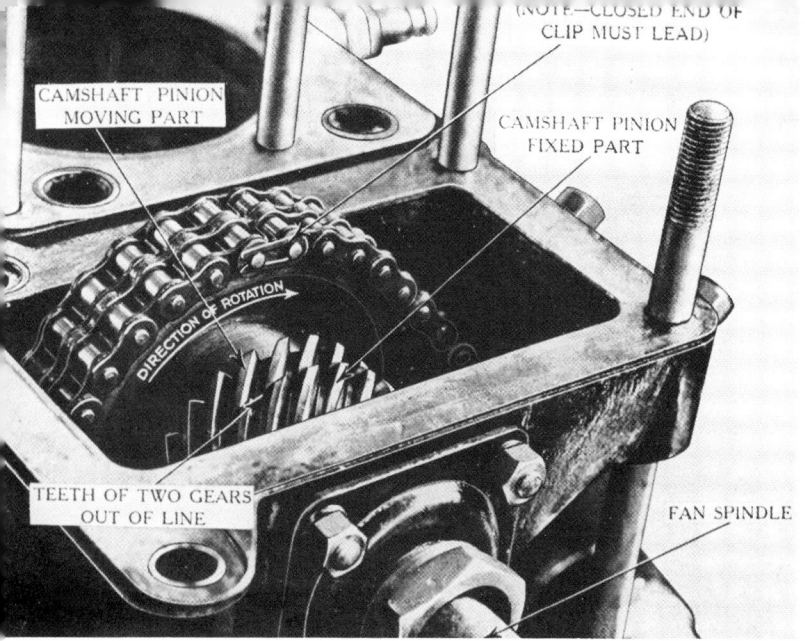

CAMSHAFT PINION MOVING PART

CAMSHAFT PINION FIXED PART

DIRECTION OF ROTATION

TEETH OF TWO GEARS OUT OF LINE

FAN SPINDLE

(NOTE—CLOSED END OF CLIP MUST LEAD)

Left: Removing the camshaft indicator cover revealed the very ingenious split camshaft pinion which was designed to take up back lash and also to accommodate differences in the thickness of the cylinder-head gasket. Again Leyland engines of the period were similarly equipped.

Below: The method of timing the valve gear of the overhead camshaft AEC engine is demonstrated in this illustration taken from a circa 1930 maintenance manual. The layout of the Leyland version was almost identical for very obvious reasons.

more or less rested until 1939 but that state of affairs was not really surprising.

As I said at the outset, I had no direct experience with these AEC products so I had to turn to some of my older colleagues one or two of whom, alas, are no longer with us, and ask them how they managed with the 1929-1934 Halifax examples, a series of buses that began with the very first of these new Regent wonders.

Apparently, the municipal managers were in conference in Great Yarmouth of all places when MT 2114 which as chassis number 661001 had been completed in February 1929 for demonstration purposes rolled into the town for the purpose of promoting a few sales.

It was actually en route for Glasgow where demonstration number one had been arranged but in Yarmouth it caught the eye of the then Halifax general manager, Walter Theodore Young, who asked if it might have a stay in that Yorkshire metropolis on the way home, and so it came to pass. An order for more was also quickly passed to Southall as did one for MT 2114 which officially entered service there as fleet number 57 on the 1 February, 1930. For 45 years after a reminder of its appearance remained clearly visible for with the bus came the distinctive orange, green and cream livery that was to survive until 1974 but I often wondered if the colours would have been adopted had Walter Theodore not been a Scotsman but, of course, by such coincidences is history made.

The ex-Red Bus Regal incidentally is a member of a later tribe for the first of this model as chassis number 662001 did not reach its operator, Plymouth Corporation Transport, until the end of 1929 when it took to the road sporting a two-door body built by Mumfords, a then wellknown local coachbuilder, so the builder must have been initially concentrating on the double-deck market.

I must digress for a line or two here and mention that sales war for both AEC and Leyland were doing

extremely well at this time and if the latter company could exhort transport managers to 'Buy a Titan and bury a tram' then Southall's spectre must also have been present at a lot of funerals as within two years of this Rackham range of vehicles being introduced, over 1,500 examples had been delivered which is a lot of buses.

To return to this story, though. My old colleagues had, of course, cut their teeth on Karriers and so after I had gently steered them away from that subject they came to the conclusion that those early Regents were good buses but there were a few matters of doubt or contention.

Most of their criticisms concerned the magneto and the associated plug leads for the former was situated close up to the exhaust pipe and as a result became well cooked which did not do the windings a lot of good even after a shield was added later to the pipe. You could

Left: The Regal Mark I chassis was equally at home on either local or long distance services, and this evocative picture which is redolent with the atmosphere of the 1930s shows one of the breed about to leave London for Cromer and Sheringham. Presumably the luggage in the foreground will come to be stowed away on the roof mounted luggage rack which represents another period piece, as does the forwards hinged front passenger door. Travelling on long distance services at this time was always something of an adventure, but an 'on time' arrival on this occasion was virtually a certainty thanks to the performance and overall reliability of the Regal.

remove this component quite easily for servicing or replacement but when it was back in situ a good view of the rotor was impossible to obtain with the net result that it was very easy to fall into a trap. The firing order was the conventional 1,5,3,6,2,4 but you could time 1 correctly and then run off the rest of the leads from the distributor to the plugs in reverse order. It was then quite easy to start the engine which would run reasonably happy albeit with sundry bangs and misses but as we have seen back fires and cold engines were almost synonymous so the fault could be missed until a service driver had one well warmed up when he would achieve the same condition. History has it that more than one apprentice had his leg pulled in this way as did the driver of a certain preserved Regal who could not understand one fine afternoon why his steed was apparently suffering from a very trying ailment.

There was, though, something else to look at first. At each end of the induction manifolds are two screwed-in plugs. There should be a sealing washer under the head of each but if this should fail, air is pulled in and the resulting weak mixture has to be experienced to be believed.

The plug leads as the photograph on page 23 shows, are carried across the engine in a nicely designed tube but again the heat caused their natural rubber insulation to perish at a fairly low mileage and then replacement was necessary.

Plugs were another continual source of trouble as they would oil up at regular intervals even though stocks of hot or cold running components would be maintained and then the job of changing and cleaning them fell to the apprentices who very quickly learned how not to burn themselves on a red hot engine and let me stress here that the exhaust manifolds could and still do glow cherry red at times on VO 6816.

Like its confreres it has an autovac mounted on the front bulkhead and these could give trouble through the

needle sticking up in the inlet valve when no fuel would be delivered and progress thus came to a dead stop. The answer was to dismantle the valve, spit accurately into the seating, put back the needle, twirl it around a time or two, add some petrol into the header chamber and restart when nine times out of ten a cure would be effected.

With an average life expectancy in Halifax conditions of 60,000 miles, the engines were good but within this period the cylinder head would have been off two or three times and the piston rings replaced once. In part, the work required from the unit was to blame but equally important was the quality of the lubricating oil which seemingly had a doubtful ancestry. It also 'benefited' from being reclaimed within the depot which like so many others of the time had an oil centrifuge whch was ostensibly supposed to remove the dirt and sludge to give a percentage of usable material but despite very frequent oil changes carbon production continued apace.

Taking off the head was a difficult task for, as already mentioned, it was very long and very heavy and all too often apparently welded thanks to the carbon to the block. It was impossible for one man to lift it out so most buses had an eye bolt or lifting ring built into the under canopy framing over the engine. Various methods would be applied to lift the head once the stud nuts had been removed from the official spinning of the engine on the starter with the plugs still in through the use of the built in jacking nuts to more unconventional forms but when the head was ready for lifting you fixed a set of chain blocks to the overhead device and swung it safely out over the nearside front wing.

You were here rejoined NOT to take out an engine in complete state this way, and when odd and not so well-informed characters ignored the warning some very odd body shapes could result, but what if the builder had omitted to provide the 'sky hooks'? Well, you set up two trestles one in front of the radiator, the other by the nearside front wheel, put a substantial plank across the two, slung the chain blocks from that and carried on regardless. After dismantling. though, came re-erection and with it the task of timing the ignition and the valves. If the former was difficult the latter was absurdly simple. There was a locking pin provided that after release was spring loaded to engage in a hole drilled in the flywheel. This automatically positioned Nos 1 and 6 pistons at the top of their strokes. Then you put the head on partially and turned the gear wheel which drove the overhead camshaft until a line scribed across the teeth coincided with two lines on the retiming indicator, and that was all there was to it. It should be emphasised here that the gear wheel on the end of the camshaft meshed with one mounted at the top of the cylinder block whose shaft also carried a timing chain sprocket. There was here a neat piece of design for as we have seen the cylinder head could be removed without having to dismantle the chain which in turn made the use of the crankshaft locking peg possible. The timing chain was tensioned by an idler wheel mounted eccentrically on its shaft on the slackside of the chain and this idler wheel contained a stiff clock spring which by loading up the wheel against the chain made sure that the correct degree of pressure was always applied.

There was also another very clever device incorporated in that camshaft gear wheel for this at first sight consisted of a double set of gears but they were double gears with a difference. If you want to make sure that gears are noiseless and have no back lash then accurate mating of each pair is essential but between this wheel and that on the camshaft came the thickness of the cylinder head gasket, a thickness that could be surprisingly variable. To account for any difference here and prevent binding, the teeth on the two wheels were cut rather deeper than was normally desirable but this factor plus their extra 'thinness' would have certainly given rise to some chattering that would have affected the valve events so one of the double gears took the drive whilst the other being internally spring laden automatically took up any unavoidable variation in pitch. Generally speaking, the whole arrangement worked very well unless the components were worn well below acceptable limits or incorrectly assembled when a series of loud rattles would become manifest on starting up.

The full length cylinder head was essential to carry the camshaft but this in turn gave rise to another trouble as the heat generated in the engine and length of mating surface could result in the fairly early demise of the gasket when you had all the problems of head removal but, fortunately, these petrol engines had a fairly low compression ratio which helped. The later diesels had a similar layout and with their arrival the science of gasket development took on a sudden urgency that had not been previously apparent.

The larger petrol engines that followed these first designs were also well received being easily distinguishable from their ancestors by having the throttle control rod passing through the centre of the cylinder block and the top nearside edge of the cylinder head machined, but they began to come into the fleet at a time when the depression was losing industry jobs and the undertaking some passengers, so economy was the order of the day. Thus, although electric starters were included, the staff was exhorted to use them as sparingly as possible and in those days no man dared disobey the

Below: Starting a Regal. This posed shot shows how the choke control on the former Red Bus Regal is virtually hidden between the radiator and the nearside front dumbiron where it could never ever be manipulated by the driver when the vehicle was in motion. It does though mean that starting on a cold morning is a process that requires two pairs of hands.

commands of the All Highest and still expect to keep his job.

Provided, though, you did as you were told, a job on the buses in that period meant security and a regular wage and these factors gave the undertaking the sort of stable staff that general managers of today dream about with longing but the stability in turn had a surprising effect upon some of the uninformed personnel. The men concerned were a group of conductors who, being friends, decided upon the outbreak of the war to join the Army en masse and so reported to the recruiting office. Included within the formalities was a medical examination and whilst they all passed, the doctor involved had immediate recourse to his text books until all was revealed. His clients were not exactly lopsided but it was a fact that whilst their left biceps were miniscule, those on the right side would not have disgraced a top class wrestler. The explanation lay in the fact that they worked on a group of routes with long layovers and AEC petrol-engined buses, and always on arrival at the outer terminals the engines were switched off. When the time to depart came around, the drivers being men of high principle, ensured their mates did the cranking and certainly the task of spinning even a warm power unit is not to be undertaken lightly unless it was being accomplished by one of my former engineers who would say 'Look, you hold the starting handle and I will turn the bus' and he was almost strong enough to do so.

Legend asserted, however, that a cold AEC was very much worse in this respect than a Karrier of Volume 1 fame but at least the Regal or Regent would fire eventually, their Huddersfield predecessors only sometimes. Cranking still is a dangerous occupation with a petrol engine of bus size if you forget to retard the ignition by the cab side lever and so if the starter wouldn't work or couldn't be worked, it was preferable to tie a tope to the handle and have one or two workmates pull on it at the appropriate times. Here, most shed men had a small piece of wood or metal handy which being of suitable size and form could be inserted in the choke control wire to bring that gadget into use.

There were other ever present hazards, too. On the Leylands, for example, was an open tray beneath the carburettor which collected any petrol which ran out of the induction port when the fluid was run off to ground via a small bore pipe which ran from one side. If an engine being started backfired, the petrol could easily ignite and I once saw this happen when one of the team bent over to blow the flames out. As he did so, the engine gave a second cough, out shot a sheet of flame and it was only the prompt action of another bystander in rubbing out the burning hair on his head that saved the would be fireman from some very nasty burns. This was something, though, that was impossible on an AEC of the period – another improvement here as the carburettor intake was turned through 90° so it faced the crankcase and to it was fixed a cast pipe that curved down behind and under the water pump drive shaft so that any overspill was drained safely out of harm's way.

Starting handles continued to be fitted to buses as standard right up until production ended for the duration in 1939 but no one in his right mind would have used them to start the diesels that came into stock from 1933.

Below: After trying out the very first Regent MT 2114 Halifax Corporation purchased a batch of four numbered 53 to 56 inclusive. Here numbers 53 and 54 pass in the lower part of Pellon Lane. With Hoyal bodies they dated from November 1929 and like most buses of the day were only 7ft 6in wide. Even so, passing one of the 3ft 6in gauge trams than ran up and down this length of road until 1938 must have called for a high degree of driver care. The buses were withdrawn in the same year as the trams, thus having a nine-year service life. They cost new just £1,778 complete.

These had 12V starting equipment and represented the second generation of AEC oil engines the first which were produced between 1930 and 1932 having the Acro head and a capacity of 8.0litre.

Series 2 was the famous 8.8litre unit still of the indirect injection pattern but having Ricardo Comet Mark I heads based on aluminium castings which carried both the injectors and a range of heater plugs. The plugs were connected in series by a continuous copper strip and if all the connections were not kept scrupulously clean, starting was not an obtainable event. Even if the necessary spots were polished bright, you could not assume that all would be well for the plugs dwelt in a harsh environment and technology had yet to solve the problem of producing elements that would not burn out, so an additional aid was provided.

This took the form of a butterfly valve in the induction manifold which acted like the choke of a petrol engine, so with the glow plugs on and the valve in, you had fuel oil in sprays, plus heat, plus not too much air. The trick here was to restore the valve to the off position as soon as the cylinders showed some signs of life otherwise solid blocks of carbon shot out of the exhaust pipe and worse the garage disappeared in a cloud of dense smoke which was bad enough when there was only one experimental bus in the fleet. With a batch all coughed for the good old petrols.

In actual fact, none of the garage staff had a good word for those first 8.8s as they were so dirty and unreliable. Much of the dirt came from the fuel which was then being purchased from the local gas works at around 4d/gal, but the gm was delighted for a gallon covered around 8 miles of operation whereas a like amount of petrol costing 11d was only good for 5 to 6 miles.

The staff, therefore, had to learn the tricks of the trade and starting was quickly aided by popping a snort of petrol down the induction pipe or having a flame device often a firebrick in a wire holder held in front of the intake after it had been soaked in paraffin and then ignited. There was also a patent coke stove with a flexible connection that could be poked through a hole on the bonnet side, the stove being mounted on a trolley so that after firing up it could be wheeled along the lines of booked out buses in the grey light of dawn as the depot came to life.

Once a series of desultory explosions announced that combustion had been accomplished, the governor came in and this piece of equipment was remotely mounted at the front of the engine and so not included within the pump casing as became usual later. Here it was not only very visible but it was also very erratic and whilst it did control maximum revolutions at somewhere about the intended figure of 2,600rpm, its effect on the idling

Below: A Ranger. No 132 one of the pair of infamous Rangers acquired by Halifax in October 1932 at a price of £1,270. The 20-seat front entrance bodies were built by English Electric. Although they officially survived until March 1945, they were to do very little work in their later years apart from decorating the driving school. A kerbside guide will be noted on the front offside wing hard by the sidelamp.

aspect was about nil. This meant that hunting at tickover was all too often manifest when the passengers and the body suffered somewhat. The engine mountings also suffered but here was an area where Southall never seemed to come up with a really good design.

The very first oil engine into the Halifax fleet replaced a petrol engine in an existing Regent and was fitted for good measure with TWO dynamos as it was perhaps wisely felt that one would never cope with starting demands on the battery, and the feature continued on the first production batch. The drive was taken off the timing chain which had the sort of tensioner already described only it could not stand the extra loadings so oft times the chain would jump a tooth or two which quite put out the timing but, in later days, a much stronger clock spring – that could give the fitters some fun – did away with that problem.

Much more serious, though, were the bottom end troubles. These engines had electron crankcases which like later Crossleys could and did go out of alignment. Overhauls were a must at around the 60,000 mile mark when the engine would be dismantled and parted from its cylinder block. The case was then bolted to a substantial piece of steel plate and line bored with the new thick wall bearings fitted in place. After boring it was mated up with a reconditioned block and the crank could be added but if you didn't do it that way, adding the crankshaft would induce a whole series of distortions and the crank could well lock up.

The method of fixing the block to the crankcase also had some inherent vice, for the lugs through which the back bolts passed often broke when these two major components went into a dance that was both visible and audible. The remedy was to change the block but not by taking out the complete engine, so an apprentice would be detailed off to remove the cab side plate and then all the back bolt or stud nuts. There wasn't a lot of room in the cab, the steering column prevented anything more than a low crouch being adopted, and the nuts were invariably nicely seized as was the back of the unfortunate operative when his stint finally came to an end 'But it was good training for "t' lad" ' as was the job of replacing a rocker feed oil pipe. This was of small bore and quickly became choked with carbon thanks to the inherent properties of the fuel and non detergent lubricating oil. This fault would register if you started a cold engine and the oil pressure gauge pointer shot right off the scale only to settle down later when running temperature was attained.

One by one, though, all these snags were eliminated but AEC lagged behind Leyland in one important

Below: Very different in every respect from the Ranger was the revolutionary 'Q' bus. As fleet number 7 'Queenie' went to work on 1 March 1934 and possessed preselective transmission and a petrol engine. Body work was by Park Royal and the assembly cost £1,614. Here, manager, George Frederick Craven, and his bowler hatted chairman, Alderman H. Gledhill, inspect the location of the power plant which to say the least was not ideal for local gradients. Observe how the body is chopped off short at the rear wheels due to the then overall length restrictions.

Left: Later Halifax AEC double-deckers were to employ the 8.8litre 130hp oil engine. This photograph shows the general arrangement of a most successful piece of motive power which scored over the Leyland engine by having two separate cylinder heads. The 8.8s were, though, inclined to be rather noisier.

Below: Later Regents also had fluid transmission. This cab view shows clearly the conventional gear lever like preselector lever and the foot stop cast into the change speed pedal that could and did make painful contact with an ankle bone if one's gear changing tended to be lazy.

respect, and that was in the retention of the indirect injection principle possibly because at the time the 7.7litre unit was introduced in 1935 an engine with this form of combustion processes could still attain a higher speed than a direct injection one.

In many respects the 7.7 which actually, with bores of 105mm and a stroke of 146mm, had a capacity of 7.58litre was similar to its predecessors only now separate cylinder heads, each covering three bores, a high mounted camshaft, and short push rods to actuate the valves figured in the new design. This part of the assembly was quite reliable but the same could not be said about the earlier crank shafts that expired at low mileages. Despite the separate heads, it was also prone to blow head gaskets and it was almost automatic that whenever the cylinder heads were lifted, the air swirl venturis which were cast in brass and fitted into the heads, would fall out. The fitters then had to remember to replace them along with the heads on reassembly when a neat 'pop' or two with a centre punch would help retention at the next dismantling.

The 7.7 engine was quite satisfactory if used in a single-decker but its limited power output of 115bhp at 2,000rpm was obviously not going to make it an ideal double-deck mover away from the plains. Nevertheless, more perhaps in hope than in real expectation, the management decided to fit one into a petrol-powered example but the results were predictably disappointing in the extreme and it was soon removed.

At last, in 1936, AEC followed Leyland and introduced direct injection engines. With the change came better starting and fuel consumption and a drop in governed speed to 1,800rpm gave in its turn a better engine life so from this time onwards the 8.8 and 7.7 units

began to achieve mileages of up to 100,000 before overhauls were needed and thus attained excellent reputations.

Additionally, both these engines set a pattern for good accessibility and here was a characteristic that remained for as long as Southall continued to design and produce oil engines but in the late thirties more development work was being undertaken on the existing range and as Halifax had both hills and an all AEC fleet, it is not surprising that two most interesting experiments were conducted under Skircoat Road sponsorship.

Experiment one concerned the oil-engined 8.8 chassis number 0661-6351 which with Roe bodywork took the road on 18 November 1938 as fleet number 64.

A Rootes supercharger was mounted on the side of the frame and belt driven from the long shaft connecting the fluid flywheel to the gearbox. This alteration was made because the 8.8 in standard trim had the reduced maximum speed already referred to and more than a suspicion of diesel knock. The resulting combination had a very impressive power output and a performance to match but as always a price had to be paid and, in the end, it was all too obvious that the crank and bearings were incapable of standing up to the higher pressures for more than minimal periods, whilst the belt drive also proved to be a source of trouble.

Experiment number two was even more drastic. Petrol engines were smooth so from this basic fact was sprung the idea of making an 8.8 engine run on that fuel. The resulting assembly was known as the type A165 petrol conversion engine and came complete with twin Zenith carburettors and twin sets of coil ignition. It was also bored out to have a revised capacity of 9.6litre. How these started on a cold morning was not recorded but

Above: This group of Yorkshire transport dignitaries had just been treated to a ride up a local alp on the supercharged 8.8litre Regent No 64 in August 1938. Mr Craven in the centre with touching fingers looks very pleased but the two technical staff members on the left of the radiator seem rather more solemn. The outer member of the Skircoat Road team is J. G. Timpson who in later years became manager of the Plymouth undertaking.

what everyone around at the time remembered was the way in which the four buses which were so fitted from delivery brand new as fleet numbers, 200 to 203, in the April of 1939 could perform. They were placed rather naughtily on the No 43 Halifax to Huddersfield route which then, and for many years afterwards, was worked by four buses in the ratio of three to Halifax and one to Huddersfield without any form of receipts apportionment being involved. You simply kept what you took. Now Halifax had done very well until on 27 May 1939 the parallel Huddersfield tramway from Elland into that town was replaced by trolleybuses and with the locals flocking to ride on this new and quite fast mode of travel, Halifax takings declined. Additionally, where a Huddersfield trolley and a Halifax 8.8 left Elland simultaneously, they were immediately faced with the tremendous climb up the Ainleys and there was no doubt which would reach the top first – and it wasn't the 8.8 – not, that is, until those petrol-engined double-deckers came on the scene. They outclassed everything else on the road and the trolleys didn't get a look in. In fact, Halifax Passenger Transport could well have done what Jowetts did later with its Javelin car and had a poster put on the backs of these new toys reading 'Take a good look

31

Left: A 1939 Weymann-bodied Regent that was one of four fleet numbers 84-87 to be purchased by Halifax Corporation. Three survivors were renumbered in 1952 and it was the last of these that is mentioned in the text as being returned from a much cannibalised condition to working order.

Right: At the same time that Halifax was taking the bus shown on the previous picture into stock, Leicester Corporation Transport was acquiring 24 three-axle Renown double-deckers. Eight (321-329) had Northern Counties bodies, the larger batch (330-345) MCW bodies that had a decidedly Wigan look about them. With 64 seats, an unladen weight of around 8ton 4cwt and only a 7.7litre engine, performance could never have been 'rocket-like' only the drivers never seemed to complain about the available power. Needless to say, however, the maintenance staffs had much more decided views.

as it passes you'. Yet again, though, there was a price to pay in this instance – a consumption rate of around 3mile/gal so once the Hitler war had hotted up, standard oil engines made their appearance in these remarkable machines whilst the engine design went on to be modified for use in certain tanks. The oil was modified too as will be noted later.

Up to this point I have concentrated on the power plants but let us now turn to various chassis aspects.

The basic engineering employed was of a high order but on early Regents and Regals the brakes were oft times one degree under because of a lack of friction in the rear assemblies. This was caused by the oil seals in the semi floating axle hubs leaking when oil would find its way on to the linings with inevitable results but the subsequent adoption of fully floating axles put an end to that annoyance.

Crash gearboxes remained standard to the middle thirties when an AEC pre-selector box based on Wilson patents together with fluid flywheels became available as an optional alternative. There was here an unusual feature as the change speed lever was not as in the Daimler fitted into a quadrant below the steering wheel but looked and worked just like a normal crash gearbox gear lever and so sprouted some three feet up from the cab floor. I quite liked the idea as it was rather more positive than the competitive arrangement where one could easily overrun one of the quadrants notches but the change speed pedal was a beast. It was hard to push down, had a metal foot pad and on the side of this was a raised cast in lug the purpose of which was to prevent a driver's foot slipping off sideways. With all non-powered gear change mechanisms of this form, it is essential when changing a gear to push the pedal right to the bottom of its travel before allowing the return stroke – a controlled return stroke, that is, to occur. Fail to do this and the band operating strut will fail to engage in the bus bar and back will come the pedal like a rocket with all the force of a very strong gear band holding spring behind it. At such times, one found the painful way that the lug on the

pedal and a left ankle bone were neatly in line when the resulting encounter would bring tears to the eyes, as did one or two other famous or infamous models, depending on your point of view and standing in the undertaking.

Many of the AEC buses that went into use in Halifax came in part exchange for redundant Karriers that Southall then sold off to various London coal merchants or local would be haulage entrepreneurs but someone in authority must have had fond memories of their erstwhile charges for all at once in 1932 two Rangers fleet numbers 131 and 132 chassis numbers 665036 and 665037 arrived which followed the tradition for bonneted awkwardness that had been so ably set by those notorious WL6s. The Rangers were 26-seaters with normal control, the big 110mm bore petrol engine and were intended for one-man operation up country. It was a condition of use that any driver should be large in stature and strong in the arm as the pedals were widely spaced, the steering wheel and column mounted at odd angles beneath a high dash, and the front end tin wear was of such proportions that those 1930 period wing guides that had the appearance of belisha beacons had to be fitted to the outside edges of the front mudguards so that the pilot could navigate up to the kerbside.

They had another engaging feature, too, and here they did differ from the Karriers because if you had the knack you could change gear without even having recourse to the clutch which was fine, only one still required what is known in technical circles as a 'boarding house reach' as the gear lever was set in an almost inaccessible situation.

Needless to say, they were not the most popular of buses and after a short period gravitated to peak-hour use only to vanish completely after the war began but, in the meantime, they had to run up some mileage so the driving school received a couple of unwanted reinforcements. Now and again some hero who had perhaps attracted the unfavourable notice of the chief inspector as a result of some sad escapade was presented with one for the purpose of taking the psv test, and one of my former staff was thus favoured. He told me that he

passed first time but the examiner had a few misgivings as at the end of the ordeal that worthy gentleman exclaimed, 'Thart non sa bad, but wilt ta use gearbox lad a bit more'. As his candidate remarked to me at the time, it wasn't lack of desire on his part, simply that he couldn't reach the 'blxxxy' thing, because the steering was decidedly on the stiff side and, in any event, driving an overlarge form of private car is rather difficult when you have never had one and done all your previous driving on a forward control vehicle with reasonable all round visibility. Had it not, of course, been for all the power available, he would never have coped at all.

Fortunately, perhaps for other drivers of the times, the Ranger was not built in quantity only 101 RHC models plus a further 71 with lefthand drive being produced in the years from 1930 to 1938 against 7,892 Regent 1s and 5,286 Regal 1s in the period up to 1947, according to official figures.

The AEC catalogue of the period also included the equally vastly proportioned Renown of three-axle fame and 1,250 of the 663 variety with a length of 27ft were built up to 1937 with another 345 single or double-deck examples of the 664 version which took the roads up to 1939. These latter machines were 30ft, the maximum then permitted but only with three axles.

Leicester City Transport took 25 Renowns in 1939, numbers 321 to 329 with Northern Counties bodies and numbers 330 to 345 with MCW coachwork to a basically similar specification and appearance. So what had the senior members of my present engineering staff got to say about them? Well, surprise number one was that all these had the 7.7litre oil engine which in combination with an unladen weight of around 8.5tons and 64 seats, plus the Halifax experiences would have suggested that the batch were very pedestrian vehicles. Here, though, one comes back to the operating aspect as there are virtually no substantial gradients in or around the city and so there was no exceptional trouble here and life between overhauls compared favourably with that obtained from the Regents in the fleet. These buses,

Above: The simple layout of the orthodox transmission equipped Regent or Regal is amply demonstrated by this unorthodox view of Halifax Regal No 30. New to the corporation in 1935, it later passed to the joint committee. Alas, something nasty happened as it was descending Brookfoot Hill on the Brighouse via Southowram route and it ran out of road at the bottom of the gradient with unfortunate results.

though, had pre-selector gears so bruised ankle bones were not unknown locally and the even stiffer steering, thanks to the greater weight, brought on driver sweat but so did the braking system. The familiar single large frame mounted vacuum servo cylinder and a series of operating rods as found in that 1931 Regal were reproduced here only there were more rods as each of the six road wheels had a set of brake shoes. The brakes from a service point of view were adequate but when an emergency stop was required and the pedal was rammed down, a heartstopping pause would follow until the message was relayed down the frame and retardation became gently noticeable. Adjusting up the brakes was carried out via the old under cab wing nuts but setting up the system after a complete reline was a time consuming task sufficient to try the patience of a saint.

Why the then popular vacuum hydraulic layout which AEC was also using by this late date was not employed is a mystery shrouded by the mists of time.

The job the fitting staff really dreaded, though, became noticeable when the ride went hard. This quickly affected the conductor who would object to standing on a platform that had all the attributes of a well-designed liver shaker and what this meant was that the pivoting trunnion that carried the central mounting of a rear road spring had seized up. I am assured that it would take up to three slogging days to rectify that fault which continued to persist even when the whole area was saturated in oil at every fortnightly dock.

By 1933, any six-wheeled bus was really a hangover from a bygone era although some of the bigger cities with heavy traffic, such as Leicester, wanted the extra capacity their legal length of 30ft could provide but in that year came a leap ahead with the arrival of the revolutionary Q bus.

Sadly, I never knew G.John Rackham but a friend who met and talked with him has told me that the Master regarded this as his favourite design but, alas, only 23 of the 761 model double-deck and 318 of the 762 model single-deck version were ever built, perhaps because the industry was too conservative to appreciate where the Q path could lead. Here was an enigma for only 18 months after those Rangers arrived in Halifax came fleet number 7 which costing £1,613 10s 0d had a shapely front entrance 59-seater Park Royal body, a side-mounted petrol engine, fluid flywheel and pre-selector gearbox.

Alas, the engine and radiator were too well shrouded by the rearwards ascending staircase and so gasket after gasket failure ensued. Fluid flywheels in conventional buses were also a problem at this time as bellows glands had yet to be invented so keeping a pressured up Q series flywheel which had a packing gland oil tight was, thanks to its unfortunate location, a virtual impossibility. Lose one pint of oil and slip in all gears will be reported, lose two and you have a casualty on your hands. If, though, the design warmed up the engine and transmission, the same could not be said about the passengers and crew for despite the front doorway, there was no door. It can be cool in Halifax and the draughts that raced through the vehicle in mid-winter can only be described as invigorating. There was, too, another midwinter hazard for, as the longest two-axled bus permitted at the time was one of 26ft and the front wheels were set well back to give room for the entrance, there was nothing left in the form of overhang behind the rear axle which due to the reduced weight it had to carry only had single wheels. Lack of weight and lack of rubber meant little or no adhesion for traction or braking and more than one driver was surprised to find that what should have been behind him in the shape of the rear of the vehicle was suddenly over toward one ear or the other, and still skidding.

Queeni, as she was known to the staff, was virtually unusable in either winter or summer and one cannot really keep a bus for spring and autumn excursions, so after doing less and less mileage she was finally sold back to AEC for just £25 6s 8d when only five years old in the February of 1939 after being out of service for eight months previously.

February 1939, though, saw the arrival of more buses of the Regent form which were intended for the last stage of the tramway replacement scheme and a few of this intake remained when I first took up the position as head of the engineering department in the early 1950s.

They were initially standing disused in the depot but as the newer Regent IIIs were suffering badly from a road which was sadly in need of repair we brought three of them back to life much to the chagrin of the drivers. The fourth which had not a Roe but a Weymann body was really only half a bus but that, too, received the call when in no time at all the end result of 12 months of steady cannibalisation had to be made good. Thus it was that I had my first and only encounter in the flesh as it were with prewar oil-engined Regents and, needless to say, I took fleet number 32 as it then was out for a test run. Run – no, endurance test – yes. The engine which used oil at the rate of 104 miles to the gallon had a note of its own. The steering was stiff as was the gear selector lever, whilst the change speed pedal showed me that despite its long sleep it had not forgotten how to fly back when the driver was never expecting anything of the sort to occur.

The engine note was, though, in part excusable for during the war someone had cooked up a so called fuel consisting of one part coke distillate to two parts diesel. This gave the members of the fleet chronic indigestion as the cetane value must have been about zero and in addition produced an aroma that gave our services a smell that once inhaled could never be forgotten. What happened when low compression engines of another make came to be fed on the mixture is quite another story but if some of the early AEC oil engines had been filled up with that stuff, then they never ever would have started.

Looking back, I am rather sad that those prewar buses were so worn when I came to know them for in their 15 years of life they had repaid their purchase price of £1,871 many times over but now they have all gone, and so too has the organisation that gave them birth.

This chapter has dealt up to this point with failings but, in retrospect, they were not all that many when judged against the standards of the time and it is only right and proper that in these closing lines I should pay a tribute to GJR for without him our industry would have been a much poorer place, and to his name must be coupled those of the men who for so many years kept AEC and thus the British motor industry in the van of vehicle development. They provided bus engineers with a Company which as its own 1950 Commercial Show advertisement so proudly proclaimed truly was 'A Radiator of Confidence' and long may its memory be honoured.

3

Some Daimler chassis and Radford power

Gottlieb Daimler was one of the founders if not the founder of the motor industry for he was assistant to the very Dr Otto who evolved the four-stroke cycle now almost universally employed in automotive internal combustion engines that bear his name and when that maestro turned his attention to the development of gas engines took a gasoline unit and fitted it to a cycle, thus becoming the first ever motorcyclist. From this point it was a small step to build a motorcar and by 1882 he had in Cannstatt near Stuttgart his own workshop.

Some years afterwards he met an English engineer called Frederick Richard Simms and that gentleman then acquired the right to manufacture engines in the United Kingdom to Daimler patents.

From this event there followed in 1893 the setting up of the Daimler Motor Syndicate of London and three years later, in 1896, the Daimler Motor Company was formed which then acquired a disused cotton mill in Coventry as its manufacturing base.

Within the decade the plant had been moved to nearby Radford and in no time at all an interest was being taken in the passenger vehicle market, an interest that was maintained and steadily developed until 1926 when, as was mentioned in Chapter 2, the Associated Daimler selling organisation came into being but, after a life of only two years, enthusiasm for the joint approach completely evaporated and so Daimler and AEC went their separate ways.

Daimler in 1928 was certainly a force in the automobile world producing a range of high class motor cars and, of course, some corresponding bus chassis which as was only to be expected in view of the early history of the company incorporated Radford designed and built power units, most of which utilised sleeve

valves, and these were often known as 'Silent Knight' engines in tribute both to their originator (an American called Knight) and quietness in running, the first being introduced in 1909.

The first new design to be produced after the ending of the merger, namely, the CF6 chassis was so equipped, but perhaps its major claim to fame was that the radiator cowl bore for the first time ever on a bus chassis the fluting that for years had been the hall mark of the Daimler car.

This CF6 machine was obtainable with a wheelbase of either 17ft 4in or 16ft 3.25in depending upon whether single or double-deck bodies were to be fitted but the former version could also be supplied with either normal or forward control.

Without any doubt, the most complex part of the assembly was that 5.76litre 100bhp petrol engine and the models instruction book contained on page 25 a set of sleeve valve timing instructions that make quite nostalgic reading half a century after they were first written, particularly as the maintenance staff were advised to remove the sparking plugs and prime each cylinder with half an egg cupful of oil whenever an engine had been left standing for any length of time to ensure sufficient sleeve lubrication for this was really the problem area, and the passing of any sleeve-valve-engine-powered vehicle was invariably marked – and scented – by a tell-tale cloud of uniform density blue exhaust smoke.

The rest of this chassis was quite conventional consisting of an open clutch, frame mounted four-speed crash gearbox, fully floating worm drive rear axle, and four-wheeled brakes, the stopping assistance being provided by a large frame mounted Clayton Dewandre vacuum servo motor. There were, however, two features

Right: Daimler was another old established bus builder with a double and single-deck constructional history that commenced well before the outbreak of the first world war. This Y type with Brush body is typical of the sort of chassis being turned out in the immediate prewar era by Radford and immediately thereafter. Originally purchased by British Automobile Traction in 1920, it was transferred to North Western Road Car Company upon the formation of the latter concern in 1923.

that were by no means common at the time, namely, an engine oil cooler housed in the bottom portion of the radiator and an oil filled vibration damper mounted at the rear of the engine.

The model sold reasonably well. Chassis No 7000 was delivered to Wrays Bodies and Motors of London on 2 November 1928 whilst No 7998 went to Edinburgh Corporation on 9 April 1931. This meant that about 990 chassis were completed in 29 months (for the records book shows a few of the intermediate numbers allocated but then not built), which averages out at about eight per week.

Sales were made to a variety of customers including the municipalities of Newcastle, Lancaster and Wallasey, Elliott Bros (Bournemouth), Glenton Tours, United Automobile Services, West Yorkshire Road Car Coy, and the best purchaser of all, the Lanarkshire Traction Company.

The records book also shows, though, that there were not as many orders being received towards the end of the above period as was the case at the beginning, and the reason wasn't hard to discover because by 1931 the AEC Regents and Regals had joined their other Rackham-inspired Leyland cousins in the market, and who wanted a sleeve valve engine when such modernities were available at the same sort of price, so not surprisingly Daimler had to produce something new, or rather two things new, for in 1930 the CG6 and CH6 chassis were announced. Both incorporated the sleeve valve engine initially but the basic frame layout was improved by being lowered to give the sort of loading facility the Titan and Regent, etc could provide, whilst the track was widened to promote better handling characteristics. The CG6 retained the previous type of crash transmission but the CH6 struck a very new note by combining for the first time ever a fluid flywheel and Wilson preselector

gearbox, and it was not long before the components for both of the latter were being manufactured at Radford. All that was wanted now was a more modern six-cylinder poppet valve engine and this appeared on the scene quite quickly when to provide some additional power the swept volume was increased to 6.6litre.

The first preselector fitted chassis was CH6 number 8000 which passed to Edinburgh Corporation on 20 March 1931 whilst the first CG6 went to the same undertaking as number 8013 on the 8 April, and if the book is correct it must have been involved in some quick body construction for it is shown as entering service on the 20 August. These had the sleeve valve engine for the new poppet valve received the CP identity and chassis number 8004 which was the first such, went to the West Yorkshire Road Car Company in March 1931 but it was not until a further 12 months had elapsed before the next two similar machines were acquired by the Lanarkshire Traction Company as numbers 8009 and 8010.

The last CP6 to figure in this series is chassis number 8171 which was the second of a pair that went to Bullock and Sons of Featherstone in the January of 1936 but, fortunately for the Daimler sales organisation if not for the historian, this does not represent all bus production about this time for a second series of numbers was opened with the CG version at 9000 that particular example going to Duncan of Edinburgh in July 1932 when it seems from a reasonably detailed inspection of the records book that a total of 168 CP6s, 126 CHs and just eight CG types were built in the period up to the completion of those two Bullock machines and one can only wonder in view of their late date if they were made up out of surplus parts which remained around the factory, for by 1936 Daimler was building one of the old time 'bus greats' in some quantity.

This was the Gardner-powered COG5, the first ever

Daimler purchased 5LW being engine number 30486 which was supplied to Radford on 29 June 1933, and the order card which is still contained in the Patricroft files clearly shows this as being destined for fitting in a CP6 chassis, the card incidentally indicates that the engine was fitted with a dynamo left over from an LGOC order, and at this stage further reference to Daimler records is required but these, alas, are not very informative.

They suggest that chassis number 9064 was given engine number 30738 and turned out as a COG5 for County Motors as early as 1 January 1933, whereas the Gardner files (which I would believe) say that particular engine was the second to be supplied to Daimler and didn't leave Patricroft until 23 September of 1933, being followed six days later by numbers 30742 and 30746. My guess is that 1 January 1933 should read 1 January 1934 and that the first engine plus the third and fourth found their way into Daimler chassis number 9131, 9132 and 9133. All these are shown as CP6 conversions and against each is a little note. For 9131 the wording is simply 'records destroyed', for 9132 'originally CP6 type converted to COG5 type for Olympia Exhibition 1933. Sold to Coventry Corporation 31.3.34' and for 9133 'Converted from CP6 for demonstration. Sold to BSA Tools Ltd 2.6.38'.

Quite a number of CP6 earlier chassis were converted around this period to Gardner 5LWs including several for Edinburgh Corporation but the first such change of all, also for that municipality, must have been that which involved chassis 8077 formerly a CH6 that was given a Tangye VM4 oil engine and it is interesting to speculate just how that one went for there weren't any more of these but there was a single batch of buses built for Newcastle-on-Tyne which had the Saurer engine. Thanks to the combination of economical oil engine (Gardner style) and an almost foolproof transmission

system that even former tram drivers of long standing could manipulate without suffering from an acute dose of knotted feet (Daimler knee was quite another ailment though), Daimler sales began to rocket but these sales involved a chassis content only and the more bus you can sell, the more profit – well, at least in theory – one should be able to make.

Daimler petrol engines had by 1935 virtually disappeared from the bus market but if customers didn't want the somewhat noisy 5LW they had by this time two other choices open to them as the larger and more refined 6LW became available from engine number 33580 despatched to Coventry for inclusion in a COG6 destined for Edinburgh on 21 May 1935 and if you wanted a horsepower producer of a very different colour then there was the 7.7litre AEC unit that materialised in chassis number 9196 completed for Coventry Corporation at the end of October 1934 and maybe it was a later version of the COA6 that set someone thinking.

Not surprisingly, once the Maudslay company of that city lost interest in the double-deck scene, the Coventry undertaking turned to the other local builder and began to virtually standardise on Daimler chassis in the remaining years up to 1939 when conditions changed somewhat. Now in this prewar period, the overall dimensions of double and single-deck public service vehicles were severely restricted and so was the overall weight which was limited to ten tons for double-deckers. These facts in combination meant that if you wanted more than about 52 seats in a double-decker, it was necessary to pare down the weight and reduce to the absolute minimum the space taken up by the engine.

The general manager of the day, one Ronald Fearnley, was though looking for increased capacity and set his sights on achieving 60 seats on a two-axled chassis and in July 1939 he accomplished the miracle with the

bus numbers 230 to 233. These were based on a specially adapted COG5/40 single-deck model and were given the new designation COG5/60. In the design the radiator was mounted vertically, the 5LW engine and bulkhead were pushed as far forwards as possible – to allow 31 seats to be placed in the lower saloon, five of these being built up to the bulkhead to give their occupants a rearward facing view when the area in the cab left for the driver could only be regarded as being of minimal dimensions. Eventually 21 vehicles of the type entered service up to October 1940 by which time they had been joined by five virtually standard COA6 chassis which also carried 60-seat bodies but these were to a new MCW design that set the pattern for the lightweights that came out of that stable in the early 1950s. These machines, fleet numbers 234 to 237 and 246, took the road between November 1939 and January 1940.

It would seem from comments made by Mr Groves and other friends who knew these vehicles in their heyday that the Gardner-powered versions were very unpopular with the crews, that cramped cab and the general lack of sophistication being the base of their various complaints but the AECs were well received so here we are obviously back in the easy operating conditions mentioned in Chapter 2, and equally obviously the Daimler design and sales staff had been watching these developments closely for the directors of the firm had come back to the conclusion that what Coventry now wanted was a Daimler oil engine and as they had a car engine designer already to hand, what could be more easy than to instruct Mr Bill Harrow – for such was his name, to see what he could come up with. There are, though, a few essential preliminaries to be thought out before any drawings are begun and number one is, 'What shall the capacity be?' Was it any wonder that the answer to this question turned out to be 7.8litre?

Daimler was following AEC thought here but the general appearance of the first such engines also suggested that a Dennis lead had been followed for the timing gear was mounted at the rear of the engine where it was said it was less affected by any tendency the crankshaft might have to suffer from torsional strains, stresses and vibrations, and the Guildford-designed engines which predated Daimlers experiments already possessed this feature but I have been told that a close personal friendship existed between two engineering executives who were employed by what in certain fields were two competing companies.

Left: After the bombing of Radford Works in May 1940, chassis production ceased until 1943. Then the wartime design emerged initially utilising the Gardner 5LW engine but later being fitted with the 7.7litre AEC unit. This illustration shows the basic layout of this resulting CWA6 assembly. The way in which the engine is solidly bolted to the pressed cross member which surrounds the fluid flywheel can be seen as can the large aperture in the dash plate. These vehicles had a vacuum hydraulic brake system.

A few test engines were actually produced but then came the blitz on Coventry when large proportions of the Radford works were virtually raised to the ground and all work came to an abrupt halt.

The events of the period are written large in those chassis record books. Chassis number 11169 a COG5 went to the Swan Motor Company in May 1940, the next ten numbers are labelled Stockton Corporation not built. Then come further cancelled batches for Sunderland, South Shields, Capetown, Rhondda, Newcastle, Coventry, West Hartlepools, Potteries, Aberdare and West Wales Motors until we come to numbers 11301, 11302 and 11303. The first two of these final three COG5s are shown as becoming Daimler works buses, the last of the trio going to J.T. Smith of Upper Heyford near Oxford as a completed bus in April 1941 but then comes number 11304 a CWG5 indicating that Daimler bus production was resumed again by March 1943 and this bus incidentally went to Cumberland Motor Services.

This wartime chassis followed its peacetime predecessor in many design respects but was rather heavier due to the enforced use of cast iron as a replacement for the light alloys normally used for gearbox casings, etc for these materials were now completely unobtainable.

The CWG5 chassis production run then continued unbroken to number 11403 of September 1943 that also went to Cumberland and then came the first CWA6 which marked a return to the AEC 7.7litre engine that then became the one and only Daimler bus engine until we reach 25 May 1945 when chassis number 12074, one of a batch of three for Birmingham City Transport, was finally completed and here for the first time was a Daimler oil engine in a brand new chassis.

Externally this engine looked very much like the 1939/40 experimental units but internally there were a number of design changes not the least being an increase in capacity to 8.6litre presumably to provide extra horses for these heavier wartime buses and the fact that the production engines which followed were known as the Mark IVA gives an indication as to the development work that had been done despite all the difficulties wartime conditions must have imposed on the engineering department.

The new engine had a bore of 4.5in and a stroke of 5.5in giving an actual capacity of 8.601litre. The maximum governed speed was 1,800rpm, 100rpm more than the corresponding Gardners but the same as the AEC 7.7 engine, and the maximum power output was 100bhp. The engine was very compact and had a number of what were then very modern features. There was a combined cylinder and crankcase casting fitted with removable dry liners and seven bearings supported a hardened crankshaft that had neither counterweights nor a harmonic vibration damper. The rear timing gear drive pinion was machined out of the crankshaft forging and the 2.8in diameter big end bearings carried the connecting rods, these being drilled along their centre lines to provide an oil feed to the little ends.

The drive from the crankshaft timing wheel was taken through a train of gears consisting of alternate metal or tufnol composition so there was no metal to metal contact. From the timing case on the near side of home market power units ran two parallel driving shafts, the lower one being connected to the water pump and the upper one to the exhauster, and thence the fuel pump, so that access to these essential auxiliaries was quite easy. Other design features were two separate and interchangeable cylinder heads, a six-bladed cooling fan belt driven off the end of the cam shaft and last, but by no means least, some resilient engine mountings.

These mountings consisted of a pad located high up on a bracket at the forward end of the crankcase and two vertically mounted 'sandwiches' fixed to the ends of flat metal arms bolted to suitable machined surfaces on each side of the crankcase. These mountings were so arranged that a line drawn from the centre of the front pad to the centre of the rear mountings passed through the centre of gravity of the engine, a little matter of useful development that others were to adopt later when at least one competitor widely advertised the fact but strangely Daimler never did.

The later CWD6 chassis also were modernised. The internal form of the fluid flywheel was modified from the circular to an oval shape that reduced slip and a non-adjustable gland was fitted. The gearbox continued as before with the preselector lever being mounted above a quadrant fixed in an almost horizontal plane just below the steering wheel and the steering system also incorporated a new touch as thrust buttons were to be found beneath the king pins whereas nearly every one else at the time employed taper roller races to take the loadings.

The remainder of the chassis followed the usual Daimler lines with 3½ in wide road springs, a well-braced frame and brakes which incorporated either manual or triple pawl automatic adjusters being powered by the Lockheed hydraulic vacuum assisted system.

For city work the CWD6 chassis was, in my view, the best available in that late wartime period and for two years after the ending of hostilities until it was surpassed by the AEC Mark III Regent that had the benefits of a bigger engine, air brakes, and air assisted gearbox operation for the change speed pedal could be stiff to push on any Daimler, and after working a shift on a busy route a driver would find that his right leg and knee would be painfully expressing their displeasure at the day's activities. Those pedals could also fly back if a gear change was made carelessly, but one was only careless once if the pedal caught you first time on the shin.

A few engines were fitted into existing chassis for test purposes and one of those 60-seat Coventry buses

Above: As the war came to an end it was possible to produce some wartime style chassis with the Daimler engine that had been in the process of gestation since 1938 but had grown up in that time from a 7.7litre unit to one having a capacity of 8.6litre. This Daimler CWD-6 went into service with Rochdale Corporation in 1945 and could well have been the first Daimler powered to be boarded by the author. It ran beautifully, but alas that wartime timber did less than nothing to promote a long and healthy body.

Right: The Daimler engine was a compact unit and rather unusually had the timing gears mounted Dennis-like at the rear of the crank case. It was without doubt very quiet in operation but in its early days at least was never able to attain the standards of reliability and low fuel consumption so ably set by that other Daimler engine choice – the Gardner 5LW.

40

number 240 was employed in this way but eventually sufficient material came to hand to allow larger scale production to take place and Daimler-powered CWD6s began to make their appearance in all sorts of places.

My very first encounter with such a bus took place one evening in 1945 on the No 9 Ashton to Rochdale service when Rochdale Corporation produced a brand new Massey-bodied example to a relaxed utility specification and I wondered at first just what sort of an engine this marvel possessed as it purred up the hill from Hathershaw into Oldham with a noise factor that was in marked contrast to the sounds of the Gardner-fitted Daimlers owned by the same authority, but a quick word with the driver soon satisfied my curiosity.

This smoothness of operation was certainly an asset for here was without any doubt the quietest bus engine of the period, and as buses were in very short supply, sales were quite buoyant, a total of 178 being constructed, production ending in August 1947, with chassis number 13541.

The new CV range of vehicles which were to an improved specification and brought back light alloys appeared with the first CVG6 of December 1945 number 12414 which was exported to South Africa, the first CVG5 number 12555 of May 1946 also went overseas actually to Bombay, but the first CVD6 built as chassis number 12691 of February 1946 went to that old Daimler customer Messrs Tailby and George of Willington, near Derby, a partnership that ran the Blue Bus concern, whilst later the same year another famous independent Venture Transport Ltd acquired the first large batch of the single-deck version of the same chassis.

During the next five years I would estimate from a cursory examination of the chassis records that roughly one-third of all Daimler production incorporated a Daimler engine and that half of these were utilised in coach chassis or went for export, in which event the left hand version of the 8.6litre unit known as the Mark V would be employed, but from 1951 more and more Gardners came to be specified and the CVD6 slowly faded from the scene, until in February 1953 production ceased, 1869 normally-aspirated versions being recorded with the last chassis being numbered 18629.

Here we come to one of those intriguing possibilities that could have given the Daimler engine a much more important place in road transport history for one was supplied to the Atkinson commercial vehicle concern of Walton-le-Dale and then fitted into an eight-wheeled goods chassis. The resultant assembly was then used on trunking work and from all reports the Daimler engine did very well but for one reason or another, despite some very serious discussions, the project failed to develop.

I could never truly discover why the CVD6 almost died in the early fifties. As I have said, it was a quiet engine which performed surprisingly well although one municipal undertaking that had a batch found them to be somewhat seasonal buses. The exhaust pipe was on the off side of the power unit and ran downwards and backwards in very close proximity to the cab side sheet. This became very hot, and so did the driver in hot weather with the end result that if you put out a CVD on a hot day, it was sure to be the subject of a changeover request before it had been out for very long. On a cold day the reverse applied and woe betide the garage foreman who tried to bring one off the road and into depot for servicing if the replacement sent out wasn't another Daimler, for that replacement was also going to figure on the changeover sheets ere long.

Left: In immediate postwar days many municipal undertakings that had not previously favoured Coventry with orders began to acquire Radford-built chassis and often Radford engines appeared as well. Leicester Corporation was one such concern that purchased 30 CVD6 units in 1948 for tramway replacement purposes. Ten (66-75) had Roberts bodies but the remainder (76-95) were given Willowbrook coachwork. Here the first of the latter series is seen at the time of initial delivery. These machines were sold out of stock between 1961 and 1963 but are still not forgotten for they, too, had a certain type of high pressure hydraulic brake.

The biggest fault with the engine was that whenever a gasket fault developed and the heads were removed, it was essential to carefully examine the top of the cylinder liners. Almost invariably cracks would be discovered in at least one of these when the liner would have to be withdrawn and replaced but as a job it wasn't all that difficult. There was, however, never any doubt that a Daimler of this vintage couldn't match Gardner standards when it came to fuel consumption but doubtlessly further development could and would have wrought an improvement here.

When Daimler did announce what had been happening, though, in that direction, it was to reveal the appearance of a brand new 'super' chassis type coded the CD650, and within this was an equally super 650cu in engine with a 5in bore and 5.5in stroke that could produce 125bhp at 1,700rpm.

As I have mentioned, Daimler at the time was involved in a great deal of export work and one of the most important overseas markets was the South African one but various customers there indicated that they would like rather more power than either the 8.6 engine or the Gardner 6LW could provide and so this new design was intended to satisfy their requirements and also provide a home market competitor to the AEC 9.6litre engine or its 9.8litre O600 Leyland counterpart. Consequently, a CD650 chassis was shown at the 1950 Earls Court Exhibition, and there it was seen and admired by two gentlemen whose decision to purchase a batch of six at £1,900 each was to give this author one or two interesting moments in the days to come.

These not to be identified individuals wanted a bus that could stand up to the rigours of a number of almost mountainous routes which came complete with miles of indifferent road surfaces so their thoughts were fixed firmly on the massive and in this respect at least they couldn't go wrong with a CD650.

The massive aspect started at the front with a radiator that was deeper, wider and thicker than anything Radford had employed before and the cost of these as a spare even in 1951 when ours were completed bordered on the astronomical. Behind the radiator was the engine which had all the looks of the 8.6 and about twice the size. Behind the engine was a large fluid flywheel and thence the drive was passed through the usual preselector gearbox to a strengthened rear axle which had 8.5in gear centres whereas the dimension on the CVD6 was 8in.

The front axle was of similar generous dimensions as were the 4in wide road springs and the whole was contained within an extremely robust chassis frame that was doubled so as to form a box from the front of the assembly to well behind the front spring rear shackle bracket. This was never ever going to sag in old age even if you had a triple decker body mounted but now we come to the bad news.

One correspondent has told me how in his Karrier days the test drivers prayed before they ever took one of their charges up a certain test hill that the beast wouldn't boil and they would reach the summit without undue

Above: Oldham was another town to take Daimlers after World War 2 of the CVD6 type. Of 25 such buses, fleet numbers 312-321 had the almost invariable Roe body, but fleet numbers 322 to 336 struck a very different note in possessing Crossley bodies with their Manchester style contours. Here 325, photographed by Bob Mack, leaves the former Shaw Wrens Nest tramway terminus on the long route 8 to Hollinwood. The Hollinwood cars were superseded by buses in 1939 after the war had begun; the standards unlike the rails were to last for another 25 years.

difficulty. Had they been in charge of CD650s no such appeal to heaven would have been necessary for it was at the top that they should have sunk to their knees for these buses had a high pressure hydraulic brake system that has soured for all time my attitude to such devices.

There was under the bonnet a large horizontal drum like container that held numerous gallons of best quality and highly priced hydraulic system fluid. This was drawn on starting the engine by a seven plunger radial pump and forced under pressure into one of two frame mounted accumulators that looked like bombs and had all the pent up explosive force therein of overripe gelignite. These hollow forged accumulators contained a rubber bag with a very special air line connection at the open end only of course it wasn't open the edges being securely fixed to the end cover of the accumulator so you could take out and renew the bag whenever such action became necessary which it did at very frequent occasions.

These air bags were then inflated to a pressure of 500lb/sq in by an outside air line, when after the engine was started, they were compressed by the fluid being forced in by the pump through an oil connection at the

Lockheed fluid pump unit included in illustration as an example of additional driven auxiliary.

Left: After the CVD6 came the fascinating CD650. The 10.6 Daimler engine that powered these highly individualistic buses was generally similar in appearance to the earlier 8.4 unit but gave a 10-league boot performance. These air filters with their dubious inners are prominent above the rocker box covers as is the dipstick in its long supporting tube.

Below: One of the CD650 buses acquired by Halifax Corporation in 1951. There were six of these numbered from 81 to 86 and all had very attractive East Lancashire bodywork. If only these vehicles had had a well-designed air braking system they would probably still be running for mechanically they bordered on the indestructible. The size of the radiator will be noted. Doubtlessly designed for tropical climes, it could have been reduced for use in Yorkshire, but, as it was, it gave the assembly a very distinctive and impressive appearance.

other end until when both accumulators were charged to a limit of 1,200lb/sq in the cut-out valve cut out and there was your potential braking force all ready and waiting.

It waited until the brake pedal was depressed when a fiendishly ingenious valve was supposed to match the fluid pressure in the brake lines to that being exerted by the driver's right foot on the pedal so as to provide a fully proportional and progressive stop. 'Ha, Ha!' When, of course, the pressure had fallen off somewhat 900lb/sq in was the designed figure in would come the pump again and restore the full working pressure, but pressure went elsewhere than down the brake lines.

Wanting to produce a thoroughly modern bus, Daimler had included a fluid power steering system and for good measure power assisted gear change and hand brake servo motors – in fact, about the only thing the power system didn't do was to blow the driver's nose, but that individual was certainly going to experience other sensations – hair raising being just one of these.

I leaped into the cab of my first CD650 one morning and drove it out of the depot yard and along a level road towards the town centre where I came up to a rather tight traffic island. I wound the lock on easily, thanks to the powered system, but when I came to straighten up – consternation there was no self centering action at all! I left the roundabout but not by the intended exit for it needed another 90° of turn to wind the lock off and when I returned to base I duly reported the fault only there was no fault, this was a characteristic of the design. The steering was actually quite easy to operate and as you did so there was a steady hiss from the column as the fluid went around and around only the lack of response certainly provided a trap for the unwary, but the brakes were a bigger trap as they simply came and went in a quite remarkable fashion.

One night I went out on safari, had a bus ride or two, and at about 20.30 on a late spring evening found myself

by the Rugby Ground. There was a match on and a line of double-deckers were waiting to take the faithful back home – the first bus in the queue being a 650. I paused to have a word with the driver who was propping up that imposing radiator when the match ended and the fans streamed out about 90 scrambling on board so I told the driver to give his overwhelmed mate a hand at the back whilst I took the vehicle down to town. Consequently, I started the engine, engaged second and pulled away along the level approach road to the main street about three hundred yards away. As I approached the junction the brakes were working beautifully but then as I began to make the left-hand turn, the pedal suddenly went solid and we began, thanks to gravity, to accelerate. The road from that point dropped down quite steeply and very close to the bottom of the hill was a concealed right angle junction controlled by traffic lights. The more I pushed

43

the pedal the harder it went so I stayed in second and took a firm grip on the hand brake lever 'just in case'. The buses behind were all AEC air-braked Regents and they began to shoot past much to the chagrin of my passengers who began to express their lack of appreciation of their driver's lack of speed by some very basic words and gestures, but if I had let go we could well still be travelling.

As we came to the lights, thanks to the preselector feature I managed to engage first which didn't help the lot of the odd forty or so standing passengers, but this must have shaken more than those individuals for suddenly the brakes came back from wherever they had been when the equilibrium of the fans was disturbed yet again.

We had the vehicle minutely examined the following morning but no apparent fault was discernible but this was by no means unusual. What was unusual was to have none of the six on the brake pits at any one time for all

sorts of problems were encountered. We even had high pressure pipes blowing out of their connections and the usage of hydraulic fluid began to equal the amount of gallonage taken on by way of fuel and at 6.5mile/gal that was by no means inconsiderable.

In the end we operated on the system firstly taking out the power steering column and fitting a standard CVG6 assembly which was re-engineered to fit. Then we took off the change speed servo motor and rejigged the linkage to provide a reasonable pedal loading. Then we did the same with the handbrake servo only here we had a problem as one needed an efficient brake to give the almost mandatory 30% efficiency demanded by the MoT vehicle examiners only increasing the overall leverage only reduced the period that could elapse between brake adjustments being required. We eventually made up some relay levers that fitted nearly into the old servo mounting brackets and found to our delight that we had success on a plate.

Then came the interesting part as those old bag type accumulators came off, and piston ones went on, in which the incoming fluid had to push up the cylinder a spring-loaded piston which somehow seemed a whole lot safer. We then threw away every remaining oil seal, flushed out every valve tank and pipe and refilled the reservoir with a specially formulated mineral oil that was a fraction of the fluid price which had been costing some £150 pa, per bus in 1955 coinage.

After all that, they did not see the brake pits but just as often instead we had an engine problem to investigate.

Now these engines had seven league boots, so much so that I found a driver one night doing something quite

Below: In 1957 a Birmingham bus was fitted with a turbocharged CVD engine and then despatched to Halifax for trials against one of the native CD650s. Here the vehicle which was laden with test weights prepares to leave Halifax Bus Station for Sowerby when it would follow the service vehicle, stopping and starting as it did. The writer who was involved in all this came to the definite conclusion that if he could have had his choice, more naturally-aspirated 10.6litre engines would have been the order of the day.

incredible. An ex-tramway man with the nickname 'ONE NOTCH' which apparently referred to his former tramway style of driving, he started away from rest in TOP gear and when the bus was moving then changed DOWN TO THIRD. I sat in a seat in the middle of the lower saloon on boarding and couldn't immediately understand why things sounded wrong. I then moved to the offside front seat and saw our pilot manipulating the selector lever, a lever which on the CD650 was now housed in a neat box complete with positive gate à la Regent or Regal and here was the first departure from the original Daimler quadrant arrangement that in my view was nowhere near as satisfactory. This action of the driver would never have been possible on any lesser breed but that CD650 took it all in its stride and never made any complaint, unlike the fleet engineer – but that's another story.

Now the engines had some inherent vice at first but we had begun to believe all this had been eliminated, which was foolish. We initially had the air filter packs being sucked down into the inlet manifolds and hence the cylinders which didn't do a lot of good and the connecting rods neatly opened out along the hole drilled down the middle to feed oil from the bit to little ends when some very nasty noises resulted but the new noise was the worst of all.

One vehicle was running light down a hill but couldn't have been going fast for as we have seen the stopping power didn't encourage speeding in such circumstances. Two elderly ladies were chatting on the front nearside seat when there was a 'swoosh' a sheet of flame and as the bonnet flew up and off so did the dipstick leave its crankcase side tube and head in a Bradford direction. Needless to say, the ladies became a little excited as did the driver who telephoned in for a replacement and a spot of garage assistance. The wrecking crew arrived to find the engine smothered in oil from which we promptly deduced that we had suffered a crankcase explosion so the bus was towed back to base when the sump was dropped. All seemed well within so we replaced it, added some new oil and a replacement dipstick and started up to be greeted with a quiet steady tickover that did your heart good to hear.

Then we patted this erring member on the flanks and sent it off to work once more which it did for a day or two and then we had a repeat. This was serious for dipsticks were expensive so we refilled the sump yet again and hammered that bus over every available Pennine gradient that bordered on the impossible but without any repetition occurring. Then we took the engine out of the chassis and stripped it down but all we could deduce was that the oil vapour in the rear mounted timing case had been ignited by a suspect bearing so we replaced the lot to be on the safe side and never again did that engine repeat the exercise.

At this point in time we were very lucky for we had a certifying officer who did not seem to care for CD650s and he vowed that the legal weight shown on the side was a complete fabrication and that when they came due for recertification he wouldn't pass them as they must be over the limit. Now a certificate had certainly been issued when the buses were brand new but the gentleman who had signed his name to the documents operated in another traffic area where perhaps it was usual to take a

Left: A late model 8.4litre turbocharged engine. The installation was well-engineered and the assembly gave very little trouble, making a quiet engine if anything even quieter, but by this time production of the Daimler engine had almost come to an end.

Left: Potteries Motor Traction took delivery of this Northern Counties-bodied Daimler that came complete with turbocharged engine. This was one of the last new chassis to be fitted with a power unit of Radford Works design and manufacture.

Right: In the late 1950s, Daimler began to offer a synchromesh gear box when a 'bought out' David Brown unit was fitted to produce the CS type chassis. Here such a gearbox is coupled to a naturally-aspirated Daimler engine to give a CSD-6 model but such machines were produced only for experimental purposes and so were very few in number.

more liberal view of such trifles. Anyway, we had to take heed of the warning so we sent a specimen down to the nearest public weighbridge which was handily situated at the local abattoir and then minutely inspected the resultant weigh ticket. Alas, our area's official had a point so we settled down to calculate what we would have to do to lose the odd half ton and began by prescribing smaller batteries that cut out a useful hundredweight. We had reached the stage of chopping a foot or two off the fuel tank and fitting lighter seats when the regulations were helpfully revised and so the proposed process of busparing never had to be practised.

The CD6 engine was mounted not only in the CD650 chassis but also in an export straight framed single-decker and, of course, in horizontal form in the equally weighty Freeline which also in the early days was blessed with that continuous flow brake system which resulted in at least one coach taking a short cut OVER an island and at this stage one can only speculate why Daimler didn't do the obvious which must have been to have fitted air brakes to all CD or Freeline models and produce in addition a medium weight underfloor chassis powered by a horizontal version of the 8.6 engine. This could well have rivalled the AEC best selling Reliance but neither line of approach was followed although some later Freelines did receive air brakes. Total Freeline production numbered 634, and 515 of these had Daimler engines.

Instead, quite a deal of effort was put into the turbocharging of the 8.6 engine when a Birmingham bus that had been so fitted was run in a series of tests which were conducted in our area against a local CD650 that was in normal condition – well, not quite normal condition, as it was loaded up with sandbags to give a maximum weight condition – which poses another

question, by making a considerable number of journeys over what was undoubtedly one of our most difficult routes.

The turbocharged machine did very well so we obtained a second engine of the type (the turbocharger by the way was then being developed by BSA Ltd) and fitted this into one of our heaviest CVG6 chassis a variety of bus that had not been noteworthy previously for their performance (well, not in a power output sense, that is) and we were all quite surprised at the outcome. One or two other operators also took turbocharged buses eg Potteries Motor Traction and Glasgow Corporation, the latter undertaking acquiring five such CVD6s as late as August 1959 chassis numbers 19573 to 19577 which were the last of the type to be built.

Even more surprising were the results of taking a second turbocharger and applying it to a Gardner 6LW in a way which did not receive the blessing of the Patricroft authorities but performance-wise it was breathtaking. It was the first Gardner I ever drove that made the back of the driver's seat smack into the back of the driver whenever one depressed the power pedal but what happened eventually had better be shrouded in mystery.

The Daimler version suffered from one problem in that the main oil supply pipe to the turbocharger failed once or twice which had a sad effect on the bearings. One such occasion took place after BSA had lost interest and sold its development programme to CAV so we removed the apparatus and the engine continued to work without any fuss for a goodly number of years thereafter and was last seen as the bus in which it was then installed disappeared through the depot door at the end of its career with us, but I must mention here that we had been provided with a revamped Mark VII unit which had

different cylinder heads and exhaust manifolds. There never was by the way a production version of the Mark VI.

I must, though, at this stage digress from chronological sequence and mention the second CVD6 engine we came to acquire.

Around 1967, our fleet of CVG6s was becoming somewhat reduced in numbers and we had reached the stage where only about five were left in service and five more were in the garage awaiting disposal. It then became all too clear that next year's new buses were going to be delayed and as the only spare 6LW had been used up some time previously, it was obviously politic to take the best out of one of the redundant machines. At this stage however the engineers ran up against a parsimonous gm who was of the firm view that a Daimler with an engine was worth a lot more than one minus that fitting, so he elected a conscripted reconnaissance party and gave the leader thereof certain instructions which were – 'Take £20 from petty cash and do a round of the scrap yards not coming back until you have both an engine of the CVD6 form (for he knew of the interchangeability factor) and some small change'.

Off went the party to their favourite establishment where the owner lead them through and over the piles of junk located in his extensive acres until right at the back of the establishment they encountered one of the most dubious-looking Daimler products ever seen by man. Now it was the Yorkshire monsoon season at the time and that yard was knee deep in a very glutinous mud, a mud which came up to the top of the sump, so no one could say that the engine wasn't well bedded. Our leader knew full well that his gm had meant not just an engine but a working one when he gave those instructions, so he

Below: If the CD650 was the fastest double-decker on the road then the corresponding Freeline single-decker with the 10.6litre engine in horizontal form must surely have taken the single-deck honours. It was a heavy chassis and the engine was somewhat thirsty but my how they would motor. Again, the Achilles heel of the model was that unfortunate brake system. This plaxton-bodied example was owned by Burwell & District Motor Services.

tentatively asked 'Does it run?' The scrap man replied that it was a belter and called for a minion who towing a battery trolley through the mire coupled up some almost bare leads to a starter that still hung loosely on the engine, added a small fuel supply tank, bled the pump and flicked the switch. The engine promptly burst into life when, as there was neither exhaust pipe or silencer, flames shot from the exhaust manifold as did a tremendous amount of noise.

In something of a daze the Führer bartered away £10 and so became the proud possessor of a CVD6 which was then ferried back to headquarters. There it was inspected by the gm – who had some engineering connections – when it was decreed that it wasn't any use spending any more money on it. If it would start under those conditions, it would in a chassis and get one old bus through the garage door, so just clean it up and pop it into a now vacant space. In this manner doeth the Lord act.

Instructions were instructions and had to be followed, and so into an ex-CVG6 it went without any attention whatsoever except, important this, the starter bolts were tightened up, so goodness only knows what the internal condition was like.

At this stage a call came from another sister undertaking which had embarked on a trolley bus replacement programme but was a bit short of motorbuses with which to do the wherewithall. Had we any working Daimlers? Certainly, and all in FULL running order too! The villain then sold the lot at some

Below: Godiva never had transport like this! With the statue of that very lady in the background one of the three Coventry Willowbrook-bodied Freelines, fleet numbers 401, 402, and 403 pose when brand new in May 1959. At the time Coventry Transport was one of the few municipal concerns that had the necessary powers to enable long distance private hire jobs to be undertaken. This was the reason behind the coach style body, but these Freelines had the Gardner 6HLW engine, and so never displayed the zest that was apparent in the Daimler-powered versions.

highly inflated price and about 18 months later had the termacity to ask the incumbent of that parish how they had done. Our Scrooge was so pleased with the result that he actually invited the purchaser to have a drink for the reply was to the effect that the Gardner-engined ones were a bit uncertain but the one with the Daimler engine was indeed a belter and WAS STILL RUNNING, but nevertheless he still dolefully contemplated what could well have been a rather low asking price when the Conference at which this hospitality was dispensed came to an end.

The other offering of the day, to return to the story, was much more acceptable, for one afternoon a demonstration chassis arrived for a short stay. This was the forerunner of the CVG6LX-30 model and was the first 30ft long home market double-deck chassis to be produced, but under the Manchester style fibre glass bonnet was not a 6LX but a late version of the 650. I liked the chassis both for its size, simplicity and air brakes, and took it out over various rural lanes where no 30-footer had trod before, (although they do so now) when thanks to the absence of a body it was possible to see exactly what clearance one had. I was so impressed that I tried to persuade my Chief to invest in one or two for test purposes but he had his eyes set on something quite different so my efforts were wasted and so, too, were Daimlers for when the 30ft bus chassis was made available for general sale, Gardner 6LW or 6LX engines were the standard power units but there were actually two of these particular chassis produced, the one I tried which eventually as number 30,000 was sold in February 1962 to Leon Motor Services Ltd, and the 1957 Scottish Show chassis number 30,003 which was subsequently acquired by Glasgow Corporation Transport.

These two vehicles almost marked the end of Daimler powered Daimler buses but there was one last fling which also must be one of those 'might have beens' of the bus world.

When the very successful Fleetline chassis was being planned under BSA group direction, top brass came back to the conclusion that more bus equals more turnover which should equal more profit, and so decided that there should be a return to a naturally aspirated 8.6litre engine but in part the decision was prompted by the fact that there was not a lot of room in an 8ft wide vehicle for a transverse engine and the associated transmission components and lack of room seems to have lead to the preference for the 8.6 rather than the CD650 that would have given much more power.

A new version of the Mark VII was produced which as the Mark VIII had better main bearing material, a heavy weight governor to bring down idling speed and hence reduce both flywheel drag and fuel consumption, and plain but pressure fed bearings in the timing train because the roller bearings previously used had tended to suffer more from corrosion than actual wear. A handful of engines to this specification were built and used either by the experimental shop or a few selected operators (I believe Coventry bus number 281 had one for a time) and, of course, in that first ever Fleetline the famous 7000 HP which appeared at the 1960 Commercial Show complete with MCW body and Birmingham CT livery.

By the time Earls Court opened its doors, the BSA interest in Daimler was no more and the new Jaguar management wisely decided to use the show as a product sounding board when the more influential customers were asked which they would prefer, a Gardner 6LX or a Daimler engine. The latter was by no means completely rejected but even though it could have been from £200 to £300 cheaper than the 6LX, the latter topped the poll and so the decision was taken to standardise on what Patricroft had to offer.

As a result, 7000 HP was the first and last CRD-6-30 but when in 1967 it was sold to the Tailby and George concern that has figured in these pages before a Cummins Vee 6 engine was to be found under the bonnet but this change had been dictated earlier by further experimental work and not through any failings of the Mark VIII which earned a justifiable reputation for longevity with mileages of 300,000 being recorded before any major attention was necessary and if the fuel consumption still couldn't match that of the Gardner, it was now no more than a whisker away.

The genuine Coventry Fleetline continued from that first chassis number 60,000 of 7000 HP until that sad day on the 30 September 1973 when the last Fleetline left the Radford Works destined for Hong Kong and so ended the bus building activities of a firm which from the twenties until the BMC/Leyland merger had played such an important part in the development of public service vehicles, having produced over 25,000 buses in its life span with 7,224 of these being single or double-deck Fleetlines.

It would have been very appropriate if that last chassis could have had a Daimler engine in it for old times sake but instead there was a Gardner 6LXB one of 1,088 that were delivered to Coventry in the years 1967 to 1973. The 6LX deliveries numbered no less than 5,392 covering the period 1958 until 1973 thus beating the 35 year intake life of the 5LW that came to total 3,230 units whilst the 6LW which started two years later in 1935 and lasted a year longer until 1968, accounted for another 4,429 engines. Finally, in 1937, Daimler took a single 4LW for some reason and issued a repeat order for one more in 1938.

I do not have the Daimler engine production figures, simply not having the time to wade through page after page of the record book, but I do have memories of the quiet murmuring of an 8.6 or the 'get up and go' performance of the 650, and here without doubt my favourites for smooth running were the Roe-bodied, Oldham examples numbers 312 to 321.

I also have less happy memories of those CD650 brake pedals but there must be a moral here for when after a none too long a life that batch of buses left the depot for the breakers yard, each one had a gleaming radiator in absolutely pristine condition for despite all the miles the buses covered collectively, none was ever involved in a front end accident.

4

A Scotstoun
sunset

For some still undefinable reason, I was always fascinated in my younger days by the sight of an Albion passenger vehicle. Perhaps it was because there were in such short supply in my part of the world, perhaps it was due to the radiator shape that was so different to that of the local corporation's almost 100% Leyland fleet, or perhaps it was due to the exotic flavour of the names bestowed upon the various models that were around in those prewar years for certainly Valkyrie for example has a much more intriguing flavour than the prosaic Mancunian, but whatever the cause of the attraction its strength was such that I would happily make quite long detours to seek one out and here, thanks to the relative distribution of sundry relations, I was able to make the acquaintance of a reasonable number of examples of the marque.

It was not, of course, until I reached an appropriate age that it was possible for me to travel around alone and almost at will but this freedom came in the year before the outbreak of the war and from then onwards I made among others a whole succession of journeys between Oldham and Doncaster.

The accepted and certainly the fastest way was to board the LNER push and pull train that about eight times a day traversed the 5 miles of track that lay between Clegg Street Station and Guide Bridge, where reasonable connections for Sheffield and beyond could be made but even if the main line trains were then horsed by such true Gortonians as a Black Pig or a Jersey Lily, which certainly possessed some attraction, the purchasing of a railway ticket meant that one was not going to see many, or indeed, any Albions that way, so if you wanted to ride on a Scotstoun product, a longer road journey was going to be the order of the day.

Now this road journey could be undertaken in a variety of ways depending upon the available time and the size of the purse and consequently when both the cash and hours were readily available I would start off in completely the wrong direction and take the jointly-worked number 9 service from Star Inn to Rochdale changing in that town on to the Hebble service which ran hourly to Leeds never ever dreaming that in later years the buses working over the associated roads would carry my name on their sides, or that even more incredible, I would drive the first Halifax vehicle to cover the route for over 40 years following the Hebble takeover of 1971, but in 1938 Hebble was going strong and so were the Albion single-deckers which then formed a high proportion of the fleet.

This Albion purchasing policy continued into 1939 when three Valkyries of the familiar CX11 form with Gardner 5LW engines and two CX9s took the road being numbered 156, 157 and 158 or 159 and 160 respectively. Registration numbers were in the series JX 6889 to JX 6991 and JX 7327/8. All five possessed attractive bodywork by C.H. Roe and as I was always strongly attracted to Crossgates products of the day, the combination made an interesting ride all that more pleasurable.

Then the year after the outbreak of hostilities, Hebble bought eight more CX11s fleet numbers 163 to 170 (registered JX 7993 to JX 8000) only now there was a change of coachbuilder, the 35-seat front entrance bodies coming from the Lowestoft shops of Eastern Coach Works Ltd and with their arrival the Rochdale-Halifax-Leeds workings were almost invariably in the hands of Albion machines, but in and around Halifax were to be seen even grander Albion vehicles for Hebble

Right: The Hebble company of Halifax was an enthusiastic Albion purchaser up to 1939/40. Both buses and coaches came to be based on Scotstoun-built chassis and so one must wonder how often No 4 actually worked on the long-distance Halifax to Blackpool service. This bus did not survive the war unlike later examples.

also had two Victor coaches of 1937 vintage numbers 139 and 140 with Duple 26-seat bodies and a sister vehicle of 1938 that carried the identity 154, and this trio along with numbers 163 and 164 were the last Albions to continue in daily use being withdrawn in 1950 shortly after I travelled on one working a Saturday evening duplicate from Odsall Top into Halifax.

I could, though, never anticipate these events as on arrival in Leeds I would plod across the city to the Central Bus Station taking in the sights and sounds of the trams as I did so, often wondering as the Bus Station rejoiced under that 'Central' label why the Hebble service wasn't 'centralised' into it but in later years I discovered that an hourly frequency from Rochdale to King Street would take just four buses when no grass could ever grow under the back wheels. In later years after various amalgamations, the PTE did introduce an extension which involved the allocation of an extra bus and it would be interesting to know if the takings have ever warranted the expense thereof but that's all another matter.

Certainly the Hebble Albions, 5LW engine or not performed sprightly but perhaps not so much so as the vehicles of Albion operator number two, namely, South Yorkshire Motors Ltd whose blue buses did, and fortunately still do, connect Leeds with Doncaster.

The South Yorkshire company was then under the management of Mr E.P. Bullock who acquired the original assets from the Winder family on 26 July 1929, assets which included a miscellaneous collection of 13 buses involving six different makes of chassis. The first Albion a PMA type registered number WX 1533 was purchased only a month later as fleet number 30. Four more, numbers 33 to 36, followed in late 1929 and between the arrival of number 30 and the commencement of the war in September 1939, a total of 16 Albions were either taken into stock new or rebuilt. Later deliveries had Gardner 5LW engines the last such

prewar machine being number 49 LWW 374 that had a 35-seat front entrance Burlingham coach body and was new in August 1939.

All these buses were intermingled with the green machines of West Riding or the red and brown liveried B&S vehicles, the red ones of Yorkshire Traction or the multicoloured and multifarious offerings of sundry local independents and I only wish that I had then been fortunate enough to have possessed a camera, but even if I had, obtaining film must certainly have been a wartime impossibility.

A journey of the above form took all of from six to seven hours but you could reduce that time up to late 1939 by taking the Leeds-Newcastle/Middlesbrough long distance buses to Leeds when you still had the walk from Wellington Street Coach Station to Eastgates, but even after this service had vanished for the 'duration', there remained the two-hourly Hanson service frequency from Oldham to Huddersfield and here was yet another Albion customer which rather tended to confuse me as it then owned a large number of goods vehicles also painted in a red livery and these carried fleet numbers in a series that also seemed to embrace the buses so I never was sure just how widespread the passenger operations were. Hanson buses, though, then had a reputation for reliability and speed and there was no doubt that the latter attribute, for one could say that nothing much passed an Albion on the way up to the top of Stanedge and nothing ever on the way down, not in the commercial field that was.

Eventually, though, one reached Huddersfield and could then continue either via Wakefield or Barnsley but it was depressing to find that neither County Motor Services or Yorkshire Traction or West Riding ran Albions most by this date having standardised on the ubiquitous Leyland. One wondered why?

I dare say, on reflection, that the Albion management asked the very same question for the company had been

Above: The postwar Valiant 32/36 seat passenger model was powered by an Albion 120hp six-cylinder engine. Chassis of this type were quoted at a level £2,000 each in 1950 when the delivery offered was just 14 days from receipt of order. The bonnet design is a nice blend of pre- and postwar features.

quite active in the passenger field in the late 1930s when it offered the CX9, CX11 and CX13 single-deckers with a variety of engines and seating capacities, and much more to my liking the CX19 Venturer double-decker that had been introduced as recently as 1939 and could have either a Gardner 6LW or the chassis builders' own 9.08litre six-cylinder engine, but, alas and alack, neither Hebble, Hansons or South Yorkshire had the initiative to buy any, at least not until after 1945.

My trips continued after the latter year when bus spotting became more interesting than ever for every concern was trying to replace as much old rolling stock as possible and as there was quite a wide choice of chassis and body builders quite ready to take orders – delivery was oft times quite another matter – you could never be certain just what bus would turn up as you waited at the stop and who prior to their appearing, for example, would have expected to travel on a Hanson Albion with a Pickering body? Certainly not me, I'd never heard of Pickering of Motherwell.

Such a creature, though, materialised one fine day when the Albion company had three chassis available on the home market. There was the CX9 Valkyrie which still featured an Albion four-cylinder oil engine but enlarged in this postwar form to 6.61litre against the 6.01 of earlier days, the larger CX13 that had a six-cylindered power unit and, finally, for double-deck work that elusive favourite the CX19 Venturer.

In 1947, this had the 9.915litre engine developed from an original 1937 design so from a cubic capacity point of view it was as large as anything else then on the market. Bore and stroke dimensions were 4in and 6in respectively, maximum horsepower was 120bhp at 1,700rpm and the maximum torque of 495lb/ft was produced at 1,000rpm. There were two separate cylinder heads, renewable dry liners and renewable valve seats plus an unusual engine mounting system. At the front of the power unit was a rubber pad interposed between the

starting handle bracket and the tubular front chassis cross member, but at the rear a special bracket was attached to machined seatings on either side of the flywheel housing and pivoted on each bracket was a bell crank suspension arm. Extending at right angles to the lower end of the bracket on each side was a journal portion to which was cottered a spherical member, bearing a corresponding bracket bolted to the frame side member. At the upper ends each of the suspension arms extended at right angles and terminated in a boss pivoted to a fork end bolt having rubber buffers and loading springs between it and the frame cross member. All this was intended to firmly locate the engine fore and aft whilst allowing torque reaction to be accommodated by the buffer springs.

The idea was new but the rest of the chassis took a traditional form with an Albion single dry plate clutch, an Albion four-speed gear box with a crash straight toothed bottom gear and helical constant mesh trains for second and third (top was of course direct), a worm drive rear axle with 8in centres, an Albion worm and sector steering box the whole assembly giving 'centre point' steering, and triple servo brakes with drums of 16½in diameter. One will note the high Glasgow content for in those days Albion made most of its own components for its larger vehicles.

This Albion chassis never became very popular, the Red and White concern being, perhaps, the largest user but some found their way into other fleets and one of my friends has told me of his experiences with the design, although it is only fair to add that there were only two Venturers of this vintage in his care, so the problems mentioned below may not be truly typical.

He indicated that both the clutch and braking systems were light in operation and totally satisfactory from a life point of view but he was not so enthusiastic about the engine. Despite its size, it quickly lost power so constant tuning was the order of the day, thanks in the main to the vagaries of the timing chain. This wove a long and tortuous path around its case and stretched alarmingly so that after 10,000 to 12,000 miles from new the automatic adjuster had used up all its available adjustment and at that stage it was necessary to reset the camshaft. Oft times, though, the chain would break and then a new one had to be fitted which was a difficulty in itself, but completion meant rivetting up the links through an aperture in the timing case that was roughly 4½in x 2in and so not really large enough for the purpose. The water pump/dynamo drive was also very noisy as this came off the aforementioned chain and additionally the lubrication arrangements were by no means totally satisfactory but there was another sad feature in the lubrication system in the form of a tap that was fitted so one could check the engine oil pressure by using a loose

gauge and flexible pipe. Drivers could and did mistake this tap for one intended to drain the water from the cylinder block and being helpful would when leaving their bus at the depot on a frosty night, set it in the open position not waiting to see if any water then flowed out. If the early turn man didn't check carefully before starting the engine, all the lubricant would be quickly pumped away and a seizure promptly resulted so in the end all the taps had to be wired up.

Cold morning starting could also bring another problem as the engines were fitted with decompressors but the operating levers were exceedingly short and located down between the cylinder heads where access was difficult.

Below: The Albion chassis was soundly constructed but the same could not always be said about some of the postwar bodies they came to carry. Welsh Metal Industries built this angular assembly whose constructional features were in several respects as unusual as the appearance with the almost inevitable result that its life was to be rather shorter than the operator – Bedwas and Machen UDC – would have wished.

His biggest chassis grouse, though, centred on the fuel line connectors that were a constant worry but nothing Albion had produced was anything like as troublesome as the bodywork which was to say the least somewhat unusual. This was constructed by one of those immediate postwar 'mushroom' concerns that had lots of enthusiasm and very little experience, and this deficiency led to the radiators and bonnet assembly being firmly tied to the cab structure instead of being allowed to float. The net result was that the radiator did the floating – into its component parts, at very low mileages but this was not the only piece of original thought for the main saloon window glasses were not glazed up in some special section rubber or through the medium of wooden fillets but instead by the old house building method of sealing them in putty. House windows, however, seldom vibrate – bus windows seldom don't, and despite that special engine mounting system, the ones in these vehicles came firmly into the latter category. It isn't every bus that leaves a trail of broken glass along its line of route but as I have remarked, these were unusual vehicles.

Despite the low sales figures of the CX19 and friends Albion persevered, and in 1948 brought out two new passenger models. The CX39 Valiant was a 17ft 6in wheelbase single-deck chassis that could accept bodywork with a maximum of 36 seats on the 22ft 7in frame length available behind the bulkhead whilst the CX37 was the corresponding double-deck version. Both continued to feature the 120bhp 9.9litre engine plus the spring loaded bell crank style mountings, but various detailed improvements had been incorporated the most noticeable of which were a new and quite majestic radiator design with a fascinating method of securing the filler cap, and neater bonnets and nearside front wing. A five-speed overdrive gear box was also offered as an alternative to the four-speed version and the former was, or so Albion publicity proclaimed, able to raise the road speed by up to 50%.

South Yorkshire took one CX19 which as fleet number 56, registration number GWT 631, had a Strachans

Below: Shortly before the Albion/Leyland takeover, Albion designed and built two highly unorthodox underfloor-engined bus chassis that incorporated an eight-cylinder horizontally-opposed diesel engine. This photograph clearly shows all the more interesting features. The radiator was mounted at the front partially due to lack of space under the frame and partially as a result of the extra cooling provision demanded by the engine layout.

lowbridge 55-seat body and first entered service on 17 December 1947. This, needless to say, soon became a firm favourite but it was displaced in my affections when South Yorkshire's last Albion purchases took the road as fleet numbers 70 and 71 on 2 February 1950. They, too, had Strachans 55-seat lowbridge bodywork but this was to a much more luxurious pattern and being based on the CX37 chassis which was complete with the five-speed box gave a much more sparkling performance. A ride along the Great North Road when on the long downwards gradient into Doncaster was invariably most exhilarating and so I always looked out for JWR 874 and JWR 875. Both buses were withdrawn on 25 May 1967, 70 being broken up and 71 being preserved, and in my view the Leeds to Doncaster route was from that time very much the poorer for their disappearance particularly as the next double-deck acquisitions were the almost inevitable Leylands.

These last Albions were despite their conventional specification somewhat expensive for in February 1950 the Scottish company quoted my engineer friend £2,000 each for a batch of three chassis which were to have the five-speed gear box, 24Volt electrics, 39gal fuel tanks and drop framed chassis extensions. The quote also indicated that delivery could be made in a record time of THREE WEEKS from receipt of order so presumably they were then standing completed in stock but, in the event, the business was placed elsewhere.

The CX37 and the CX39 were the Company's swan song for in 1951 the concern was taken over by Leyland Motors Ltd as a first step in the process that was eventually to lead to the formation of the British Leyland conglomorate and, as a result, we were deprived of

Venturers (Glasgow taking the last 25 examples to be built), individuality and unorthodoxy for Albion was then actively experimenting with a new and most unusual chassis. Known as the KP71NW it had an Albion 9.76litre 4.25in bore 5.25in stroke eight-cylindered horizontally opposed oil engine that had banks of four cylinders plus the four plunger fuel pump therefor mounted on each side of the split crankcase.

I never met one of the two prototypes which after construction were used on very different types of work, for FYS 495 received a two-door Scottish Aviation body and went to work with Glasgow Corporation whilst BSD 470 was fitted with the last Scottish Aviation body ever built and as a quite luxurious 30-seater was operated by Western SMT on the overnight Scotland to London services until late in 1955 when it was returned to the makers and then used on the Scotstoun to Yoker works shuttle.

Little or nothing was ever published about them but a former chief engineer of the company who was involved in their development on hearing of my interest kindly presented me with the accompanying photographs and told me something of the automotive engineering thought that lay behind them.

The strength of the chassis side members will be noted together with the neat way in which they were splayed out behind the rear wheels to accommodate the spare tyre. Then to provide the desirable straight running propellor shaft an overhead worm rear axle has been utilised and presumably this was based on the design used in more conventional passenger chassis of the day. There was the usual Albion five-speed constant mesh gear but again the engine was very far from conventional

Right: One of the two chassis was given an Alexander body and then was used experimentally on the London service of Western SMT. The vehicle was later returned to Albions and used on a Scotstoun workers service where it was snapped by Bob Mack. The other was bodied by Scottish Aviation and used for a time on stage carriage work by Glasgow Corporation Transport. Here the ex-Western SMT machine BSD 470 is seen in its later Albion days in Glasgow.

for not only was it horizontally opposed but possessed on the offside at the front a remotely mounted combined oil reservoir and cooler for sump temperatures in all horizontal engines are invariably higher than in similar vertical types, but make that horizontal engine horizontally opposed and oil gets hotter than ever. The unorthodox postwar Jowett Javelin car suffered from not having any such provision and here we have what could have been the Javelin of the psv world, but if fitting a crank and bearings was anything like the interesting occupation that Jowetts gave one at engine overhaul times then the bus depots were spared a deal of suffering thanks to the non-appearance of this design on general sale for this engine had a built up crankshaft and *roller* bearings.

It is, however, obvious from the photographs that very great care had been taken to provide a supply of cold and clean air on the induction side for the intakes which (on these pictures are minus the necessary flexible hoses) are clearly visible both on the cylinder heads and on both sides of the chassis adjacent to the places where the side members were broken to provide space for the cylinder heads. The experimentation aspect was continued on completion for whilst one engine fired in a conventional manner, the other had the ignition timing so arranged that firing took place simultaneously in each pair of opposing bores so that there was in effect a balanced four cylinder unit but this arrangement tended to overstress the clutch so it was eventually converted to standard.

With the Leyland takeover came a form of rationalisation and so Albion for a time only produced an export type single-decker, the Victor, a very few coming onto the home market, but one day a visiting representative from a component supplier who usually had his ear very close to the ground told me that things were stirring again at Scotstoun and before long I should be hearing about a new underfloor engined passenger chassis that was close to being launched. He was proved right, too, only having my mind filled with thoughts of a new style Venturer, or eight cylinders, I was not expecting the sort of bus that was displayed under the Albion banner at the 1955 Scottish Show for here was the first Nimbus type MR9N. I immediately became rather disappointed. It seemed, too, I was not the only one in this frame of mind for the *Buses Illustrated* reviewer in the January 1956 issue commented that he also was not impressed and went on to wonder why the 'Sure as the sunrise' motto should have been affixed to a vehicle labouring under the name 'Nimbus' for was not that the definition of the noun a raincloud?

The new chassis was very much a lightweight being derived from the Claymore 4ton goods vehicle of 1954 and was intended for use on feeder services or on routes

Below: South Yorkshire Motors of Pontefract purchased three postwar Albion double-deckers. Seen here leaving Pontefract bus station is No 71 – JWR 874 one of the last two to be obtained in February 1950. Both had Strachans 55-seat lowheight bodies. The other bus No 56 also had a Strachans body, was based on the CX19 chassis and was new in 1947. No 71 was withdrawn from service on 25 May 1967 but was not sold for scrap until February 1971.

having a low traffic density and in its initial form included a large number of proprietary parts, eg rear axle, gear box, etc with a view to reducing costs.

The engine, though, was Glasgow-built and had four cylinders with a cubic capacity of 4.1litre (251cu in). It was, in effect, two-thirds of the engine which powered the Leyland Tiger Cub range of chassis and incorporated in general appearance much of current Leyland thought. There was also a nitrided crankshaft, strip bearings, etc. Governed to a speed of 2,200rpm it could produce 72bhp and also offered a very level torque curve peaking at 190lb/ft at 1,300rpm.

The wheelbase was only 11ft 10in and in order to allow a propellor shaft of reasonable length the engine and unit mounted gearbox were carried well forwards in the 7in deep frames, frames that were swept down at the front to give steps of minimum height a feature which in turn necessitated the radiator being mounted at an angle so as to reduce overall height without restricting the cooling area.

The engine drove through a 12in diameter clutch into a David Brown four-speed constant mesh gearbox and then into the BMC spiral bevel rear axle that seemed titchy to one who was used to looking at rather more robust buses. The same feeling arose after an inspection of the front axle but there were hydraulically-operated two leading shoe brakes working in 16in diameter drums which was a credit but then came a very black mark for these vehicles had no exhauster and the vacuum assistance was produced via an Albion automatic bypass valve that was fitted alongside the throttle butterfly and so designed to shut off completely with the throttle on overrun to reopen when engine revolutions fell to idling speed.

Apart from this sad feature, the rest of the layout appeared to be well-conceived except that the hydraulic clutch operating slave cylinder was actually located INSIDE the clutch bellhousing so when it needed

Left: The Albion/Leyland Lowlander was another vehicle designed to combine the advantages of the conventional central gangwayed body with a low overall height dimension, a dimension which in this case could be brought down to a little over 13ft 4in.

The front part of the chassis was based on that of the PD2 but behind the cab structure were very many frame differences. This picture illustrates most of these and also indicates the rather different form of dropped drive arrangement that was employed. The gearbox was positioned well over to the near side so as to bring it away from the lower saloon gangway and under the seats. There was a dropped centre rear axle and an exhaust system layout that was decidedly similar to that employed on the prewar Crossley Mancunian. Model LR1 had a pneumocyclic gearbox, Model LR3 one of the synchromesh form when a 16.5in diameter single-plate clutch was employed.

Rather unusually twin interconnected fuel tanks were fitted on the offside having a combined capacity of 38gal.

The nationalised Scottish companies were the principal purchasers although some went to work with ex-BET concerns, odd municipalities and a very few with independents such as South Notts Bus Company.

attention (there never could be an IF here), rather too much dismantling was going to be called for.

The first Nimbus to be completed was given a 31-seat Alexander body and was finished in the livery of Scottish Omnibuses but as I did not go to Glasgow that year I had to wait until the 1956 Earls Court Show in order to see a Nimbus in the flesh as it were and then I met ROW 700 which complete with Willowbrook body was finished as number 256 in the fleet of Southampton Corporation Transport an undertaking that took two more of the model as numbers 257 and 258 in May 1957. I spent quite some time looking over the bus and this did nothing to dispel my initial feelings for I did my apprenticeship in a place where an overgenerous provision of inbuilt strength was as natural as night following day and after noting the chassis 'featherweight' of 2ton 17.25cwt I quietly mourned the days of truly Albion Albions although at the same time I recognised the logic behind the inception of the design.

I was not, however, the only one to carry out an appraisal with the result that more important eyes than mine saw, approved, and bought, so the day dawned when a certain engineering department found a little bevy of Nimbii standing in the depot awaiting licensing day and the start of a career on two brand new services, plus two more which had been or were to be simultaneously converted to one-man operation for by now we were at the end of the 1950s and economy was beginning to be the order of the day. It did, though, seem to be a shame to see them quite unemployed so one or two of the bolder spirits tied on a set of trade plates and went out for a practice run to return with very mixed views as to future prospects both for men and machines. At last, though, the day dawned and the first thing to become very obvious was that these Nimbii like certain earlier Leylands would not stand up straight, in fact they leaned badly downwards at the nearside front and had a decided tendency to bounce when in motion, faults later cured by fitting heavier goods vehicle type springs.

Before those springs went on, though, brakes were going off thanks to that automatic bypass valve. No four cylindered engine is ever very smooth but if one does vibrate all one normally has to do is to put up the idling speed until any apparent vibrations are smoothed out, only this just wasn't possible with a Nimbus for if you put up the speed you reduce the degree of available brake assistance and if you reduced vacuum production until you had a good brake the engine was nearly leaving its mountings. That was bad for one-man buses usually spend quite lengthy periods at some stops and neither the passengers nor the bus liked the resultant idling characteristics and as a little by-product, certain chunks of chassis bracketry began to go adrift. We lost several bits and pieces but the almost unbelievable happened one night when a waiting passenger rang the depot from a phone box hard by the Town Hall. He had been waiting for his bus when a Nimbus stopped to load and as it pulled away he was sure something had dropped off. Something had, too – it was the dynamo – again, thanks to a mounting failure, but there are several sorts of

mountings and the most important are those which keep the engine in situ.

The Nimbus engine had a three-point fixing there being one large bonded rubber bush at the front and at the rear a pair of studs screwed into the rear engine cross member. One of these began to break off with a nasty degree of rapidity, the fault first coming to light when the garage received another road call this time from a driver who alleged he could not change gear. He, too, was right – in fact, it did seem that only the gear selection lever was keeping the engine in place but I might be exaggerating there. I am not so doing, though, when I comment on the basic aspects of gear changing. The selector box was again mounted forwards so as to be by the driver's left hand and from it a very substantial tubular member ran backwards to a relay beam and thence another similar tube took the striking and selecting movements to the gear box itself. When new, all was well, but before long all the pins in the assemblies wore and a great deal of free play resulted. All this meant that you had to swing the gear lever around before the various ratios could be engaged and if the wear became a trifle too much, then before one could successfully locate reverse it was necessary to open the half cab door in the driver's partition. I had never previously seen a gear lever that worked OUTSIDE the cab that housed it but we live and learn.

This condition could be cured fairly simply but far worse was a gearbox problem we encountered from time to time when one gear selector seemed to overrun another and one then had two ratios in at once when nothing worked. When this occurred the gear box had to be removed from the chassis and stripped down but quite often the cause of the fault was indiscernible.

The buses had, of course, some good points as the fuel consumption was very low, around 11mile/gal on stage carriage services, and as they were fitted with 7.50in x 20in tyres, the entrance steps were easy for elderly or

Above: The concept behind the introduction of the Nimbus was admirable but once again time was to prove that almost every form of stage carriage duty even on routes that are not over endowed with passengers rugged construction is essential if bus maintenance problems are to be avoided.

This three-quarter chassis view demonstrates the lightweight nature of the frame, the angled radiator, to give maximum ground clearance with the lowest possible floor height plus as much cooling area on the block as can be obtained, and the gear selector rod with its relay mechanism referred to in the text.

The 70bhp Albion built engine gave plenty of power and so with 31 passengers and an all up weight of six tons, there was no lack of urge – but there were other difficulties, so one bus engineer was far from sorry when the 16 examples he had to deal with over a period of about six years found other homes. Nevertheless, with more development and some judicious stiffening, the Nimbus could have become a useful traffic tool.

disabled persons to negotiate. Another very good point was the attention paid to our various grumbles by the Albion service department but some of the difficulties were inherent in the component mix and only a substantial specification change could really effect anything approaching a cure. It must also be added that these vehicles were being employed on quite level routes so one wondered how they would perform in more difficult terrain but before long I found out.

Albion went on to produce what was really a Series Two Nimbus reference NSR retaining the original 4.1litre engine but dropping the David Brown gearbox for one of two Albion alternatives which had either five forward speeds or five forward speeds plus an overdrive to give a total of six alternative ratios, and with the new gearbox came an improved selector linkage. A further improvement was to be found in the brake system for the automatic valve had been replaced by a belt driven exhauster so engine idling could be adjusted at will whilst

Left: Two of the aforementioned vehicles were when about two years old refurbished, given semi-luxury seats and a revised version of the green, orange and cream Halifax livery.

In this guise they were employed on various private hire duties when thanks to their six speed gearboxes, fuel consumptions in excess of 15mile/gal were not unknown.

There were ten buses in the batch numbered from 250 to 259, all possessing Weymann bodywork but all were sold out of service by 1967. Nine went to other operators but the tenth was transferred to the Halifax Social Services Department and was altered to accommodate wheelchair confined passengers when a lift was fitted to the nearside.

the engine itself had more robust mountings, so yet another source of major complaint should have been eliminated but those who had had Nimbus maintenance experience were not cheering yet for this second series was to be put to work in rather hilly country where anything might happen. In the event, everything did.

The first crop of failures involved gaskets. The buses went to work late in the year when the heaters were turned on and the faults would first be noted by the drivers who would book these equipments as not operating. The bus had then to be put on dock and there the cylinder heads would be removed and a new copper/asbestos gasket fitted. Before very long after a return to traffic the replacement gasket would also fail and so it went on until various alternatives came to be tried. When summer came around the heaters naturally were turned off but then came a spate of 'engine boilings' and so it was back to the gaskets once more. Now usually gasket fault occurs because either the cylinder head studs are insufficient in number or location, or the machined surfaces of the block and/or cylinder head are insufficiently robust and warp under heavy operating conditions unless, of course, a totally wrong type of gasket has been specified at the outset but in the case of the Nimbus it went far deeper. Quite often removing the head would reveal a cylinder block with a piece burned neatly out of the metal forming that upper face so that anyone who had not known the case history of the bus would have imagined that some malicious person had deliberately applied an acetylene cutting torch to the area. Whenever this occurred, the whole crankcase was scrap and a new one had to be fitted which in effect meant a reconditioned engine and one or two failed at mileages in the order of 8,000 miles which made it all somewhat expensive. Eventually a gasket with a built in weakness was prescribed, but the root cause seemed to be firmly located in the design of the combustion

chamber although it must in all fairness be said that later engine life did show some worthwhile improvement.

Next on the list were rear axle oil leaks caused by the half shaft seals cutting into the sealing surfaces when lubricant would start to seep along the groove thus formed when if something wasn't done quickly, a differential failure could occur due to oil starvation.

This was new, but failures of various chassis brackets continued as of old and spring pins oft times wore badly thanks to the presence of an automatic lubricator and at this point the reader could be forgiven for saying how could this occur if the pins are lubricated on a strict mileage basis. The answer was simple. The Nimbus has a cable driven speedometer and the lubricator was driven by an extension of that same cable. The cable would break beyond the speedometer head drive take off and as the miles per hour still registered, no-one knew that the lubricant poured into the supply tank was staying there until the bus was found to have a full tank after a full day in service or sundry rattles and squeaks prompted an investigation to be made.

The original layout of the clutch slave cylinder, too, was sadly retained and as some of the loadings on those hilly routes were quite heavy clutch faults ensued, so it was advisable to change the whole slave cylinder for a reconditioned one every time it was necessary to renew a friction plate until an appropriate campaign change ensued, and here a word must be said about those friction plates for they were none too large and being well shrouded by the clutch housing would burn off their linings at quite a rate. Here the fact that one-man operation was the rule didn't help for if a driver failed to select neutral when more than two or three people wanted to board and instead let his foot ride on the clutch pedal, the run off rate became even more excessive. That six-speed gear box was also a mixed blessing for it was not as positive from a selection point of view as one would have wished whilst finding overdrive was quite a teaser for the gear lever had to be 'joggled' into the relevant position. The Albions were intended to replace a batch of elderly AEC Regal Mark III preselector single-deckers that had the traditional half cab layout but had been adopted for one-man operation. Needless to say, the drivers did not appreciate all the head twisting that working one of these buses entailed but there were those who would nevertheless ask for an old Regal when offered a Nimbus when any garage man in hearing range would give a cheer. An Albion might have been much better on fuel consumption but when it came to reliability, it just hadn't a look in. A Regal on this type of work would return around 8.5mile/gal whereas a Nimbus could sometimes complete a full day's work on a consumption of around 12/13mile/gal and do even better on a route where the overdrive could be engaged for reasonable periods, but nippy and economical though they were a heavy town centre route was no place for a Nimbus.

Management toyed with the idea of amending the services on which they were mainly employed by cutting them back to suitable inner suburban terminal points and turning what were then through facilities into feeder services when either inward or outward changes of vehicle would have been necessary but in the end wisely concluded that the passengers weren't going to accept the higher fares a break in journey would entail (unless some form of transfer ticket was utilised) with the inconvenience such a break must mean with a burst of cheering, instead a new local sport of management head hunting might have become popular – did I say a new sport? Whilst it also began to be appreciated that a 31-seat Nimbus still figured on the stock return as a bus and so the batch formed a part of the operational fleet but when peak hour buses were in short supply and an Albion did happen to be spare in the depot, it had to go out when its low capacity was appreciated neither by the passengers nor the traffic department.

In the end, the decision was taken to cut the department's losses and withdraw the lot but in so doing it was appreciated that they had been purchased as an experiment that could well have worked and one was in the end asking a boy type NSR chassis that cost around £1,351 new to do the sort of work a man-sized Leopard or Reliance then priced at around £2,100 should have been doing.

As a lightweight rural bus, though, a Nimbus should have been a worthwhile proposition and thanks to its underfloor engined front door layout, a much better buy than most of the lightweight chassis of the day then being favoured by the independent operators but strangely very few found their way into such situations, total production coming out at 124 of the first MR9 variety which were built between 1954 and 1957, and 217 of the later NSR version which continued in production up to 1960.

The Nimbus was also given a larger sister, known as the Aberdonian, that had a 16ft 4in wheelbase, was built to 30ft x 8ft dimensions, and included a Leyland 350cu in engine, this being the first time a Lancashire parent power unit had featured in a Scotstoun passenger chassis, but despite the low unladen weight of a completed vehicle (in the region of 4ton 6cwt) it was underpowered and only 471 were built during the 1957 to 1960 production period.

We never looked at an Aberdonian but we did size up the next Albion chassis to appear, not that it was a true product of the Scottish firm for the Lowlander which was designed to carry a 72-74 seat double-deck body and simultaneously provide the low height single step entrance features of such competitive machines as the AEC Renown or the Dennis Loline was really a modified PD3 or PD2. With a suitably contoured frame, stepped drive line, O600 engine and a stepped double reduction axle, a Lowlander 30ft long 18ft 6in wheelbase chassis turned the scales at 5ton 8.5cwt, pneumocyclic or synchromesh transmission being available to choice, but again the Lowlander was not chosen by operators in any significant quantities, 274 being constructed.

Most were taken by the Scottish Bus Group when Albion badges were affixed but if the vehicle was ordered for an operator south of the border then it left Glasgow as a Leyland whilst, as the reproduction of a sales leaflet shows, publicity attributed it to the Leyland stable. At the time we were contemplating buying a small batch of buses of the type for a particular traffic reason so we borrowed a Lowlander from a neighbour but in the end came to the conclusion that something with a Gardner 6LX engine was to be preferred for sundry reasons, not all of a purely engineering nature.

The Lowlander came out in 1961 and the last example of the design was acquired by the South Notts Omnibus Company in 1966 and so we come to the virtual end of Albion production for the home market for apart from the odd small Viking, the only offering thereafter was the rear engined 16ft 2in wheelbase chassis that was powered by a Leyland O400 engine but had an Albion five-speed gear box and an Albion hub reduction rear axle. Again Scottish Omnibuses took almost the entire output and again the design was not to have an overlong life span, even though the self change box was offered at the end of production.

Very few passenger vehicles carrying Albion badges now survive but I must confess here that I never felt any twinges of nostalgia as our Nimbus machines left the garage on that journey of no return but now and again I find myself driving along those roads which connect Leeds and Doncaster and as I pass the vehicles of what is now South Yorkshire Road Transport Ltd in their new livery which to my mind is not just as dignified as that once borne by numbers 70 and 71, I find myself wishing that I could park the car and have yet another ride on one of those outstanding Venturers, although it would be even better if I could beg a drive for here is what is now the biggest gap in my bus handling experience.

Perhaps, though, the sun will rise again one day in the future to reveal a brand new Albion double-decker all ready to delight the eye of one who always enjoyed looking at 'different' buses.

5
Some Guys
I've known

Guy Motors Ltd of Wolverhampton was brought into being in May 1914 following the resignation of the founder of the company from the position of works manager he had held with the then world famous Sunbeam Motor Company of that same West Midlands town. Looking back on the period one can only wonder at the pioneering spirit and obvious self confidence that Mr Sidney Guy must have possessed for his fledgling concern could in no way be compared to the influential organisation he had left in order to put up his own plate on the door of the somewhat restricted buildings at Fallings Park that came to house Guy Motors design and constructional activities.

The results of activities soon became apparent with the appearance of a 30cwt light capacity lorry that had a pressed steel frame but later in the year attention was turned to the passenger field and a combined mail and passenger vehicle was sold to a Scottish operator. Hardly, though, had this entered service between Achnasheen Railway Station and Aultbea when World War 1 commenced and so for the next four years no further orders of the sort could be undertaken but as the firm was making aeroplane engines and depth charge firing mechanisms after the ending of hostilities, there was a large backlog of new vehicle requirements to be made good and so Guys contemplated a little diversification. Fortunately for the shareholders, however, a projected entry into the high class private car market failed to develop after 1924 and so commercial vehicle manufacture again became the order of the day after a Vee 8 engined sports car had been introduced in 1920.

The year 1921 saw the marketing of a 30-seat charabanc chassis and a year or two later a small one-man type saloon was achieving limited success but then came the almost incredible leap forward with the introduction in 1924 of the first ever British passenger vehicle to possess the now universal dropped frame contours but the welcome this received must have prompted visions of wider horizons and so in 1926 Guys began to offer the first 60-seat three-axle pneumatically tyred double-deck chassis which like certain Huddersfield products of Karrier fame have, although long since gone, never ever been forgotten by those bus men who made their acquaintance or, indeed, by the more transport-minded passenger, a race that actually included this scribe. Wolverhampton and Morecambe were the first undertakings to put these buses into service.

I didn't go to either town but I did meet a whole variety of 1920 style Guys thanks to the fact that I had numerous relatives living in the Oldham area and so we visited that place on very frequent occasions before going to live in the area with the result that by the time I was about seven, I was able to ascertain that the Oldham fleet included around that many different types of Guy buses within a fleet of 26 vehicles of Wolverhampton manufacture and even now almost 50 years later, I can still clearly recall certain of their characteristics and seating layouts.

The oldest of these, three in number, were born some 18 months after I was entering service in November 1927 and they were decidedly quaint for they were virtually the only normal-control double-deckers that I ever encountered. This meant that about five feet of bonnet projected beyond the driver's seat, only that worthy had no cab of his own, instead he occupied a portion of the lower saloon that was partitioned off for his use. Now,

Right: The first Guy double-deck buses purchased by Oldham Corporation were of the forward control type. No 20, (BU 4511) was one of three (Nos 18-20) acquired in 1926. Roe 54-seat bodywork was fitted. One wonders if this was the vehicle allocated to Wilfred Beckett for his first duty as a bus driver. This particular bus based on chassis number 22180 went into use on 13 November and lasted for about seven years.

Below: Later Oldham Guy double-deckers were built to substantial proportions. No 54 was one of a series of three (54-56) that went into service in late 1928 or early 1929.

The 66-seat bodywork was by English Electric and was virtually identical to that fitted to some contemporary Karriers. These buses were usually employed on the Market Place to Denshaw or Lees routes that bore the identities H and O respectively. They survived until 1935.

being modern buses, they had the pneumatic tyres, the aforementioned three axles, two very high steps up to the rear platform and open staircases which meant that a seat towards the rear of either the upper or lower decks could be very draughty but if you sat at the front things were much more different for then you could not only see the way ahead but also the pilot himself at work, or rather HARD at work.

The driver's attitude to their charges can best be summed up by the story the late Wilf Beckett told me during the time he was my traffic superintendent at Great Yarmouth in the early 1960s for Wilf started his passenger transport career with Oldham Corporation. He had previously been in the grocery trade where he had learned to drive a delivery van but when he reported to the bus garage for work on 5 October 1928 his licence was inspected, he was asked to confirm that he really could drive and then he was issued with a Guy BX and a Manchester service route card and told to get on with it. So much for training! Sadly, it began to rain (as it does in that part of Lancashire), a day long persistent drizzle which made the setted roads wet and slippery but although this was a bus of less than two years of age, it had neither a windscreen wiper nor an electric starter, and on that day it was the first of these now essential items that he missed most for the only way to clear the glass was to swing the pivoting frame over – a wonderful source of draughts – and then wipe it down with a rag, only the insides of the cab window also continually needed the same wiping treatment for they steamed up as soon as two or three passengers were on board but should he have worried? Well, not really, for he was only the driver – the mechanics experienced much more trying times.

It was generally agreed that enginewise the four cylinder 5.1litre units could perhaps have been worse for this type of motor was to be found under the bonnet but double-deck series two had an 'IMPROVED' six-cylinder version which did tend to make things more difficult. They started off with duralumin connecting rods which soon began to fail when a piston assembly would leave the engine via the side of the crankcase or worse through the cylinder head when all the engine was virtually scrap. The pistons too had no oil control rings so the lubricating oil usage bordered on the extravagantly extravagant whilst plugs that don't appreciate over-oiling would quickly fail to spark. Then there were engine cooling problems that dictated the fitting of successively larger radiators and modified water pumps whilst the violent temperature variations across the engine which were set up, turned nicely rounded cylinder bores into ones which had a 'D' like cross section that didn't exactly help progress. Progress wasn't exactly helped either by the type of water pump drive adopted. There was a skew gear on the end of the cam shaft that drove both the water pump and the magneto but it was far too tishy, end float quickly became apparent, and then the gland of the water pump would leave its seating and yet another bus began to boil.

All this meant that spare parts had to be called for but

there was a bit of difficulty here for such things as the engine mounting bolt holes could vary on centre to centre distance by up to $\frac{1}{2}$in which made fitting a mite interesting.

The engine was splash lubricated each connecting rod being equipped with a dipper that took its lubricant from oil trays fixed beneath the crankshaft but dipper clearance had to be carefully set by adding or removing shims from the tray securing bolts for if a tray was too high, more overlubrication followed and if it was too low, oil starving was a foregone conclusion. Incidentally, it was usual for the trays to be set at a slight angle to the horizontal to ensure the big ends were fed when the bus was negotiating a rising gradient and here is a long vanished facet of automobile engineering practice. Mounting engines and gear boxes in sub frames comes into the same category only these Guys had sub frames carried on three ball joints one lying at the centre of the front frame crossmember and the others at the tail end of the gearbox. Alas, although designed to rock, they did not do so evenly with the result that the gearbox mounting feet would shear off and all sorts of truly horrible disasters then ensued.

The biggest disasters, though, lay in the clutch assembly. This was an innocent looking single dry plate version that was open in almost every sense of the word. When new they were stiff to work but became even stiffer as flats wore in the operating levers three in number of the 'multiplying' type. When a certain degree of wear was reached, the original lever holding studs would shear off and then about three pounds dead weight of operating mechanism would depart from a segment of the engine flywheel with such force that one such lump I am assured was later discovered around half a mile from the point where it must have become airborne but it didn't need the enlightenment offered by such a missile coming up through the cab floor to tell the driver his bus had a malfunction. Take such a weight off a segment of the engine flywheel and the resulting vibrations make the departure more than plain.

You had, of course, to line up the gearboxes and engines carefully in the sub frame or more vibrations surfaced and oftimes the sleeve bearings within the gearbox itself would seize but this was as nothing compared to what could and did happen in the region of the rear axles. There was no third differential so if a half shaft broke in one assembly, the other would continue to give a drive but not for long. These axles were very small for the work they had to do and so would hot up until an internal bearing failed and then the bus became a complete casualty and some mechanic then found that the failed half shaft that was the prime cause of the days misfortunes was so chewed up that extraction bordered on the impossible, but if you want to read about the impossible jobs, let us pass on to the suspension system for here was a dilly.

The axles on each side were located by two springs of the familiar semi-elliptic form, one looking upwards, the other down. These springs had a common trunion mounting in the centre and pins at either end passing

Above: The Oldham single-deck fleet in the late 1920s included three 39-seat Roe bodied examples that could only be described as being long, lean and rangy.

Dating from 1927, No 30 shown here and her two sisters were usually to be found on the limited stop services and the author has distinct recollections of sitting by the road side awaiting a replacement when his Gatley to Uppermill transport had failed en route. Reliability was, to say the least, suspect.

through suitable brackets carried top and bottom on the inner sides of the axle casings, and so the ends of the springs had to carry all the accelerating and braking torques plus the weight of the bus. They didn't! It was as simple as that, so when a spring eye sheared a second would quickly follow and then the axle would literally turn over when the companion flanges, universal joints, brake rods and sundry other bits and pieces would be promptly reduced to scrap, but if an end had to fail, one hoped and prayed it was never a top one for then everything dropped downwards and then there was fun. I have been told how one night a Leicester vehicle of the same type was heading back towards the depot on the last inwards run of the day. It hurtled over the then Saffron Lane level crossing when the jolting set up by the first of the four lines of railway line caused an immediate failure of a top spring eye. The intermediate axle dropped and turned over when the end of the axle drive shaft jammed between the next line of rail and the sleepers that formed the roadway. That axle then stopped dead but the bus went onwards until the rear axle came to rest somewhat displaced under the back platform. For the next seven hours all railway traffic was suspended or diverted and it is on record that the LMS took a very dim view of a Guy's disruptive abilities.

The sort of delay the railway suffered, though, was almost equalled by that inherent in the brake system for there was a long thin pipe connecting the exhauster with the vacuum tank and the main servo. A driver would press his foot down on the stopping pedal, obtain no reaction and press down still more. By the time the second and larger force was registering gently at the linings the servo would suddenly come alive and wheel locking would promptly follow, all of which must have given Wilf and his colleagues some very nasty moments and, of course, this in turn was relayed to the spring ends with the sort of results already described.

One can only wonder at the way in which these completely undeveloped vehicles were let loose on the industry but, of course, business was booming and so most undertakings could afford to experiment with what hopefully might turn out to be very satisfactory machines. Here, I come back to Chapter 1 for buses of this sort were on display at Olympia at the same Commercial Show that witnessed the arrival of the Titan, and with the arrival of the AEC Regent in 1929, the writing was on the wall for the sort of Guy buses that had been produced in the two years up to that time.

The range had been quite extensive commencing with a small 20-seat single-deck chassis of 12ft 3in wheelbase which was powered by a four cylinder 20hp engine. Next up the scale was a 15ft 3in wheelbase chassis designed for 26-seat bodies also with a four pot engine that was rated at 28.9hp. These two chassis were of the normal control type but there was also a forward control single-decker with a six cylinder engine that could accommodate 35 seated passengers and then came the big stuff, six-wheelers with a variety of frame lengths and a choice of the 43.4hp engine that was also to be found in the larger single-decker or the 56-96hp unit that gave these bigger buses that extra 'urge'.

Left: Another Guy operator was Blackpool Corporation which acquired two FCX three-axled chassis in 1927. One of these as No 52 received a Northern Counties body whilst the other – 54·– sported Short Brothers coachwork. As was so often the case neither of these buses was destined to have a long life and both had been withdrawn by 1933 the year that the undertaking's last Guy double-deckers, a pair of Gardner-engined Arabs that became 82 and 83, were purchased. Here one of the original pair undergoes its tilt test.

For the 1929 Show, Guys produced an improved four-wheeled double-deck chassis having a 16ft 7.5in wheelbase, the 43.4hp engine and servo-assisted brakes. The weight with electric lighting and starting equipment was 3ton 15cwt and it was marketed under the type name of Invincible. There was also a corresponding single-decker known as the Conquest and the show stand also included a Guy trolleybus with the usual Rees Stevens electrical equipment.

Guys was by this time an established builder of trolleybuses having made a first excursion into the battery-powered field in 1922 and going on to build a three axled double-decker for Wolverhampton in 1929 and in actual fact trolleybus production continued when the building of full sized psvs came to an end in 1936.

Before this date was reached, however, Guy Motors realised that a diesel bus was the bus of the future and so in 1933 the first Arab was sold which could be had in one or two deck chassis forms and had a Gardner 5LW engine as standard. The firm was the first to standardise completely on the fitting of oil engines in bus chassis but despite the recent design of the Arab, very few were built in the three years to 1936, Leeds, Blackpool and the West Riding Automobile Company figuring amongst the double-deck purchasers.

By the outbreak of the war, full sized Guy buses were very much a rarity and it was not surprising here that most of the six-wheelers had very short lives, their demise often being hastened by the requirements of the Construction and Use Regulations which were introduced under the authority of the 1930 Road Traffic Act. The Oldham vehicles had their last outings on Silver Jubilee Day in May 1935 when they were used to ferry the crowds to and from the bonfire held at Bishops Park Grains Bar and so from an enthusiast's point of view the local scene was much the poorer for their disappearance.

I had, in consequence, to make do with the district diet of Crossleys, Leylands and the odd AEC, Dennis or Daimler owned by other local municipalities, or the Bristols and Tillings-Stevens favoured by the North Western Road Car Company until one never to be forgotten night in the early nineteen forties.

I was working in the Gorton area of Manchester by now and the quickest way home was to use the rather sparse train service that linked Guide Bridge with Oldham but this particular night I missed the connection out of Gorton and so had to make the journey by road. One started off by trolleybus to Ashton but invariably the through vehicle would be full so then I would catch one which took the detour via Guide Bridge or take a short working to either that place or Audenshaw (the Snipe) and then made a change on to an Ashton-bound vehicle. Then on arrival in that town a walk across the Market Place was necessary to the Rochdale bus stop where again the through bus would be packed solid so it was an Ashton Crossley to Hathershaw (they were never allocated to a Rochdale turn except in the direst of emergencies) and there came yet another change on to an Oldham local. To sum up, it took about 36 minutes by train with a change or up to two hours by bus with from one to three changes.

This night the worst was happening so I was not in the best frame of mind as I trotted across Ashton Market Place to see on the Smallshaw stand a most odd looking grey-painted double-decker. I was so intrigued I failed to join the Oldham queue but instead dashed across to see just what this was and was amazed to find a brand new vehicle with the single word 'Guy' on the radiator but that was more than enough.

I took a ride to Smallshaw and wondered as I did so.

This vehicle was spartan. The seats were of wood but surprisingly comfortable, there were minimal opening

Above: The prewar Guy Arab double-decker was a very rare bird and one of the largest fleets was that operated by Southampton Corporation. No 12 (OW 7234) was one of ten in the series 12 to 21 that entered service between December 1934 and September 1935. All had Gardner 5LW engines and Park Royal H30/26R bodies. They survived en bloc until 1949 or 1950 by which time the Arab had been adopted as the corporation's standard bus chassis.

windows and none at all in the upper salon emergency door. The interior was single skinned, there were no heaters, very few bell pushes and little in the way of noise insulation, and noise there was for the driver seemed to be having fun with the gearbox. We never reached a canter let alone a gallop, and it was all too obvious all too soon that whatever engine was powering this startling innovation was not really large enough for the purpose.

What I had encountered was, of course, Bus No 13, the first Ashton utility, registration number FTC 715 that entered service in February 1943, to be followed later that year by numbers 14, 15 and 16 with numbers 41, 42, 43, 44, 67, 68, 69, 70, 71, 72, 73 and 74 following between May 1944 and January 1945. All these 15 buses originally had Massey bodies (being rebodied by Crossley or Roe in the case of 72 and 74 between 1950 and 1955) and as a result of all this I soon became very well-acquainted with wartime utility buses but, again thankfully, they were not usually seen on the Rochdale service which was normally left to the four all-Leyland TD5s of 1939 vintage, fleet numbers 17, 18, 19 and 20 that were without any doubt the best buses Ashton Corporation possessed at that

time. Of the rest, the few later Mancunians were not all that bad and the remainder decidedly suspect.

The Guys, though, soon began to acquire a very reliable reputation and the story of their birth is worth repeating. The Ministry of War Transport rightly came to the conclusion that some new buses were a must and originally intended that Leyland Motors should produce them but Leyland was heavily engaged on war work and just at that moment an order on Guys for searchlight trailers was cancelled because of the widespread introduction of radar. Consequently the frame layout of this wartime Arab Mark I owed quite a lot to Leyland thought but there the Lancashire influence ceased and Wolverhampton took over.

The motive power was provided by a Gardner 5LW engine with provision being made for the engine bay to take a 6LW only very few of these were installed in practice although surprisingly for a wartime production the engines were fitted with resilient mountings. Behind the engine was a Guy two-plate clutch and this drove into a remote mounted constant mesh gearbox also of Guy manufacture which confused everyone by having the gear lever selector positions reversed to those on any other bus of the day. Top gear on a Leyland or Crossley meant second gear on an Arab, so no wonder that first driver was producing various unfortunate noises. It happened to me later but more of this anon. The axles came from Kirkstall Forge of Leeds, the brakes were of the vacuum hydraulic form and cab instrumentation was conspicuous by its absence, speedometer and vacuum gauge excepted.

The assembly was solid, simple and thanks to the few horses available, far from overstressed but the same

Left: The sight of a postwar 38-seat Brush bodied Arab of Northern General on the long distance Newcastle-Leeds-Liverpool service always gave the author heartburn, the effects registered on other parts of the anatomy came later. Here KPT 267 on such a duty turns into the Leeds Wellington Street bus station, doubtlessly to the relief of the passengers but in 1947/8 such a bus was better than no bus at all.

Below: It was the Guy Arab I in wartime utility form that formed the basis of Guy's later bus business. Here the author's fourth 'foster child' ex-Swindon Corporation 51 prepared to take part in the Halifax 1968 Seventieth Anniversary parade. The chassis can only be described as being virtually indestructable but the bodywork was a very different matter. By no means the sweetest bus to handle, 51 must have given Reggie Baggott who drove it in 'one hop' from London to Halifax a most uncomfortable day but at least it kept going – and still does. Behind 51 is the ex-wartime Huddersfield Daimler CWA6 that had a much more sophisticated specification.

Above: The Guy Arab Mark 4 double-deck chassis was a well-engineered vehicle that came with a variety of engines and either orthodox or pre-selector transmission. Here a later version with the Birmingham style 'tin front' poses in the Fallings Park works yard.

could not be said of the bodies. The basic specification was drawn up by a select band of coachbuilding types who evolved the 'Lobster back' front and rear domes, the dimensions of those wooden seats and the rest of the equipage but even if the appearance was in my view very acceptable, they could do little about the sort of materials employed in the building which certainly were not. Strachans, Northern Counties, Duple, Roe, Park Royal and Masseys were all involved in building these standard bodies which also went on to Daimler or Bristol chassis and I well remember Arthur Tyldesley of Masseys telling me in later years that the utility bodies his firm built did less than nothing to enhance its reputation for the wood from which they were assembled was so green that if an operator had that colour for his fleet livery, paint was not really necessary. There was nothing here that the bodymaker could do for if he was told to produce a batch of, say, 20 bodies, he was allowed to obtain just sufficient materials for the purpose, and another old friend told me of the rumpus in which he was involved when he made a mistake and actually turned out an extra body over and above the specified number. As he said, he came to the conclusion that the offence was treasonable at the last, but those designers had sowed a seed that would later bring much trouble for by evolving a chassis that would take a long body and a Gardner 6LW engine, they overran the then legal length of 26ft by 4.5in so a special wartime length dispensation of 26ft 9in was granted and when it was withdrawn after the end of the war much heartburn followed.

The Guy Arab continued to be built throughout the wartime emergency period, 500 chassis running from FD 25451 being produced in the four years from 1942 to 1946. An improved Mark II version followed with chassis numbers commencing at 25951 and runners up to 28450, but then an even better Mark II began to be delivered.

This latter bus chassis still used a Gardner engine but a constant mesh gearbox (still remotely mounted) replaced the crash version and now we had standardised selector positions and a red knob at the top of the gear lever to prove the point, a single plate clutch took over from its double plate predecessor, full air brakes could be had instead of the original vacuum hydraulic system as could RP type automatic brake adjusters, the springing was improved as were the shock absorbers and last, but by no means least, a new cab assembly and radiator gave both a much lower bonnet line and a greatly improved front end appearance.

By the time we had reached this stage some of those original utility bodies were beyond redemption but as the chassis were virtually indestructable and not all that old, there were those who felt that it would be useful to undertake a spot of rebodying and at this point we meet up with those extra 4.5in. If you did what Ashton did and retained the original front end, added a Crossley body and kept the original registration number, all was well but try putting on the new bonnets and radiator plus a new body and then want a brand new registration number. It wasn't possible unless the vehicle was shortened to come within the 26ft limit for fortunately for all concerned the regulations were subject to some speedy amendment.

The later Mark III series took all this into account and soon began to achieve an even better service reliability factor although the price asked was by the standards of those days by no means inconsiderable, but now we had reached the bigger engine era and not everyone was satisfied with the 102bhp put out by the Gardner 6LW of the time (around 1954 the K type engine was produced which offered 112bhp at 1,700rpm which did improve things a bit in this respect) so an alternative had to be offered.

This was the Meadows 6DC 630 of 10.35litre which could offer 130bhp at 1,900rpm and which in appearance resembled the Dennis and Daimler oil engines of the period in having the timing gears mounted at the rear of the cylinder block. Like them also it was a compact unit but perhaps had rather more sophistication as it also possessed a built-in advance and retard mechanism that varied the injection point with crankshaft speed. An Arab so equipped was dearer than the Gardner alternative, there being a £70 difference, with a constant mesh chassis coming out at £1,789 and the fluid drive version which had a four-speed self change gearbox costing £1,909 or at least these were the figures that my then undertaking was quoted.

Now I never met a Meadows engine professionally but I did spend some days in a touring coach so equipped in the summer of 1949 when at the first sight of the word

'Guy' on the radiator I felt like going home instead of on holiday. The reason for this attitude was due to my having had a few journeys on a long distance service when the Northern General Company had allocated a 5LW powered Arab with a spartan bus body for a 100-mile ride and on the level or when climbing it was almost as quick to walk – we went downhill whenever possible in neutral which did speed things up a bit, but this coach type Arab was far, far different.

We actually set out from the Manchester area in a prewar Albion which sadly developed a fault so the Guy was acquired from a quite small concern which surprisingly released what must have been its newest coach. I wondered if, or when, we would ever reach our destination Bournemouth but how my eyes were opened. It was a beautiful day, we had the sun roof back, the radio – ah, a modern miracle on – and we swept easily past everything else on the road, including one or two petrol engined Leyland Tigers that never could be regarded as being slowcoaches. We had a rest day on Sunday, another Guy excursion on Monday, and the Albion back on Tuesday which really was a considerable disappointment but despite the excellence of the performance, the Meadows engine simply didn't catch on. Perhaps the basic cause lay in the combustion characteristics for a 6DC 630 on full power setting was a very thirsty beast and even when the fuel delivery was restricted so as to give the 112bhp of a K type Gardner it did 1.5 miles to the gallon less than the Patricroft competitor and after the fuel tax increases of 1950 when fuel came off the ration that was a matter of some significance. There were, however, mechanical problems as well. Sundry oil and water leaks would, I am told, develop without any apparent cause, lubricating oil consumption was also on the high side and crankshaft failures were also experienced at perhaps too frequent occasions.

The net result was that when the Mark III Arab came on the scene in around 1951, the Gardner engine was adopted as the basic power unit but a few were given Meadows engines and as these were produced at a factory in close proximity to the Guy premises, it is not really surprising that Wolverhampton Corporation Transport obtained a batch of 12 in 1957 which achieved up to 230,000 miles between overhauls but the fuel consumption after derating to 112bhp averaged 7.81mile/gal as against 9.13mph for the Gardner-engined Arabs of similar vintages.

Left: The Wulfrunian was as different to the Arab as cheese is to chalk. This panoramic view shows clearly all the complexities involved in this model. Note particularly the twin front engine air intakes, the fluid flywheel and inclined transmission shafting, the rear axle radius rods and the rear-mounted fuel tank. No wonder it was studied with interest when it first appeared at the Commercial Show – and not purchased in quantity.

Right: One of the two unique rear entrance Wulfrunians of Accrington Corporation photographed by Mr Roy Marshall when en route to Clayton-le-Moors. The background is typical of Lancashire as is the somewhat damp atmosphere. No 156 has a distinct list towards the bows but the air suspension would level things up once a few passengers had boarded.

Some of these engines also came to be hidden under the so called 'new look' bonnetry which originated in Birmingham (although to be fair both Midland Red and Foden were the first manufacturers to tread this path) when the traditional radiator and front wings were replaced by a set of pressings that certainly did eliminate a lot of odd corners that were none too easy to keep clean but these assemblies also brought various other troubles that were not usually appreciated by the garage staffs.

Dismantling was almost impossible so a minor front end accident on a conventional machine that might remove the paint from a dump iron or chassis end could necessitate the removal of the front cowl for this when distorted could in turn distort the beams of light coming from the headlamp and taking off a front cowl could be a time consuming task.

Removing an engine was, now, another one. On the exposed radiator version once the concealed radiator block had been removed a crane could be run in, the engine hook secured to the recommended studs, the weight taken and then with the front crossmembers dropped the power unit could be drawn forwards. Now, though, the drill was different if you went by the book, for that immoveable front cowl was an obstruction to progress. One needed a crane with a jib that would go over the tinware and then when the weight was taken and the engine drawn as far back as possible it had to be packed up so the hook could be disconnected, brought to the front and then reconnected. More than one instruction book of the period showed partially extracted engines poised in space on pyramids of dodgy looking packing but after one first attempt at least one workshop produced an engine trolley that at least made the job a lot safer. One had to compliment Guy Motors, though, for so arranging the design that it was possible to remove a cylinder head without having to shed both the bonnet

top and the top centre bonnet panel, something that had to be done on a competitive make of vehicle which at first sight used identical front end components.

These same components also made kerb side sighting difficult and speedily became subject to galloping corrosion but this was a fashion of the times and so had to be endured but other people must have shared our opinion for certain Mark IVs did have traditional radiators (or later the Johannesburg assembly) and others including the new thirty foot version that came out in 1956 the Gardner 6LX engine that was a tremendous improvement on the old 6LW faithful.

Despite all the foregoing improvements or rebuildings, the fleet of wartime Guy Arabs I came to know remained in their original wooden seated condition and were to say the least unloved by all. The antique does, though, possess some attraction and I always appreciated adding to my store of driving experience so from time to time I would take one for a test run or even relieve a service driver for a trip or two when any such exercise fell into two parts.

The first of these consisted of those anxious moments until one had fixed it firmly in mind that this gearchange layout was like no other, the second enduring the rest of the trip, and enduring is the only possible word. Despite those resilient mountings, the vibrations coming from the 5LW more than put your teeth on edge and especially so as speed reached a maximum which on our examples was just 29mph unless you were descending a steep downwards gradient when with a following wind and stout nerves all of 35mph might be recorded. To do half a shift on, say, a PD2 or a Regent and then find an Arab allocated to the second spell of duty was like going back into the dark ages and drivers would find every possible excuse, and some not at all plausible, to get rid which made life difficult for the depot as they formed a part of

the licensed service fleet and being virtually indestructable, gave very little basic trouble per mile run. I say 'virtually' because every now and again the inevitable would occur and a welcomed withdrawal would ensue and on one never to be forgotten day I was the executioner.

Number 22 had stood in the depot for quite some time but on that particular day we were coping with a very popular sporting event so everything that could roll had to, and so off wandered this particular Arab. It arrived at a main loading point and within seconds was laden with about 70 fans whose minds were set firmly on what they were to see that afternoon which was just as well, for my mind was on matters that were much more disconcerting. I boarded the vehicle as it pulled away wanting to see how things were progressing at the venue but I quickly moved off the dubious looking platform as the bus moved off from the stop. I would swear the chassis was 10 feet down the road BEFORE the body moved and then all sorts of very alarming structural contortions followed with the lower saloon ceiling which is when all said and done the underside of the upper saloon floor rising and falling at least two inches as we trundled up the main road. Then at the terminal the body continued in motion after the brakes were applied until the chassis and body regained their intended positions. Even the woodworms were leaving their holes, so the driver was instructed to return to Depot at once and so did our fleet lose a member but almost the same week by way of recompense we acquired a very different horse of a very different colour – in this case black and orange.

This Wolverhampton Wanderer was a Wulfrunian demonstrator and here was a talking point. We had seen the original 15ft 4in wheelbase chassis earlier but it was some time before it acquired a Roe body to become number 863 in the fleet of the then independent West

Above: The arrangement of the last version of the Wulfrunian is clearly portrayed in this official East Lancashire photograph taken before the completed Wolverhampton Corporation order left Blackburn on its first journey to Earls Court. Like its Accrington sisters, this particular machine was also to have a rather sad history. The design had possibilities but further development was not to be.

Riding Automobile Company where it formed one of an initial batch of 25 but as was only to be expected it was retained by Guy Motors for a time and exhibited at the 1959 Scottish Show where it was in almost constant demand. A quick trip around Kelvin Hall is, though, no substitute for an extended trial so we had our fleetname added to the list of would be 'truth seekers' with the result already mentioned.

There can never be any doubt that the idea behind the inception of the Wulfrunian was most praiseworthy because as I have said before rear-mounted engines may be all very well from a one-man operation/traffic point of view but they do make life somewhat uncertain for the black gang and particularly so in periods of very cold weather as many of us found out to our cost in the atrocious winter of 1979, but that's another story. Now there was available for the purchase the oft longed for combination of front entrance and front engine and if only Guy had been content to stop there with Wulfrunian Mark I, all might have been well but the company was not. Disc brakes, independent front suspension, air springs and various other advanced features were incorporated for the delectation of a notoriously conservative industry with results that should have been anticipated.

I took our specimen for a long test run and found that the riding was exceptionally good, as was the cornering capabilities of the vehicle, so much so indeed that a return to a conventional bus after a few hours 'Wulfrunianing' was frought with danger for you tended to take traffic islands and similar hazards far too fast. The steering was very low geared so that a lock had to be wound on or off and this process was rendered difficult for anyone over average size by the very restricted cab and the same adjective applied to the loading platform that was really too small for comfort. There was not much comfort either in contemplating the likely maintenance problems which began promptly during the first day in passenger service when the shutters on the combined radiator/saloon heating system stuck in the closed position and we had a boiling bus on our hands. Then we had the gear selector switch dropping in bits and followed that with a spot of brake trouble but this wasn't surprising as it was all so new.

From a service point of view, the footbrake was smooth and powerful but those brake pads cost around £80 per set in 1960 vintage £sd and it was suggested that their life was not long due perhaps to the way the discs were shrouded by the body. There was, too, a transmission handbrake and here was food for thought. One garage I knew years ago had a big frame fastened to the back of the main exit door and into that frame every seven days went a new slogan. We had 'Everyone likes a kind conductor' or 'Passengers count' and we also had 'Handbrakes are not meant for downhill runs'. One wondered if the originator of the last missive had anticipated our new demonstrator. This brake worked on the shafting at the axle end and when it was applied to a moving vehicle, the same either stopped dead or you had sundry lumps of brake scattered about the road surface. This was rather disconcerting.

The appearance of the front wheels could be described similarly for thanks to the independent suspension they either leaned inwards or outwards so more than one driver rang the foreman in a state of desperate alarm whilst the combination of high front end weight plus the suspension scrub ensured that front tyres could never endure for long.

The first Wulfrunians also set the bodybuilders some interesting problems for they had to provide all the internal bonnetry and as the front end of the chassis was somewhat unorthodox, it was not just a matter of laying some cross members over the framing and then tying up the resultant structure to the front bulkhead for due to the absence of some front chassis cross members that could not be incorporated due to the location of the engine, it was necessary to stiffen up the front wheel arches which was why a pillar was provided between the rear of the front wheel boxes which carried the air spring mounting brackets and the lower saloon roof sticks. Later models were improved here though when some very generous frame stiffening angle irons were provided and then the pillars could be safely omitted.

Most Wulfrunians were purchased by the West Riding Automobile Company, Ron Brooke, the then chief engineer of the company (he had been with Bullock & Sons prior to the 1950 merger) being heavily involved with the development work, and it must be said that the Roe bodies produced to the company specification had numerous useful features such as the access step and low mounted handles designed to make destination blind turning easy to accomplish but the need to have a low height vehicle meant that the nearside staircase, differing floor levels, prominent wheel arches and low headroom all combined to give the lower saloon a rather cluttered appearance.

The Wulfrunian high water mark occurred at the 1960 Earls Court Show when one chassis and three completed vehicles for Bury, Lancashire United and West Riding were on display with 72/73 seat bodies and unladen weights of around 8-8-0 but by 1962 the Wulfrunian Show content was reduced to a single Wolverhampton bus, fleet number 71, which in my view should have been a Mark I version rather than a Mark II for it had a much roomier cab, conventional springs, drum brakes and a normal handbrake mechanism. To achieve some of these features the front door had been sacrificed and so the East Lancashire body had a forward entrance but some more development could have produced an even better solution, something Ailsa managed to achieve a decade or so later with a design that was surely based on Wulfrunian thought but eliminated every unnecessary complexity, but if one so wished it was possible to obtain yet another form of Wulfrunian that went back, at least so far as body layout was concerned, to the ultra-traditional when a rear entrance was provided.

The East Lancashire Company produced the coach work on two such vehicles, the only ones of their type to be constructed that entered the Accrington Corporation fleet as bus numbers 156 and 157 in the September and October of 1961.

These vehicles were actually ordered in the August of 1959 but it was not until March/April 1961 that the chassis were despatched to Blackburn but these were Wulfrunian chassis (numbered 74920 and 74970) with a difference. A Gardner 6LW engine was fitted and this drove through an air assisted SYNCHROMESH gearbox. The front overhang was reduced to 4ft 6in and there was a rear overhang of 7ft 10in which left sufficient room for a platform width of 4ft 2in. As the vehicle was 28ft 6in long, a little arithmetic (allowing a 2in body tolerance) shows that the wheelbase was to the 16ft dimension and overall height was down to 13ft 5in. The buses accommodated 66 passengers, all 37 of the upper saloon seats faced forwards but downstairs eight of the 29 seats were fixed longitudinally over the rear wheel arches whilst five passengers on the bulkhead seat looked out towards the rear. For their comfort, however, a Cave-Brown Cave thermostatically-controlled engine cooling/body heating system was provided with all the intracacies so involved.

The chassis cost £2,943 each, the bodies £2,905 but it is very doubtful if they ever came to be regarded as a worthwhile purchase. Their maintenance records show that a whole series of problems arose with their entry into

Left: The Guy Arab Mark V was a much more successful model that must have become very popular had it not appeared at a time when front-engined buses were about to go out of fashion. Another Wolverhampton purchase – No 111 – exhibits its two-step entrance, a most praiseworthy feature. Bodywork was by Weymann and had 72 seats. This bus was new in 1963 and bore the registration number 7111 UK.

service beginning with heavy steering when a larger steering wheel was fitted but eventually the steering box itself was re-engineered and provided with a different ratio worm. Air suspension faults, failures of the front suspension units (the unladen weight on the front wheels was 4ton 9cwt 1qtr) hydraulic brake servo snags, excessive disc brake pad wear and cooling problems all featured in the lists until the opinion was ventured that 'the vehicles were incapable of operating town services for any length of time without developing some fault or other'.

The fact that Accrington had a fleet of Arabs could well have been partially responsible for this jaundiced outlook but eventually in March 1968 both were sold out of stock after running 78,380 miles and 83,771 miles respectively in their seven year careers which works out at an average of 11,582 miles per annum, but even then the engineers responsible for their demise expressed the view that if they had been properly developed and more of the components had been more accessible, this rather sorry story could have had a very different ending.

It is here easy to criticise with the benefit of hindsight but Guys obviously thinking it had a winner in the stable withdrew the very successful Arab Mark IV and so customers for the conventional had to go elsewhere. Additionally, as we have seen the Wulfrunian was that much more expensive for whereas an Arab IV with fluid drive and all mod cons came out at around £2,750 per chassis, the more usual front entrance Wulfrunian, admittedly with the larger Gardner 6LX engine, was in the range £3,200 to £3,450 depending upon specification, but here we had learned one thing, namely, the Gardner 6LX was an acquisition that was well worth having.

For the rest it was decided to wait and see – as did almost every other potential customer when orders for Guy buses went into a steep decline that was only partially reversed when the directors did the only thing possible and reversed their course, reintroducing that front-engined favourite, but then they went one better and brought out the Arab Mark V.

This was announced in 1962 in an era when most conventional chassis being purchased were fitted with forward entrance bodies and appropriate provision was made. In actual fact the production of the Mark IV machine never actually ceased thanks to China Bus and other export orders but its replacement was certainly a much improved design.

The frame contours were altered so as to bring the top flange some 2.5in below that of the Mark IV so that any bus built with the door behind the bulkhead need only have two entrance steps. The front engine mountings were modified, as was the suspension, the air brake operating pistons were replaced by diaphragms and sundry other detailed amendments were made but a choice of Gardner 6LX, 6LW or 5LW engines continued to be offered as did the constant mesh or semi-automatic gear boxes. The only note of regret was the adoption of the original design of new look front end structure and I often wondered why the opportunity was not taken to produce something which would retain the cleaned up appearance and still be easy to maintain. One can here only presume that the cost of any new tooling was beyond the financial ability of the company.

Again a demonstrator was offered which had a Strachans body of rather unusual design as the rear corners were squared off, a change which could have made the rear main pillars somewhat vulnerable but at least it offered a different appearance. This bus made quite a good impression. The drivers liked the way it handled, the passengers liked the two step entrance and the ride characteristics, and the maintenance staffs liked the general degree of 'getatability'. We normally put all our demonstrators and new rolling stock through a maintenance examination which had 24 headings ranging from a complete engine change to topping up the fluid flywheel with a maximum of 10 points each being awarded. The complete list made quite interesting reading but this Guy came out very well with a full mark rating in the important starter change area for this most important piece of equipment is all too often tucked away in some inaccessible spot and a 24V starter motor is a surprisingly heavy item.

The undertaking next door had also become interested in the Arab buying two for test purposes and had intended to increase the number after a successful test period but then the manufacturers ran into serious financial difficulties losing nearly £500,000 in 1960 and seemed likely to be completely liquidated. In October 1961, the assets were acquired by the Jaguar concern that wanted to break into the commercial vehicle field and had, or so it was previously reputed, been using the design facilities at Radford to draw up a Daimler truck but work on this was promptly suspended and it was announced that the Guy range would be continued except, of course, for the Wulfrunian for only 137 of these vehicles had been produced 126 of which went to West Riding, a company which then cancelled orders for a further 25; indeed, the cost of designing and developing this chassis played its part in the demise of the original Guy company.

Production of the Mark V continued but orders for this, too, faded away thanks to the change over to one-man operation and the effects of the Grant Scheme and when Wolverhampton Corporation Transport began to order Daimler Fleetlines for entry into service late in 1969, the writing for the Arab was firmly on the wall and, in fact, a 27ft version of the Mark V although advertised was never put into build. Then, too, Jaguar had to some extent already rationalised production within the group by utilising the excellent Guy constant-mesh gearbox in the Daimler range to give the CGG6 but here was another front-engined design that was not to have a long life.

The last batch of Guy Arab double-deckers was purchased by Chester Corporation and consisted of six machines that entered service in 1969. The first three of these, fleet numbers 42, 43 and 44, went to work in the March of that year and numbers 45. 46 and 47 followed in October. All were 6LW powered Mark Vs with 73-seat Massey/Northern Counties bodies. Number 47 actually had the highest chassis number, namely FD 77108 but due to a delay in the issue of its Certificate of Fitness, number 45 was the last to be put to work and so this bus must have the distinction of being the last Arab of all.

There was, of course, another Arab that was very, very different being the horizontal-engined Gardner powered single-decker that first appeared at the 1950 Commercial Show complete with a 6HLW engine and a four-speed preselector gearbox, but various variations on this theme came out later when this heavyweight was supplemented by a much lighter alternative with a 5HLW engine and constant mesh gearbox. The underfloor-engined Arab in one form or another proved to be quite popular but there were other Guys produced to a similar configuration. One such was the Warrior of 1956 which was a 16ft 4in wheelbase lightweight with a Meadows 5.5litre Meadows 4DC 330 engine and five-speed plus overdrive constant mesh gearbox. The chassis weight was 3ton 6cwt but even this was much in excess of the 49cwt of the Seal of 1959, an 11ft 6in wheelbase small capacity machine that incorporated a Perkins 5litre six-cylinder engine and also had orthodox transmission.

The Seal was not unlike the Albion Nimbus but did not sell anything like as well on the home market nor did the last Guy to be mentioned here. Another underfloor machine it was shown at the 1958 Commercial Show and differed from the Arab UF in a number of very significant respects. The Arab UF had a frame with humps to clear the engine but this bus or coach chassis had flat side members, the Arab had a Gardner engine this assembly a Leyland O600 unit, but the list of comparisons is not yet exhausted for now we also had fully automatic transmission, independent air suspension, hydraulic accelerator controls, twin system air operated front and rear disc brakes and a two leading shoe transmission handbrake.

Here were a series of components which are only now twenty years later beginning to appear on production underfloor engined chassis so no wonder the Guy advertisement of the day proclaimed that here was 'the most advanced single-deck passenger chassis ever produced'. As was only to be expected, it never sold in quantity but I cannot help wondering if this machine was not the true progenitor of the Wulfrunian for it had some very similar design features.

None of these single deckers survived the Jaguar takeover and although odd Daimler Roadliners also of unhappy memory were sold in appropriate export markets as Guys, the last true bus production of the marque was the overseas inclined front engined super heavyweight known as the Victory that became very popular in Africa and South East Asia, and is still being produced only now it is marketed under the Leyland label for neither buses nor trucks are now produced at Fallings Park under the Guy label.

The Guy company certainly had its share of successes and failures but it made a substantial contribution to the cause of British bus development and it also fostered some production innovations and here it should be remembered that a moving track for the assembly of the smaller range of Guy vehicles was opened as far back as August 1939 and a second line for larger chassis came into use in the March of 1941, and if the later vehicles that came off that line (Wulfrunian excepting) were not cheap, they had that most desirable property of being exceedingly reliable.

There are not all that many Guy buses about these days but there is one I know very well. One of the first wartime utilities it commenced life in July 1943 (chassis number FD 25972) with Swindon Corporation as registration number DHR 192, fleet number 51 and continued in use in that town until 1962. For the last ten years it has been in my charge and in that period it has been slowly renovated and refitted with a set of genuine wartime seats with their polished timber 'upholstery' which has the merit of being virtually vandalproof. Now and again we have it out for one reason or another when we suffer all the driving torments already described but when one has had a day when the latest super modern rolling stock has been somewhat troublesome, it is worthwhile going across to contemplate that Arab's total simplicity and then you realise how it was that during peak periods in days now past a Guy operator with a fleet of, say, 205 could have around 200 listed on the output board as being in service or available for work.

Could you have a better testimony?

6

A Sandbach revival?

As I have previously mentioned, I used to thoroughly read and digest my complimentary copies of *Passenger Transport* that were passed to me by the chairman of our local passenger transport undertaking each month over a period of about four years from 1939 but he then relinquished that office and my supply of journals ceased, when I simply could not afford to buy them for myself, and so for the next few years until I had access in my own right to departmental copies, I remained in some ignorance as to what was happening around the country passenger-transport wise, and here you younger readers should remember that there were then NO reasonably-priced enthusiast type magazines in existence so we truly have much to thank Ian Allan Ltd for.

You must also bear the foregoing in mind when I go on to say that a friend of mine, who was then not in the industry but now holds a general manager's post, told me one day not too long after the war had ended, that he had visited a certain Lancashire town that I also passed through from time to time and had there seen at least one brand new double-decker with the word 'Foden' on the radiator grill and here was a piece of news that I found very hard to believe. Now I knew that Fodens produced a variety of goods vehicles and I had had in my childhood several rides on a steam wagon on that make that had plied until around 1940 on a twice daily shuttle service that connected the local railway goods yard with the calico printing factory of its owners some three miles away, but passenger vehicles – never.

What, of course, I did not appreciate (and the copies of *Passenger Transport* that I had never mentioned the fact) was that Fodens had actually built a number of full size psv chassis in the decade before World War 2 started and I believe that these amounted in total to just 11.

Three of these were double-deckers, one of which was operated by the former Ebor Bus Company of Mansfield, and of the single-deck balance, there was certainly a most attractively-bodied front entrance saloon that was contained in the fleet of Wells Motor Services of Biddulph.

All these buses had conventional radiators, Gardner oil engines and Foden's own axles and gearboxes so in these latter respects they were to set a pattern for things still to come.

What these things turned out to be was something I quickly saw for myself for a quick visit just had to be made to Warrington to find 'praises be' that my friend was correct in his assertions only there was a bonus for two of these brand new buses had some decidedly quaint body architecture and here was a puzzle until I was told that these machines, fleet numbers 15 and 16, had received second-hand bodies taken from prewar Crossley Mancunians which true to form had not had just as much wear as the uninitiated might have expected.

Despite this blend of ancient and modern, I came away most impressed by what I had observed and my feelings here were substantiated when I read the 'additional' issue of the *Automobile Engineer* for the month of November 1947 for this contained a detailed review of every heavy duty passenger chassis then being marketed, but let me add that my copy was secondhand and somewhat outdated when it finally came to rest in my possession, where it still remains, for it was a mine of information with several illustrated pages being devoted to the latest PVD series offerings from Sandbach, offerings that included quite a number of modern, unusual or surprisingly ingenious features.

The most obvious of these to the casual observer was

the 'new look' front then being employed only by Midland Red on its own make buses but to my mind the Foden arrangement was, and still remains, the neatest of its type. Here, I often in earlier days wondered why other makers could not have adopted the flush and easily cleaned dash panel layout with its quickly removable front grill that was actually made of sufficient size to allow the engine to be withdrawn on a jacking trolley when the radiator which was carried on slotted mountings and the front frame cross member had been removed. The only obvious disadvantage in this assembly was the rather restricted size of the bonnet top that both hinged on its upper edge and folded in the middle but even so there was adequate room for normal servicing.

Another unique and very visible feature share with contemporary goods vehicles was the mounting of the speedometer (and horn button) in the space usually occupied by a solid steering wheel boss where it could be easily seen by the driver but it was beneath the body that the greatest differences lay and here we must start with the chassis frame. This had most substantial side members contoured on the top and bottom flanges to accept the central cruciform cross member that was like no other, was heavily gusseted in the middle and had its arms crossing each other off centre so that its centre could accommodate a nearside propellor shaft centre bearing of massive dimensions, a bearing that was encased in rubber so as to ensure that no transmission vibrations were conducted into the frame. Forwards of the end of the cruciform were the Vee-shaped gearbox steady link and the engine mountings, the latter being of the three point variety when coil springs were employed within the widespread rear anchorages whilst a circular rubber bonded bracket did duty at the front, a bracket which to save space was neatly recessed into the dished fan pulley. Also bolted to the front of the frame was the

Above: The first Foden double-deck buses to catch the author's eye were some of those taken into stock by Warrington Corporation and without any doubt the oddest looking were the pair fitted with prewar Crossley Mancunian bodies. With the registration numbers EED 15 and EED 16, fleet numbers 36 and 37, they went to work in 1948 and 1949 but in the writer's view completely spoiled the look of chassis 23000 and 27300 that had to bear the end result. Operationally, however, the combination must have been quite successful as they were to survive until 1964 and 1961 respectively. This high level depot view shows the way in which a windscreen 'peak' had to be provided.

Above right: Also to be found prowling around Warrington were the much more attractive Fodens operated by the Lancashire United concern that possessed Northern Counties bodywork. Noteworthy features of 449 and her sisters were the flowing frontal curve that harmonised with the front end 'tin wear' and the twin pairs of sliding ventilator windows employed in the four bay side frames that were arranged in such a manner that any standing passenger could easily see the world outside.

very substantial steering unit which incorporated recirculating balls in a praiseworthy endeavour to reduce effort to the minimum. Here was another Foden speciality.

There were also some unique features in the braking system. For example, the brake shoes of 16.5in diameter 7in rear width, 4.25in front were of the split segment type which was only adopted by most other bus builders years later. The segments mean that stuff moulded liners can be securely rivetted to the curved surfaces of the shoes and the intervening slots help to clear away dust but this wasn't all for the drums in which the linings were worked were exceedingly heavy and provided with helical cast ribs. The ribs help to dissipate braking heat and the heaviness prevents distortion and does much to prevent brake squeal.

Below: Other Wigan-built bodywork, only this time produced by the Massey concern of Pemberton was fitted to the range of Foden chassis acquired by Chester Corporation Transport. Again the curves employed by Masseys in the immediate prewar and most postwar productions fitted in neatly with the design of the Foden front but No 76 also has the added attraction of a plated front bumper bar. Massey body production only amounted to about one per week but every one was nicely finished, gold anodised window finishers being a standard offering. If good looks could sell a bus then the Foden PVD should have been a terrific success.

When it came to the actual method of brake operation, Fodens was again without imitators although the wheel assemblies were at first sight of the familiar hydraulic type being built into the brake carriers – it was how those brakes were powered that provided the surprise. A gear driven pump was mounted on the engine and coupled to the dynamo drive shaft. This drew ordinary engine lubricating oil from a reservoir contained in the so called 'boost box', a substantial hollow box like casing fitted directly below the cab floor and after passing through the pump the oil was returned to that reservoir but not before it had circulated through certain very important internal passages which contained a valve that was linked directly to the brake pedal. When the latter was in the normal position, the oil circulated freely but as foot pressure was applied so did the valve close when a pressure was set up in the passages. This pressure acted then on the input side of the brake master cylinder piston when the resulting movement was relayed to the hydraulic brake fluid which in turn operated the wheel cylinder pistons. This action continued until the internal fluid pressure balanced the loading imposed by the driver's foot when by a judicious arrangement of the various valve areas, a fully proportional braking boost was made available in the ratio of around 10 to 1. Originally there was only one master cylinder affixed to the boost box and the operating piston was provided with a direct mechanical connection so that if a pump should fail then the driver's right foot would have some effect but later buses had two masters – one for the rear brakes and one for the fronts, so there were in effect two different systems but that

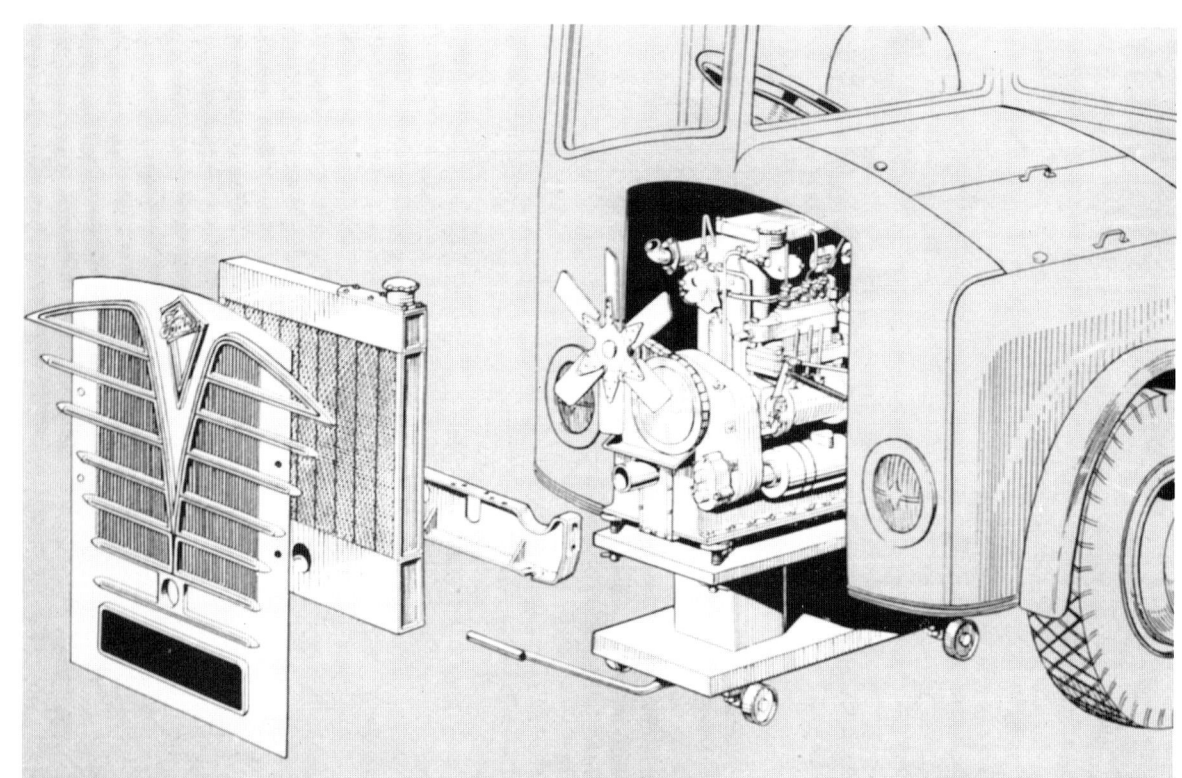

HE FOLLOWING SEQUENCE OF OPERATION SHOWS HOW EASY IT IS
TO REMOVE THE ENGINE FROM THE FODEN S. D. OR D. D. CHASSIS.   IT IS UNNECESSARY
TO USE LIFTING TACKLE OR TO DISMANTLE ANY PART OF THE CAB—A FEATURE OF
THE FODEN PASSENGER VEHICLE.

SPEEDY

REMOVAL

OF

ENGINE

1. Remove front panel, complete with grille.

2. Drain radiator and uncouple hose connections.   The radiator mountings are slotted—loosen mounting bolts and remove radiator.

3. Disconnect engine control linkage, and uncouple electrical connections, fuel pipes and speedometer drive.

4. Position suitable wheeled jack to take the weight of the engine.

5. Withdraw engine front suspension bracket bolts.   Remove front cross-member.

6. Tap out the hinge pins from the rear engine supports.

7. Uncouple the foremost universal joint behind the gearbox.

8. Detach gearbox locating link.

   The engine can now be drawn forward clear of the chassis.

Left: Despite the 'inbuilt' appearance of the front end structure, the designers had taken care to ensure that the power unit could be extracted without the garage having to resort to extremes of dismantling. This picture, reproduced from the Foden bus sales book which was a very lavish publication, shows the intended method. One could describe the layout as being the direct result of 'positive thinking'.

Right: Alas, positive thought did not extend to the pedal gear. This view of a cab interior shows how the brake and clutch pedals were not on the same line as is normally the case. Perhaps the brake pedal was positioned as it was to bring it near to the accelerator but whatever the reason drivers remained unimpressed. Housing what are normally the contents of the instrument panel in the steering wheel bus represent another unusual feature as does the existence of a reverse catch at the end of the gear lever, something more usually associated with goods vehicles.

wasn't quite all. One master had a diameter of 1.5in, the other a diameter of 1.75in so that the ratio of rear brake effort to front effort was properly proportioned but that inbuilt direct connection was still there so that the rear brakes could always provide some stopping power.

Another included safety device was the hillholder and this I would have loved to have tried on that hill mentioned in Chapter 1. Certainly no other bus of the day had one although many years later Leylands produced a pneumocyclic gearbox that contained a basically similar device only it worked on a very different principle. On the Foden, the hillholder was fitted into the main brake line between the master cylinder and rear brakes and was of Lockheed manufacture. The modus operandi was quite simple. As a driver brought his bus to a stop, he would push down the clutch pedal to disengage the drive, and of necessity apply the brake, which produced the aforementioned pressure in the brake pipes and also in the hill holder. This was a small cylinder that contained a cam, a spring loaded cage and a large ball intended to act as a sealing valve. The cam had an exterior arm that was attached to the clutch operating mechanism. The movement of the clutch pedal and linkage allowed the cage to move backwards and as it did so, the rear end that incorporated a seating came to rest against the outlet but the orifice remained open unless the bus was on a rising gradient. Then the ball ran back, thanks to gravity, prevented the fluid from draining back and so retained those brakes in the on position. The driver could then take his foot off the brake pedal and the bus would not roll back so long as he continued to depress the clutch pedal when it was, of course, exceedingly easy to select any other desired gear ratio, when as the drive was taken up again the cam rotated to move the cage, the ball came off the seat and, hey presto, off came the brakes.

Those brakes, though, had sundry other unusual features for all the wheel assemblies were of the two leading shoe pattern and had in later chassis a Foden

designed automatic brake adjuster that contained provision for the shoes to be taken back so as to increase working clearances without a mechanic having to resort to a full scale dismantling operation. To the uninitiated, this might seem to be a very unnecessary provision but, alas, bus brakes all too often heat up, the brake drums expand and the automatic adjusters doing their stuff rack up to allow the lining surfaces to follow the greater radius. Then you bring the bus back to depot, it stands awaiting its next duty, the brakes cool, back go the drums to something approaching their original diameters but the adjusters stay put. Result – binding brakes which in extreme cases make the vehicle almost completely immobile.

All these obviously well thought out points were incorporated not surprisingly for the time in a traditional chassis layout which came to be marketed in four different forms. There was, firstly, a double-decker of 16ft 3in wheelbase that had a Gardner 6LW as the standard motive power, then came the corresponding single-decker using the same engine but having the axles at 17ft 4in centres, and both of these were intended for the home market. Chassis number three was for export being 30ft 9.5in overall with a 19ft 6in wheelbase whilst also for export came version number four which had a 21ft wheelbase and could take bodies up to 32ft 6in long, both of the latter featured the Gardner 6LW. Here there must have been a change in thought for the *Automobile Engineer* clearly stated that for the home market the 5LW engine had been adopted as standard to accommodate bodywork having the maximum carrying capacity but the very fine passenger vehicle catalogue that came with a tender for double-deckers in around 1951 and is still in my possession, makes no mention whatsoever of anything other than the 6LW.

The frames were full length and so included the rear platform supports and also contained an offset 7.25in centre worm drive drive rear axle, underslung leaf springs and a substantial front axle that had taper roller

Above: What no luggage? Opening the boot lid of this Foden displayed not a pile of suitcases but a Foden two-stroke diesel engine, so as the centre doored body shows no visible signs of incorporating side lockers, where did the passengers belongings go? We do not know the answer to that question but there is no doubt about the performance that this type of chassis could offer. If there had been an extensive motorway network in existence in the early 1950s, the Foden rear-engined coach could well have become a much more familiar sight – and sound – than it turned out to be. This particular example was bodied by the long-vanished firm of Gurney-Nutting Ltd.

bearings to accommodate the king pin loadings but there was a most disappointing feature for the standard gearbox was of the four-speed constant mesh type but if you had hilly routes then a close ratio five-speed version could be obtained with the extra gears giving a super low facility. This gave a 9.9 to 1 ratio and with it any Foden bus should have been able to climb a mountain – as some did, for Llandudno Urban District Council purchased a brace of single-deckers in 1951, had them fitted with anti-run back sprag brakes and operated them up and down the 1 in 5 gradient of the Great Orme for years. There might well have been others particularly as during the boom coaching years of from 1946 to 1951 many operators seemed to take to the Foden front-engined passenger vehicle in a big way, and so they became a very familiar sight. The Llandudno vehicles had by the way 35-seat full fronted Metalcraft coach bodies.

The first postwar double-deck chassis was number 23001 which acquired a Willowbrook body and was turned out of the Loughborough shops on 21 November 1945 to be employed as a demonstrator, but the Foden/Willowbrook combination was to become something of a rarity for there were no more double-deckers to follow and only two single-deckers that were acquired by the

erstwhile West Monmouthshire Omnibus Board in the June of 1952 and the February of 1953.

The double-decker was loaned to Warrington with the results already noted but it must be added that this operator became the biggest Foden double-deck purchaser building up a fleet of fifteen starting with number 36 registration number EED 15 based on chassis number 23000 that entered service in 1948 and ending with fleet number 112 chassis number 39832 that took the road on 25 March 1956.

Within the above period only 61 double-deckers were sold with Chester Corporation taking eight, Merthyr taking six and Derby five, a figure that was also repeated in the order placed by Lancashire United in 1951 that materialised as fleet numbers 447 to 451. The balance went in penny numbers to sundry private operators such as P. & O. Lloyd, Phillips Motors, Smiths, and the Green Bus Company of Rugeley (a prewar Foden user) but with a substantial chassis and Gardner engine why did such a sorry sales picture emerge?

The answer was probably due to a combination of three factors the first of which was price. In October 1950, one of my former municipal undertakings advertised for the supply of 12 double-deck chassis and received no less than eleven different offers from six manufacturers. The cheapest of these was the Crossley type DD42 with synchromesh gearbox and 8.6litre engine at £1,630, followed by the AEC Regent III with similar transmission at £1,679. Three more chassis were available at prices below £1,800, namely, the Guy Arab with Gardner or Meadows power, or the Leyland PD2, and two more came out just over that level but these would have had the more expensive fluid flywheel/epicyclic gearbox combination (the Guy Arab or the Regent Mark III). Only then did the Foden materialise at £1,859 per chassis but surely that was a very high price for a chassis having a 270sq in area clutch and the

previously mentioned constant mesh gearbox which by that time was beginning to be regarded in the best circles as being outdated.

The transmission system could be classed as reason number two, not even an eight-week delivery time offsetting the fact, and so we are left now with reason number three, to whit, the braking system.

The triple servo vacuum arrangement was known and appreciated for its reliability and simplicity, vacuum hydraulics were acceptable even if half the working medium had to be purchased in gallon cans, compressed air systems were more expensive and complicated but were becoming more widely employed but high pressure fluid layouts were regarded with more than a little suspicion and not if the Daimler CD 650 was any pointer without good reason, but in the Foden case there was no pressure back up offered by the contents of a previously charged reservoir so if the pump stopped working where went the power assistance?

We should, therefore, at this stage ask in the interest of science and the light of subsequent running experience if this attitude was truly justifiable and here I must add that my running experience amounts to nil. I did my best to break my duck when around 1954 a secondhand Foden double-decker was advertised in the trade press and as we could then have used an extra bus, I suggested to my chief that we might buy it. I even had a fleet number ready and waiting but he, no doubt wisely, wouldn't agree so once more I am obliged to a number of colleagues for the information that follows.

The maintenance staffs undoubtedly looked upon their new charges in their early days as mixed blessings because of their unorthodox features. Front hub races did not last overlong, possibly because they were of the parallel type and so unlike the taper alternative were unadjustable. The steering boxes were also subject to heavy wear when the internal worms had to be changed

Above: The years that saw the Foden rear-engined chassis in production also saw some very unusually-styled coach bodies taking to the roads. These ranged from the distinctive Bellhouse-Hartwell productions to the Crellin-Duplex half decker. This Foden PVR/6 received a Lawton 43-seat semi-luxury body whose restrained lines would not look out of place in 1980.

VRF 743 became No 11 in the fleet of W. S. Rowbottom whose base was in quite close proximity to Sandbach.

at mileages which were lower than those attained by worm and nut or cam and roller alternatives, and these failings continued as the buses worked out their lives. Conversely, braking performance improved when the lining material was changed and that second master cylinder was introduced although in certain notable instances this alteration so improved stopping power that brake snatching was set up so odd operators restored the original layout. Several also took off the hill holder for this, sad to say, could sometimes stick on the 'on' position and then roadside surgery was the order of the day. Oil pumps gave little or no trouble but there was always that lingering thought that if ever a driver stalled the engine when in neutral and on a gradient trouble could well follow and one must appreciate here that even the most unlikely combination of circumstances could well occur.

As nearly every Foden had a Gardner engine, there was virtually no trouble in that department but the rear engine mounting brackets were prone to failure and invariably the nearside mounting was the more persistent offender. Clutch liner life was also on the low side but without any doubt the lightness of the mechanism was a contributory cause as it encouraged drivers to slip the drive rather than to take the trouble to engage a lower ratio when in traffic or when cornering and no friction material is going to stand up to that sort of treatment for very long. Stiffer clutch springs here might

83

Right: Warrington purchased a total of 15 Foden double-deckers and thirteen of these having new bodies possessed a much more normal appearance. Three, numbers 102, 103 and 104, of 1954 had Crossley bodies, the remainder East Lancashire productions. Here, one of the final Foden intake No 109 of 1956 is photographed working on the Poplars Avenue route. There were five buses in the batch numbered from 108 to 112 inclusive, the latter vehicle being the last front-engined Foden double-decker to remain in service being finally withdrawn in 1972. It was then purchased for preservation.

worsen the operating characteristics but will certainly improve the life factor by reducing abuse.

It seems from my enquiries that most drivers did not take too readily to Fodens, at least in the various municipal fleets that contained any, and this could well have been because nearly every series of buses that are acquired in small batches, irrespective of make, suffer in this way but it must be added in all fairness that the men had some justifiable reasons in so far as these Sandbach products were concerned. The driving position was set rather high and for some inexplicable reason the clutch and brake pedals were not mounted on the same floor line. The brake pedal was further forward and the pad was carried higher up than was the case with the clutch and so the right foot had to be raised up more than the left. I have yet to meet any other psv with this unfortunate feature.

Then the steering was good but the column was perhaps rather too rigid and the solid feel that resulted could be somewhat disconcerting. That other essential control, the gear lever, was also the subject of early complaint being rather too short for easy manipulation but an improvement was soon made when a longer stalk was made available.

Of all the general service complaints the most serious centred on the gearbox. It was generally agreed that lifewise it could not compare with the unit in the Guy range of heavy duty passenger chassis and at about 200,000 miles a new set of innards would be needed. Gearbox assembly was not a highly technical process but for some reason the designer had elected to allow the rollers of the clutch shaft spigot bearing to run directly on the shaft instead of in a cage so fitting was invariably dependent on the liberal use of thick grease to keep them in situ whilst the box was lifted into position and some good luck thereafter until shaft location became an accomplished fact.

This, needless to say, was always a fairly slow business as indeed was the process of gear changing when one had mobility once more and even though a clutch stop was provided (a stop is a form of clutch brake) double declutching was always a necessary part of 'cog swopping'.

These were the bad points, so what about the good ones? There never were any framing troubles, the radiator design was exceptionally good and at least one owner asked the Guy company to go do likewise whilst the standard of ride was in my book second only to that of the contemporary Crossley. Finally, Foden double-deckers could usually return a more advantageous fuel consumption than any other bus built to a similar specification, thus possessing Gardner engines, constant mesh gearboxes, solid plate clutches and comparable unladen weight/seating capacities. The reason for this desirable state of affairs can only be ascribed to the fact that Foden axles had parallel rather than taper roller bearings which are never so free running although the arrangement of the cooling system and the overall gear ratios might have been better suited to Gardner engine characteristics than those of the PVD's competitors, but at this point mention must be made of the exception to the general rule and here we are back to chassis number 23001 and that lowbridge Willowbrook body.

When that machine first visited Warrington, it was powered by a Gardner 5LW engine but rather later it made a second excursion to Lancashire when a Foden two stroke oil engine provided the horses and this it was to retain thus becoming the only British double-decker to be so powered. The corporation transport department did buy some more Fodens but continued with Patricroft power so local impressions cannot have been over favourable but eventually the bus was sold two-stroke and all to Roy Cawthorne, of Barugh Green near Barnsley, who used it on his stage carriage service into that town until he sold out to Yorkshire Traction on 26 March 1952. One might have expected such an oddity to be promptly purged from a large fleet but it continued to adorn the area until 31 August, 1959 when it was sold out of stock.

The engine fitted to KMA 570 was of type FE6 had six cylinders of 3.35in bore and 4.73in stroke which gave a swept volume of 200cu in or 4.095litre. A Roots blower was fitted for charging/scavaging purposes and the engine was advertised as putting out 162bhp at 2,000rpm. Unfortunately, all mechanical characteristics aside it cannot truly have suited the intended purpose for the maximum torque figure of 350lb/ft was not obtained until the engine was running at 1,500rpm, a speed half as high again as that of a 6LW which offered the same turning moment at around 1,000rpm, which meant that a rather different driving technique was required. My own driving experience with the Foden engine is rather limited but, nevertheless, I soon discovered that one could not 'hang on in gear' but had to make the fullest use of the available ratios to obtain a satisfactory performance. When the bus was on the move, though, the engine went very well and with its higher governed speed was very acceptable in a longer distance/higher speed vehicle which was just what Fodens went on to provide and here, fortunately, it was very smooth running in the 1,000-1,700rpm range.

There was then no two stroke double-decker placed in full production but the 1950 Commercial Show saw another Foden first, or rather three of them, in the shapes of two REAR-engined coach chassis, one with a Foden engine the other with a Gardner and a complete Foden powered 43-seat coach with bodywork by the then highly esteemed firm of James Whitson Ltd.

This chassis like its forward engined passenger counterparts had a robust frame complete with cruciform cross member (only this didn't have to

Above: Few would have expected to see the re-emergence of the Foden double-decker after 1972 when the last Warrington example was withdrawn from passenger service so considerable interest was aroused when details of the Foden/Northern Counties design were announced. One of the original prototypes was purchased by the National Bus Company to enter service with the Potteries Motor Traction Company. The last passenger waiting to board will, though, be more than usually interested in its progress for Mr Allan Collinson of Ferodo has had much to do with the design and installation of the friction retarder fitted to these vehicles.

accommodate a centre bearing any more), the four or five speed constant mesh gearbox, the recirculatory ball steering and the hydraulic brakes with engine driven pump oil pressure boost but there was yet another innovation in the handbrake mechanism as this incorporated a variable leverage device. The handbrake lever was connected to the conventional pull rods through a chain which engaged on an eccentrically mounted sprocket so that the initial free movement was rapidly taken up and the subsequent effective movement assisted by the sprocket going over centre.

The trade press had a field day road testing what was the first British rear-engined production passenger chassis but most testers obviously preferred their spells with the Foden-engined versions which had a unique engine note with a goodly proportion of the noise coming from the supercharger. More than one writer mentioned that the exhaust noise was akin to that of a high performance sports car and when a fishtailed exhaust pipe was fitted, the resemblance became even more marked. The chassis by the way had a 16ft 4in wheelbase and an unladen weight of around 4ton 11cwt and some very favourable fuel consumptions were reported with figures of some 12mile/gal being returned over quite high speed runs.

When one looks at layout of these vehicles, one can only express some astonishment at the expense and effort that must have gone into their design and production for they were very well engineered and here is one of those fascinating near misses of British commercial vehicle history for the model was, sadly, not destined to have a long production run but one must wonder what might have happened if Fodens had gone that bit further and endeavoured to market a rear engined double-deck chassis with a Gardner engine and air brakes. It would have been a stage carriage sensation.

In my view, three factors mitigated against the achievement of an acceptable commercial rear-engined chassis success. Firstly, the two-stroke engine was never really accepted by our notoriously conservative industry. Secondly, the constant mesh gearbox was not the ideal transmission system to employ in a chassis where it must of necessity be located 25ft or so behind the driver. A lengthy mechanical gear change linkage is a must and if it isn't well designed, gear changes are not going to be facilitated whilst even more to the point is the difficulty drivers must have in synchronising engine revolutions with road speeds but when the engine is an unusual two stroke then the difficulties become compounded. As it was, though, there was one surprising benefit here for the Foden engine had some rapid acceleration characteristics and this speed of response to the throttle – a throttle that was worked by a cable after some hydraulic experiments had not been over successful – did make things rather easier than was the case with the Gardner version. Thirdly, this rear-engined innovation came in rather too early for bus work and rather too late for the coaching trade. To explain this statement, let me go on to point out that in 1950 passengers still bought bus tickets in plenty and the bus business was still booming – so who was looking for one-man operational economies? Then on the coaching front, the underfloor-engined chassis was beginning to make its mark and here was a vehicle with the whole of the floor level space available within the body able to accommodate passenger seats when the resulting layout still meant that the traditional rear luggage boot could continue to be specified.

After about 1953 sales began to fall off so when I came to visit Sandbach for the first time in the early months of 1954, only a single passenger vehicle was to be seen and that was a rear-engined coach owned by the Liverpool-based Topping concern. Coaches and the coaching trade suffer from what can only be referred to as changes in fashion and so the lives of this vehicle and almost all its sisters were not overlong and it is pertinent to mention here that only one or two ever came to carry stage carriage bodywork, something that could well have lengthened the life span. Here, the double-deckers had the advantage and so most of them survived their full writing down periods of from 12 to 15 years. At last,

though, they too disappeared from passenger work when the last to continue in service with its original owner must have been the last to be built, namely, bus No 112 of Warrington Corporation that was new in 1956 and survived until 30 September 1972 when it was fortunately purchased for preservation.

After 1953/54, Fodens concentrated on the goods vehicle market and produced in the next 20 years a whole series of most attractive and successful trucks although the two stroke engine ceased to be fitted in standard 'on the road' vehicles from May 1972 being last employed in six wheeled concrete mixer trucks, but there were those who nourished the hope that some day there might be a Sandbach passenger vehicle revival and in so doing prayed that the company would reintroduce those most attractive sales brochures plus the combined and very well illustrated spare parts/maintenance manual; only, if there should be a revival, then let the vehicle involved have a rear engine and a set of air brakes.

It was a dream for the future but dreams sometimes become reality.

I went one night in 1973 or 1974 to an official transport conference function and there met a friend of many years standing who began to whisper in my ear and for the second time I could scarcely believe what I was hearing.

Now around 1974, new buses were very hard to obtain because we were then suffering from the after effects of the miners' strike and the three-day week but complete buses were not the only things noticeable by their absence – spare parts were firmly in the same category. This, needless to say, did not make certain established bus manufacturers very popular and, of course, several of these had been amalgamated in what were then very recent times into a certain large combine. It was rumoured, and I will put it no higher than that, that the said group having designed and produced an integral single-decker, was about to do the same for their share of the double-deck market when a series of conventional chassis would disappear but perhaps more serious was going to be the effect on the bodybuilding industry. What would such firms as Willowbrook, East Lancashire, Alexanders and all the other established double-deck constructors do when they had no mobile foundations available on which to base their wares and, equally important, what would the still independent operators do if and when their choice of bus was to become so severely restricted?

Fortunately, all this didn't happen but equally fortunately, and I write here as a bus buyer, nature abhors a vacuum and soon the nasty gap that had been opened up began to fill with the Volvo/Ailsa emerging as the first newcomer.

Northern Counties Motor and Engineering Company of Wigan didn't have the resources to embark on the full scale manufacture of bus chassis within the Wigan works but the company did have the resources and resourcefulness to enter into an agreement with Fodens Ltd whereby the latter concern would produce a rear-engined double-deck chassis – complete with air brakes and Gardner engine – that could be bodied by Northern

Right: The author was also involved with these first buses by sponsoring the order placed by the West Yorkshire PTE for fleet number 7250. It, too, possessed a Northern Counties body but was not placed into service until he had left Wakefield for Leicester. When this photograph was taken it was operating out of Huddersfield Depot on the Lepton route but is more usually employed on the intertown service to Halifax.

Below right: Not surprisingly in view of the sponsorship involved most of the Foden double-deck rear engined chassis have been bodied by Northern Counties of Wigan. The South Yorkshire example does though represent an exception to this rule, and as bus number 511 carries East Lancashire Coachbuilders two-door bodywork.

Counties, or any other bodybuilder for that matter, and this must have been the first time ever that such an arrangement had been entered into. Once it had been completed, the Foden design team went to work and the results of their labours were eventually placed on display at the 1976 Earls Court Show when it could be truthfully said that what was then visible was rather more of an underframe than it was a chassis for the completed Foden/Northern Counties double-decker was really a semi-integral vehicle and so possessed that degree of unorthodoxy that had figured in those postwar series two chassis.

The fabricated underframe of 16ft 9in wheelbase and 31ft 2in overall length came complete with body side members and wheel arch frames that would form the basis of the coachwork and this underframe was designed to accommodate either front or front and side door positions according to the wishes of the purchaser. Similarly, although the standard motive power proved once more to be of Gardner parentage, this time the 172hp 6LXB engine, the engine bay was arranged to accept Rolls-Royce of Cummins alternatives. The engine was mounted at a rather high level and this feature meant that any rear-engined Foden double-decker could easily be recognised from the back by the size of the engine bay doors but this position was deliberately chosen to allow the Allison MT640 automatic gearbox, the bevel drive box which carried the drive to the propellor shaft, and a Ferodo retarder to sit in a line on their subframe which was positioned in front of but at a lower level than the power unit itself. This subframe also carried the retarder heat exchangers and the gearbox coolers and also the alternator which was gear driven at 2.26 times the engine revolutions. Because the engine was placed well above the road, there was a high level offside air inlet with the ducting and fully cowled 24.5in diameter fan designed to provide a 600cu ft/min flow through the radiator which was also carried in the engine compartment and thence across the power unit to a nearside outlet.

As mentioned, air also provided the braking force and in the inlet line was a Bendix Westinghouse air dryer which actually does remove, as intended, the water vapour, dirt, oil and carbon that will invariably contaminate the system and produce frozen up brakes in cold weather periods.

At the front end were all the usual controls with a Burman power steering system being provided as standard and to take away the rather unfortunate degree of effort that normally needs to be applied to a Gardner accelerator pedal, an air-operated throttle assembly was incorporated, and here was something to cheer about for at the date of introduction competitive rear-engined double-deck chassis had either had cable worked assemblies that were far from trouble free or hydraulic systems that were not the easiest of things to bleed after any repair work had been carried out but if all the internal air was not removed, full throttle operation was never going to be achieved and so some mechanic would have a bus booked for pulling poor to rectify. Pressure charging was the only suitable remedy but even that was never 100% certain.

There was also a spring-loaded air-operated hand brake, leaf springs and that Ferodo air-operated, oil-cooled friction retarder contained in a neat cylindrical housing which was linked with the brake pedal and so designed to provide either 5% or 10% retardation depending upon which of the two working stages were brought into use. For those readers who are not too technically inclined, it must be explained that the retarder was a form of clutch unit that could be brought in whenever it was necessary to slow the bus down and by absorbing a very high proportion of the energy involved the wear and tear on the foundation brakes would be proportionally reduced.

I spent quite some time examining that show exhibit (intended for West Midlands PTE) because I had proposed the purchase of one of these vehicles literally straight from the drawing board and it is not all that easy to so interpret drawings (and particularly if they are of the initial preproduction variety), that one can become positively assured that no or, at the most, very few maintenance access problems will arise but I must confess that I viewed the contents of the engine compartment somewhat suspiciously for there did seem to be a considerable number of hose connections around plus a goodly collection of pipes and wires but it had to be admitted that in the case of the pipes, every possible union was staggered so as to allow each piece to be removed as easily as possible without having to resort to wholesale dismantling and all the wiring harness were protected by high melting point plastic conduit which was secured away from the chassis itself on plastic clips. It should be stressed here, too, that there was no doubt about the ability of the engine but what of the transmission for have we not met torque convertors here before?

Well, yes, we had, but the science had moved on since Leyland first used its back in the 1930s and this one had not two forward speeds but four, and again unlike that old Leyland design engine braking was obtainable as third and top could be held thanks to the control system provision wisely incorporated.

The underframe did look, too, to be rather on the heavy side although a weight of under 6ton was initially quoted with a design weight of 10ton on the rear axle and 6ton on the front but it was found that the back end was too heavy and so later units had a series of thinner section rear frame members whilst some weight was also pared from the rear axle.

In all, eight of these buses were built being purchased by Greater Manchester, fleet numbers 1434 and 1435, South Yorkshire PTE No 511, West Midlands PTE No 6300, West Yorkshire PTE No 7250, Potteries Motor Traction No 900 and City of Derby Transport No 101. The eighth machine was retained by Fodens although it was suggested in the early days that Nottingham City Transport might also become a Foden customer.

The seven service machines went into service in 1977/78 and were then subjected to prolonged testing procedures and for some two years thereafter little was heard of this Northern Counties/Foden enterprise and no other similar buses came to be built, but in my view this was a very wise policy to adopt for here is an area where it pays to make haste slowly and, in any event, these were a preproduction series.

Service experience seems to have been quite encouraging with such failures as have been experienced centering around the transmission line with bevel box or transfer box bearings having to be replaced. There have also been cases of the Newall Engineering Company-produced rear axle hub reduction gears being damaged by the failure of a lock washer which has allowed them to run out of line or of rear axle oil leaks but a cure has been found for these problems which are bound to become manifest in any such development programme.

The worst aspect has been the rather high fuel consumption and as a 6LXB is an economical engine, the cause must be due to the rather high unladen vehicle weight of around ten tons and/or the change characteristics of the torque convertor and here we are back to 1934 Leyland experience. In fact, when you ride as a passenger on an Allison fitted Foden, one can gain the impression that the engine is working hard but not all the effort is arriving at the rear tyre treads. Fuel figures on city work are in the order of, say, 5.5mile/gal but when one of these machines is put on to longer distance limited stop work, a commendable 9.5mile/gal figure is not unknown. When it comes to high mileages, though, the brake linings also score thanks to the retarder which has also been updated for after a period in service it was found that although the unit was sealed on manufacture, the oil contained in it had all but disappeared thanks to evaporation when internal damage could occur. Now a filler plug is incorporated and it is little trouble to check the internal level at the appropriate servicing periods when life benefits accordingly. Oil usage seems to take place at a rate of about 1 pint per 1,500 miles run.

It is pleasing to be able to record thanks to 'information received' that these Fodens are doing well for, unfortunately, I never saw the West Yorkshire vehicle enter service having left that undertaking for Leicester before it was completed and it was equally pleasing to read in the week that I completed the draft of this chapter that Fodens was open to undertake further bus production and has a suitable capacity available plus a new own-design rear axle. There has also been news of a SINGLE-DECKER in the shape of a forward-engine machine for export and home market though the latter must perhaps be regarded as a 'one-off' since it is intended to provide the very successful Fodens Motor Works Band with some very special transport.

One can only trust that the double-deck passenger vehicle attains a high degree of success in the years to come for the company's excursions into our industry have deserved a much greater commercial return, particularly as it has, as these pages clearly show, displayed an unusual degree of initiative in formulating some highly individualistic designs and it must never ever be forgotten that without enterprise and competition stagnation of design and development will be the inevitable outcome. The passage of control of the business now known as Sandbach Engineering into United States hands and a reduction in production capacity has, however, clouded the issue and made the prospects rather gloomy.

7
Dennis Dominant?

In my younger days, the sight of a Dennis bus in and around my home area was something of a rarity and so from an enthusiast's point of view they had a definite scarcity value, particularly as the few that were about had a most decided character of their own.

The most unusual were members of the small batch of Ace type models purchased by the North Western Road Car Company in the mid-thirties and given the fleet numbers 651 to 656. Four of these vehicles had Eastern Counties bodies Nos 651 to 654, the other two Harrington and with their long bonnets (not I hasten to add anything like as long or as high as those on an AEC Ranger) normal control layout and front folding doors, they were in marked contrast to the larger Bristols or Tilling Stevens that in those days formed the bulk of the NWRCC's fleet, but then these Dennis machines could only accommodate 20 seated passengers and were intended for one-man operation on lightly trafficed routes. Now it so happened that one of these services initially passed our front door for around 1937 the company opened a new local route which ran from Oldham over the Pennines to Huddersfield and originally this was worked on a two-hourly frequency co-ordinated with the much older Hanson service that utilised the same terminal points at either end but ran via Uppermill rather than via Delph. There were suggestions made locally at the time that Hansons had wanted to utilise the Delph route and that the North Western facility had been provided purely as a blocking measure but I cannot say that such was truly the case. What was true, though, was that not too many passengers could be found on the full size buses that initially appeared and so the Dennis vehicles came on for economy reasons, and if a bus route needed

'economising' in 1937, then it wasn't going to have much of a future, and this hadn't – finally disappearing around 1969 after years of slow decay.

We, though, found the service very convenient and I had numerous rides on the Dennises which made me take rather more interest in the make than had previously been the case. In actual fact, these little buses which had a 3.7litre petrol engine seemed to be very nippy and could run up to the top of the Stanedge Moors without any difficulty, and here they seemed to score over the other North Western Dennis vehicles of the Lancet variety.

There were two varieties of these. The first, of Lancet I form, consisted of 30 1934 models fleet numbers 621 to 650 and 28 1935 purchases fleet numbers 681 to 708, had the rather heavy looking radiator that was standard on those chassis and seemed almost as ponderous as those on the Crossley Mancunians of similar vintage, but batch number two, also Lancets, came into the Series II category and had the much more stylish design that certainly had modernised the overall appearance. Numbers 751 to 753 were new in 1936, and had Gardner engines, numbers 896 to 898 dated from 1938, originally had the Dennis O6 engine but came to have Gardner ones later.

There were also odd machines of Guildford manufacture that were acquired secondhand along with the services of various bought out small operators.

These, apart from a coach or two, were the only Dennis buses our side of Manchester but from time to time new vehicles on delivery, usually from Roe of Leeds, would pass the house and amongst these were buses travelling to Atherton to join the Lancashire United fleet, a company that bought quite a number of

Above: The Yorkshire Woollen District Company purchased a substantial number of the popular Dennis E type chassis in its early days. No 78 was one of a batch of 10 (75-84) that had Brush 32-seat front entrance bodies. The way in which the radiator stands proud of the cab dash plate will be noted as will the driver's highly polished leggings, perhaps a symbol of world war 1 service. Steering box maintenance must never have been a problem on this type of bus.

Guildford-made chassis in the immediate prewar period and these were also to be seen and ridden on when we visited other branches of the family who lived around Newton-le-Willows or Earlestown.

The full immediate prewar LUT acquisitions consisted of:

Fleet Nos 11-16	1936 Lancets with petrol engines.
Fleet No 17	1936 Lancet with Gardner 4LW engine.
Fleet No 240 (later No 100)	1932 Lance II. Originally had petrol engine but later fitted with diesel unit.
Fleet Nos 234-239	1933 Arrows with Roe bodies.
Fleet Nos 243-246	1934 Arrows with Roe bodies.

Family visits also gave me the chance to ride on some other quite modern Dennis Lancets as several ran on the United Services route that linked Doncaster with Wakefield, but at the time I never could decide if that was a large organisation or not and it was not until many years later when I became initially involved in its eventual sale to the West Yorkshire PTE, that I learned something of the rather involved history of what was in effect a 'federated' undertaking with three owners, two of which had Lancets.

That represented the sum total of Dennis travel so far as I was concerned but it was sufficient for me to find that the Lancets possessed either Dennis petrol or oil engines, or Gardner 5LW units, with the former giving the most quiet ride and the 5LWs the noisiest.

The North Western examples Aces apart did not normally work on the north side of Manchester but about a decade later I was Dennis riding again for LUT had returned to Guildford for some postwar buses and so 10 Lancets, Nos 346-355 began to work from around 1947 on the then recently-restored express routes from Liverpool or Manchester to Leeds or Newcastle or Middlesbrough, and so traversed some of the roads which had been covered by the 'flying pigs' of prewar memory. I was firmly convinced that the Lancets could not climb the local gradients with the same ease that their predecessors had displayed . . . back to power weight ratio again? but downhill was a different matter as an overdrive gearbox gave a maximum speed of around 60mph. I should mention here that the first five had Gardner 5LW engines but 351 to 355 had the latest Dennis six-cylinder unit.

The Gardner 5LW was not really an ideal engine for a long distance express service but it was to be found in buses allocated to the workings by five of the six joint operators (Yorkshire Woollen was the exception). Now in my view the Dennis machines were the best of this selection giving a better and quieter ride than the competing Guys or Bristol buses of the other stables but a little of my prejudice against the latter was caused by the seating offered by the LUT contingent. That on these front doored Roe buses wasn't bad originally but some were later improved by having seats fitted that were obviously taken out of prewar coaches so now we had Lancets de luxe or almost so.

Guildford products, though, remained elusive locally with only a few 1947 or 1949 LUT Lances around to

P.6403.

Above: Mention is made in the text of the normal-control Ace model developed for use on rural routes but Dennis went on to offer a corresponding chassis with forward control and set back front axle the latter feature also being incorporated in the lighter weight goods chassis of the day. This Mace, to quote the catalogue name, was sold along with others to the Southern National Omnibus Company and when complete with Brush body had a rather attractive appearance. The roof-mounted parcel luggage rack was quite common in the period but bus undertaking parcel services are now mainly conspicuous by their absence.

show that Dennis could and did offer a post-war double-decker. Nos 193 to 201 the 1947 intake had Weymann bodies and Gardner 6LW engines whilst the 1949 intake consisted of Nos 410 to 414 which had five-cylinder Gardners, whilst Nos 415 to 424 sported the larger six-cylinder alternative.

Here, one had to wonder after gaining more knowledge of the industry and its workings as to the 'stop – go' sales policy apparently adopted. I was going now to each Commercial Show and thus gazed on such intriguing beasts as Dominants or Pelicans or even in early years a Lance or two, but then after a sudden flurry of activity all would go quiet and another model gently disappeared from view before it had even entered production. I wondered why this could be and then, thanks to another flurry, I think I found the answer.

Our engineering department when wanting new buses would draw up the sort of specification documents mentioned in *Looking at Buses*, send them out, and wait for replies to come in and one day in 1953, to our great surprise, one such arrived at the office bearing a Guildford post mark. We were at the time wanting more double-deckers and were now presented with an offer for 22 LANCE chassis with of all things a Dennis O6 7.58litre four-valve head engine and reproduced here is the very picture of the power unit that accompanied the associated tender documents. We looked at it carefully for here was a design that none of us had ever come across before and we did the same with the aforementioned documents only that wasn't a task that took very long. Now most manufacturers around that time almost spent as much on their tenders as the customer spent on the bus. There would be pretty folders, photographs, drawings, a neatly typed out specification, a list of various extras, a sales brochure or two and, of course, the undertaking's own standard tender form which always had to be returned all carefully

completed and signed by some senior personage, often the company sales director.

The Dennis reply was not of this pattern. True, there was the picture of the engine, and true we did get our form back with a covering letter, a single specification sheet and one or two cuttings taken from brochures to make up weight and that was the sum total. We wondered if they were really serious and we wondered even more when we saw the proffered price. Now Guy never had the reputation for being the cheapest bus builders but their quote for a bus with a Gardner 6LW engine, fluid flywheel, air operated pre-selector gearbox and air brakes was £2,288 per chassis. Dennis on the other hand proposed the Dennis O6 engine which having a cubic capacity of 7.585litre put out 110bhp at 2,000rpm (whereas the Gardner figure ws 112bhp at 1,700rpm) a two-plate clutch, a five-speed constant mesh box with the fifth gear being a pre-selective overdrive and vacuum servo hydraulic brakes. for this assembly we were asked £2,423 each, and a quarter of a century ago there was here a quite substantial price difference, and an even bigger one from a specification point of view. Dennis did not get the order and neither, by the way, did Guy but had I been the general manager at the time I would not have recommended a Lance purchase as the engine

91

Right: In the early 1930s the best selling Dennis single-deck chassis was the popular Lancet Mark I. This three-quarter front view of Northern Western Road Car Company No 692 shows all too clearly the ponderous design of the radiator employed on this model, that could never be classed as either neat or pretty. The bus was one of 16 acquired in 1935 all of which were fitted with the operators' standard type of Eastern Counties 31-seat rear-entrance body, as were the other Lancets of Marks I or II forms.

alone would have represented too much of a leap into the unknown but was that a correct assessment?

In all fairness, I must quote from a now retired colleague who was responsible for the running of quite a number of Lance and Lancet machines, and when I asked him how they fared, he replied in the following terms – 'I recall the Dennis petrol engines were smooth and very quiet but at the time I knew the prewar machine days were numbered. The oil engines though were also good and it would have been interesting to speculate what the position would have been if superior lubricants had been available about ten years earlier.'

As it was the only recorded sale, this K4 type of Lance which had the 'new look' tin front was of a single batch of 32 which went to Aldershot and District (but with Gardner 5LW engines) and after they had been delivered in 1954 the Dennis double-decker faded from the scene for a year or two, but in 1956 the stop policy turned to go and an announcement in the trade press indicated that the Company was about to re-enter the psv field by marketing a version of the low height Bristol Lodekka, a design that could then only be purchased by concerns inside the nationalised Tilling or Scottish Bus Groups. This press announcement gave few details but before many weeks had elapsed, anyone interested had only to go along to the Earls Court Show and there was a nicely finished specimen on Stand No 75 just waiting to be inspected, a chassis which by the way incorporated both a Gardner 6LW and the five-speed Dennis box that had been offered in those Lance documents.

The bus looked to have promise only there didn't seem to be much drive about putting a sales campaign in hand, but eventually several orders were forthcoming and a number of rear-entrance Loline Mark Is began to take the road.

Then came the Mark II which could take a forward entrance (and here Dennis were ahead of Bristol) and also incorporated a greater number of Dennis components and, of course, the Guildford-built gearbox was retained. We even had the loan of a demonstrator

and I took it out for the odd trip. In some ways it seemed slightly odd for the steering wheel was at the sort of angle to be found on the Lodekka and some prewar Crossleys I once knew, and the gearbox had one or two little quirks, but once you had the knack it was quite easy to drive and the fuel consumption was amazingly low. We came to the conclusion that it would be a very useful machine if one had some inter town or longer country routes but it wasn't quite what we wanted for urban usage so, again, we decided not to make a purchase even though we were told that still more development was under way and a Mark III was about to be launched that was to offer air rear suspension and semi-automatic transmission as optional alternatives. Things were looking up particularly as Dennis sales staff began to call for the first time in the experience of the younger members of the engineering staff.

This activity though did not last. Dennis did begin to pick up various orders but then two larger competitors – AEC and Leyland, produced competitive chassis, namely, the Renown and the Lowlander and, of course, offered rather lower prices. Dennis sales declined once more and the end of the Loline was then announced. This was stop yet again but in next to no time we had yet another 'go'. Apparently instruction number one came just before a change in top management, number two just after, and this hiatus was exceedingly unfortunate as one or two potential customers had been lost by it but the Loline had by now quite a reasonable reputation and once again some repeat orders plus a few from new customers began to come, and it was at this stage that a very particular undertaking came into the picture.

It has to be remembered that at the time this part of the story began there was no bus grant nor any associated requirement that every bus should be suitable for one-man operation. There were indeed some heretics of the opinion, as there still are, that one-man operation does not represent an automatic cure for all or any financial ills the industry might have and, by the same token, the move towards rear-engined buses that was then

Above: The Lancet II single-deck chassis had a much improved appearance over that of its Mark I predecessor as this picture of an ex-Caledonian bus shows. In prewar days this Dumfries-based concern was associated with the British Electric Traction organisation through Tilling and British Automobile Traction, hence the style of the Weymann body carried by the chassis. Motive power was provided by a Gardner 5LW engine. Caledonian passed in postwar years to the Scottish Bus Group and was then wound up, at a time when it was operating about 160 psvs.

Above: The postwar Dennis Lancet also seen here in a Yorkshire setting was very different to its E type predecessor. Bob Mack photographed Lancashire United 346 leaving Leeds Wellington Street on a Manchester express working in early postwar days. These were comfortable buses to ride on in marked contrast to the Guys and Bristols of certain other joint operators but doubtlessly the Roe bodywork helped. No 346 was new in 1947 and had a Gardner 5LW engine, but it also possessed a five-speed overdrive gearbox that gave it and its sisters in the 346-350 series of 1947 a top speed of at least 60mph. Five more Lancets Nos 351-355 followed, which had the chassis builder's own O6 type oil engine. A final five Nos 410-414 come in 1949 with the 5LW.

beginning to be made on some scale was regarded (and not without some justification) as being something that was not going to further the cause of overall reliability.

It was, therefore, decided to order two batches of new vehicles which would represent the most advanced models then available, one having a rear engine, the other one at the front, so appropriate inquiries were set in train.

A trip to Guildford followed and there in one corner was noted a Northern Counties bodied Loline of rather odd design, painted in a dull red, standing forlorn and neglected. This it seemed was an export order that had failed to catch the boat and as it had both a 6LX engine and fluid transmission, both of which were being contemplated, the suggestion was made that it might be put to work. Unfortunately, the intending purchaser who was operating in the tropics had called for such items as an aluminium floor and wooden seating which were not satisfactory for home use but eventually it left Guildford for the works of Messrs Strachans and rehabilitation.

When this had been completed EPG 179B as it became (it had chassis number 1071L3AF1E1) put in an appearance in the 1964 Commercial Show demonstration park, spent some time at the manufacturers and then went into service with us.

It did not, alas, do too well for a variety of reasons. The windscreen had a metal panel at the top that made sighting for a tall driver difficult and to make matters worse there was a roof stick exactly in line wth his head that could give the unwary a nasty knock. Then the electric gear change unit was mounted not on the steering column but on the cab nearside sheeting so that every gear position was (utility Guy like) completely reversed. The uninitiated could thus start off not in second but in third and then make a change down to the former ratio with rather distressing effects upon the passengers, and transmission system.

There was also a transmission whine reflected by the metal in the floor that accentuated noise, some odd

Above: This illustration accompanied a Dennis Lance double-deck tender. It shows the layout of the O6 oil engine and also provides some brief specification details. There are double air filters mounted on the rocker box covers and twin fuel oil filters carried behind the fuel pump and above the vacuum brake rotary exhauster. The timing gear case is carried at the rear end of the crankcase.

propellor shaft vibrations, a distinct lack of urge, and according to the conductors who had a very different outlook, a lack of well placed bell pushes.

Nobody either had a good word to say about the large sliding door which was not as fast in use as the folding doors that feature in our fleet and so at the end of about three weeks it was returned with thanks to base but not before we had one surprise.

The fluid flywheel was almost hidden by a most complicated casting that carried the step down gears for the transmission and one day the gland (of the bellows type) developed a bad leak. A Dennis service fitter duly came on the scene but he had never encountered such an assembly and not having a handbook was baffled. The job possessed at first sight some first class problems but then the method was spotted and thanks to the design adopted the loosening of some nuts and front prop shaft enabled the whole to be withdrawn without anything vital needing to be dismantled. We gave that point full marks and also appreciated the air rear suspension but found the ride at the front rather poor – a feature I should add here that has been experienced on other double-decker buses that have a combined leaf spring/air suspension assembly.

All these complaints were reported in full and after investigation it was discovered that the engine power setting was not what it was supposed to be and that the transmission line did not follow the proper path being a degree or two out due to the inclusion of a faulty crossmember.

We had the bus back again after rectification and it did much better although because of the greater power output and different transmission, the fuel figures did not reach those recorded by the solid clutch Mark II version but, nevertheless, it seemed to form the basis of a promising design.

This viewpoint was reinforced after trials with one of the aforementioned competitors and a detailed inspection of the other, but fortunately neither found favour and then low-height bodies on rear engined chassis were considered and rejected, and so we were back again at the Loline and matters were consequently taken a step further when Dennis Brothers was asked to quote.

A week or two went by and then one morning the postman staggered into the office carrying two parcels having a combined weight of about 12lb. There was initially some speculation as to what these could contain but when they were opened it seemed as if the company was making amends for the scrappy effort that had been furnished those years before for now we had a copy of every material drawing plus some that did not really come under this heading, a stock of photographs (some of which have been used to illustrate this chapter) and a nicely made up data book that proved to be a mine of information.

Within the book were listed various alternatives that could be accepted to choice; for example, four different power units, three gear boxes each with varying ratios, an assortment of rear axle gears and a variety of other miscellaneous items.

It took quite a time to digest but one line of approach was obvious right from the start.

A local passenger bus needs reasonable acceleration – this is more important than the ability to run at high speed – but to obtain the former characteristic fairly low gears are essential particularly if the completed machine is going to be somewhat heavy when fully laden. Low gears though mean low maximum road speed and when the power unit, as in the case of the Gardner, is governed down to around about 1,700rpm the net result flat out on a level road with 9.00 x 20 tyres, is going to be around the 38mph mark which whilst sufficient for a bus that never leaves the town, is not sufficient for one which is required for inter-urban work as well. The double duty moral is plain. Fit another gear, and here was the ideal solution for not only was such a box offered but it was of the semi-automatic variety as well. Couple that to a 6LX engine and a most flexible performance should be assured. Here, the fact that to the best of our knowledge and belief there then were no double-deckers running in the country thus fitted was absolutely no deterrent to saying 'yes'.

This was just one example of the way that Dennis on this occasion had tried to give the customer what was wanted and, in fact, the whole specification was lavish. Even cab heating and de-misting equipment was

Left: A postwar Lance of Lancashire United heads under the trolley bus wires towards Hollins Green. No 194 was one of a series of nine (193-201) that had six-cylinder Gardner engines and Weymann bodies. New in 1947, they survived until 1964. LUT took delivery of ten other Lance double-deckers in 1949 that also had the 6LW power unit.

Below: The Dennis oil engine was subsequently modified to enable it to be used in horizontal positions and the last passenger chassis of all to be powered by a Dennis engine was sold to the Glenton Tours concern in 1960. Glenton Tours was an enthusiastic Dennis purchaser in the days when the Lancet underfloor engine chassis was being marketed and this photograph shows one of the vehicles acquired in 1957 to the company's somewhat unusual specification which always included a central doorway, something that is still called for in 1981.

included and this had been designed to go into the bonnet structure and not to be added as an afterthought with odd pipes more or less clamped to the cab sheeting. There were also obvious demonstrator benefits too for now the gear selector box was to go on the steering column and the positioning of the ratios in the gate was left to our choosing, and we needless to say chose the orthodox.

Over the following days the various decisions were made and an order placed, and then came the long wait until production was put in hand, a matter of almost 12 months. It was pleasant to see the Dennis assembly shop at that time for several contracts were in hand almost simultaneously and although Lolines were virtually hand built and usually so in small numbers, the place then had a mass production air until despatch to the bodybuilders began.

Our pilot chassis travelled first though to its intended home and was sampled by some of the engineering staff who remarked upon the smooth ride so unlike that usually experienced when seated on the temporary wooden seat fixed for delivery purposes on to bare chassis, but here the advantage of the air rear suspension and of the new design of two rate front springs was being made plain, the latter being yet another development from demonstrator days. We ran it around for a little while and then it, too, went off to join the remainder of the batch and then there was another wait until the coachbuilders had sorted out their various specification queries and had the front entrance bodies mounted on to the chassis.

Finally, they were completed, certified, and announced as ready for collection and so our career as Loline operators began on, it must be admitted, a rather disappointing note (after we had parted with exactly £7,000 for each complete vehicle) because the noise that came from the transmission was far, far worse than anything we had experienced with EPG 179B. Fortunately curing the fault was not too difficult and when some resilient couplings had been inserted in the line quietness reigned supreme, at least within the saloon. In the cab it was different for as one progressed the cranked handbrake lever beat a tattoo on the side of the offside wing until the inclusion of an off position steady settled that little matter once and for all.

We had other faults as well, needless to say. Water from the washing machines found its way into the engine air intake with some unfortunate results and the engine also suffered from a most unusual fault as the rocker gear and push rods on odd ocasions would tie themselves in knots. We couldn't quite decide why at first for Gardner 6LX engines are decidedly reliable but then we traced the cause back to that five speed gearbox. You could charge along quite happily with one of these Lolines at something over 50mph – I'd rather not say how much over – in overdrive, and then wanting a little engine braking on encountering a downward descent, rev up and drop the gear lever into fourth or third, thanks to the semi-automatic feature. At this point the inertia of the bus would be conveyed right along the locked up transmission to overspeed the power unit when you got engine breaking all right but note how the word is spelt.

The high ratio also played havoc with the fluid flywheel seals for acceleration periods could be quite lengthy when the flywheel would overheat but these failures were promptly reduced when a combined fluid flywheel/lock up clutch replaced the original unit. The gearbox mountings also had some peculiarities at first until a little modification was carried out whilst the gearbox itself was like no other ever made by Self Change Gears Ltd. This was due to the fact that the step down gear REVERSED the rotation of the front propellor shaft from that of the engine and so the gearboxes had to have reversed internal components which meant that they were very much a Loline special but the step down gearing itself proved to be almost trouble free and the basic arrangement with its easy removal facility was to reappear later in a way that could then never have been foreseen.

We also had that inevitable problem of freezing air brakes thanks to the ingress of damp air via the compressor and we had odd troubles with the air suspension system at the rear due in the main to faulty air bellows but there was one nasty job within this region that cropped up at regular intervals. There was a hefty rear axle locating rod which pivoted around a substantial bolt secured to the frame. The rod had a bush but this would wear and then there would be a continuous rattle coming from the area when the bus was in motion. A cure should have been simple and so it would have been had not those bolts invariably seized solid and then some strong arm methods had to be employed to effect the desirable separation.

The Lolines were used for a time on some long distance regular contract workings and during this period we often had local acquaintances telling us that whilst motoring 'abroad' they had been overtaken when travelling at a rate of knots by a posse of Lolines, information we always received with a complete air of disbelief, for a Loline burbling along in overdrive was an experience to be savoured, if you were the driver that is, but in actual fact the transmission system was their weakest point. We went initially through a whole gambit of troubles changing Layrub couplings for successively larger sizes and giving the propellor shafts the same treatment but one part of the layout here never figured on the defects sheets and that was the Bristol rear axle which came complete with appropriate hub caps just to confuse the unwary bus spotter.

Again we came to the conclusion that thanks to the work done these Loline IIIs weren't bad buses and with development would be very good indeed but, alas, there was no development.

We had the 1968 Transport Act and the Leyland/ Bristol link up which brought Lodekkas on to the open market at a time when bus grant requirements began to ensure that every one of the front-engined chassis then being made, irrespective of make, would soon be rendered obsolete and so up came that stop sign once more. Production of the Loline ended in 1968 when a total of 279 chassis had been built consisting of 50 Mark Is, 47 Mark IIs and 182 Mark IIIs. The following table shows where all these went and what type of power unit was fitted:—

Mark I (rear entrance)

Aldershot & District	34	(Gardner 6LW)
Tailby & George Limited	2	(Gardner 6LW)
Hutchings & Cornelius	1	(Gardner 6LW)
Middlesbrough	3	(Gardner 6LW)
Leigh	2	(Gardner 6LW)
LUT	6	(Gardner 6LW)
Leigh	2	(Gardner 6LX)
Total:	50	

Mark II (front entrance)

Walsall	15+1	(Gardner 6LW)
North West Road Car	12	(Leyland 600)
North West Road Car	3	(Gardner 6LW)
Luton	2	(Leyland 600)
Middlesbrough	8	(Gardner 6LW)
Oxford	5	(AEC)
Barton[1]	1	(Leyland 600)
Total:	47	

[1]Built with off set upper deck gangway, overall height 12ft 5in (built after Mk IIs and before Mk IIIs this is a one-off).

Left: The last version of the Loline was the Mark III that would have the alternative of fluid transmission. This photograph shows the fluid flywheel in its housing, the filler plug (one of two) and the step down gear case mentioned in the text. This gearing took the drive to the offside of the chassis reducing the height of the drive centre line in the process. The casing was heavily ribbed and had a large oil sump for cooling purposes. Dismantling was incredibly easy.

Below: Mention is made in the text of the Dennis Loline demonstrator that set out to be part of an export order, but in fact never left these shores. This view shows it after being rehabilitated to home use standards, when on trial with the Halifax Joint Committee undertaking. At the time this trial took place double-deck buses did not normally work under the Raistrick railway bridge, but when the subsequent order for five Lolines was completed, examples were often to be seen operating on the 42 Field Lane to Brighouse route.

Above: The last Lolines to be built were
purchased by the former Halifax Joint
Omnibus Committee in 1967. There were
five in the batch numbered 300 to 304
which had Northern Counties bodywork
to a lavish specification. Undoubtedly, the
fastest buses in the area in their day, they
were later sold to the West Riding
Automobile Company and are now
withdrawn.

Right: After an absence from the
passenger field of some eight years, an
operator prevailed upon the Dennis
company – soon to become Hestair
Dennis Ltd – to produce a rear-engined
double-deck chassis. Design work began
in 1975 and resulted in the appearance of
the first Dominator in 1979. Incorporating
a Gardner 6LXB engine and a Voith
automatic gearbox, the pilot chassis was
fitted with an East Lancashire body. It is
here seen in Leicester when brand new in
its ivory and blue demonstration livery.
This bus was purchased by the South
Yorkshire PTE, an organisation that
acquired a second with a Rolls-Royce
engine and then went on to place a bulk
order in 1979 for a series of 144.

Mark III (front entrance)   *(All Gardner)*

Aldershot & District	107
Belfast	1
China Motor Bus	1	(4 speed semi-automatic)
North West Road Car	35
Reading	26	(4 speed semi-automatic)
Warners of Tewkesbury[2]	1	(4 speed semi-automatic)
Luton	6
Halifax	5	(5 speed semi-automatic)
Total:	182

[2]This is the one demonstrated to Halifax, originally cancelled by CMB. It was still in service with Warners at the end of the 1970s.

The first Loline chassis was delivered to Aldershot & District on 3 October 1957, the last to Halifax on 25 November 1966.

After 1967 Dennis production went down and down, the company ceased to take a stand at the Commercial Show and it began to look as if the end of all the long-established Guildford manufacturing activities was in sight but then came 1974 and a decided turn around in the affairs of the Woodbridge works.

Why 1974?

Well, firstly, the ownership of Dennis passed into new hands and a policy of reconstruction was quickly put into train hence the new company title of Hestair Dennis Ltd. Secondly, someone, somewhere, went on a new bus shopping trip and could not obtain what he wanted – actually a batch of chassis of what was to him a standard type from another supplier. A potential buyer and a potential seller thus came together by virtue of a process that will not be commented upon further here and a new bus design was hatched. The basic format was exceedingly simple consisting of the following ingredients – Gardner engine, rear position, front mounted radiator, substantial engine mountings, bolted up frame of more than adequate proportions, leaf springs, dropped centre axle, powered steering, vast brakes, an air dryer, automatic transmission, a retarder if possible and last, but by no means least, adequate 'getatability'. There was also one other material qualification. This new chassis must be able to accept either high or low bridge bodies to designs then available without their framings having to be re-engineered in the process in order to reduce the cost of the completed bus. It was something of a tall order. So then what happened?

A team of bus engineers, and chassis designers took a series of strolls around a variety of bus garages and looked at every failure they encountered in an endeavour to find out just why these had taken place. Whilst this activity was going on, party number two began to research every potential double-deck transmission system and some that on reflection didn't enter the category at all, a process that took the seekers onto the Continent where sundry characters had a fine old time driving maximum length lefthand steer single-deckers up and down the severest gradient it was possible

to encounter or on to which some friendly but apprehensive operator was prepared to entrust a complete stranger with his best bus.

Once this exercise was over, a redundant Daimler 6-30 6LX purchased cheaply secondhand lost its power unit and preselector gearbox and received instead a Gardner 6LXB engine and a Voith transmission unit. To everyone's considerable surprise, the change was accommodated without it being necessary to resort to drastic surgery and subsequent road testing revealed that like love and marriage, the twain fitted together – to continue to quote that once popular song like a horse and carriage. The Voith is, of course, an interesting unit. It is fully automatic, gear changing being controlled by a mini-computer housed in a metal box which is usually fixed under the panelling of the driver's cab. To go forwards, you simply press the appropriate button when first, second and third gears are engaged as one accelerates away from rest, but if you press the middle of the three buttons, top gear is cut out and so engine braking is available through the indirect gear if it is wanted. There is, however, in addition, a built-in hydraulic retarder and that can and will provide about 90% of all the braking effort that will ever be required. You gently depress the brake pedal, sufficient air goes along the pipes to take up any slack in the rigging, and stage I of the retarder comes in. Press a little more and stages II or III follow in sequence until at around 7mph further pressure brings in full air and so is the bus brought to rest. There is, though, yet another benefit for the heat generated in the retarder is returned by a heat exchanger to the radiator cooling water and so the engine tends to run at more even temperatures when the bus is working on undulating routes and, of course, the passengers can benefit from improved saloon heating in periods of inclement weather. Here we have one reason why the new Dominator has its radiator at the front but there are others – better weight distribution and improved engine compartment accessibility being two of these.

The gear controls do, of course, include a reverse facility with a safety catch to prevent unintended selection, and a hidden cut out switch that renders the retarder inoperative when one wants to carry out some friction system brake testing, another very necessary provision.

In its rather short life, the Daimler convert did a tremendous amount of work but it isn't really quite dead yet as, at the end of all the testing, the engine and gearbox were removed to become spares for a fleet of Dominators that were then being introduced into service and so the true Guildford Dennis double-decker took the road once more.

It was very interesting to look over the various drawings and to see them transformed into likely looking lumps of metal for there is an old engineering saying that what looks right is right, and the Dominator did have a very satisfactory appearance – in almost every respect.

Of the engine, what can be said except that there is still in the opinion of this scribe no better double-deck bus

Right: By January 1980, the Leicester undertaking had a fleet of 39 Dominators in use with more on order or in build. The bulk of these had East Lancashire bodies but two set yet another new note in being fitted with the first ever Marshall double-deck body work. Here Nos 231 and 232 await their official handover ceremony on 8 June 1978. A 1978 Show Bus intended to be fleet number 230 failed to materialise but another five Marshall-bodied Dominators were scheduled to be in service by 1981. One of these has an alloy as opposed to a steel frame.

engine than a Gardner 6LXB. Behind the engine is the Voith resilient coupling, and behind that the aforementioned transmission unit. The drive comes out of the gearbox and then through a three-gear drop box that has all the look of the one fitted to those Mark III Lolines of old, and then the drive runs parallel to the engine to a right-angled drive unit affixed to the back of that unit. Thence, a short propellor shaft takes the tractive effort into a double reduction rear axle that allows the chassis to accommodate those highbridge or lowbridge bodies, an axle that also owes something to Loline experiences and is of Dennis design and manufacture.

The layout of the rear end is shown in the illustration reproduced here but what it does not indicate are the means by which the gearbox, etc can be removed from the frame when the engine can continue in situ.

Eventually chassis number one was complete and ready for test when all concerned wanted to be the first to have a run, and what a day that was.

About a fortnight after the event, there was a piece in a wellknown trade journal about a certain member of the operating side of the industry being seen late one Saturday evening driving a brand new design of double-deck chassis along a certain motorway when the gratuitous comment was made to the effect that 'it was some vehicle to utilise for a weekend shopping excursion' only what the author did not know was that after an early morning run of some seventy miles, the rear drive failed. This resulted in consternation and a great deal of dashing to and fro whilst various components were acquired when a full scale surgical operation was carried out in a remote country lane and here we were back again at that development aspect I have mentioned so often before.

Despite all the thought and effort put into the conception and care taken to ensure that no component could ever be overstressed, everyone had overlooked how efficient an oil pump, a taper roller bearing can become given the right conditions. These conditions do not apply during stop/start work normally associated with bus operating but given a 70-mile top speed run mainly on motorways, the final angle drive bearings very efficiently pumped themselves and their casing dry. The solution when it was reached was easy and now every Dominator has an oil pump located at the foot of the drop box giving positive oil feed to the angle drive bearings, they, having a happy time as a consequence.

Driving a bare chassis can be an alarming experience if one is not used to the task. The ride is absolutely solid, one can feel quite noticeably the flexing of the frames even on motorway standards of surface and braking, thanks to the lack of adhesion weight, is an uncertain process, whilst the weather can also make life difficult, so we really had to wait until that first chassis gained a body before it was possible to truly ascertain how the new toy handled. Not too well was the answer for the steering had some odd characteristics and this was found to be due to being actually over-engineered – there was one bush too many at the foot of the steering column plus a lack of alignment in the two universal couplings that are located at either end of the shaft that links the column to the chassis mounted box that contains the power steering assembly.

Generally, though, this first vehicle proved that the Dominator could and would work, so a batch of pre-production chassis actually 17 in number were put in hand and these were quickly followed by the first examples of the main stream series, and here more little problems began to appear, for example – the one part of the whole assembly that did look a bit suspect was the layout of the exhaust system, a matter that was confirmed when the horizontal cylindrical silencers which were affixed to the end of a vertical down pipe began to drop off. The pipe was cut, a flexible bellows inserted therein, and more dropped off, only now a part of the pipe went too. The cure was to redesign the mountings and throw in a piece of flexible exhaust piping of the conventional form.

Then we had a noise difficulty. The pre-production prototypes had a hydraulic fan motor as it was felt that no electric one would be sufficiently robust for the purpose. A thermostatically operated control was included so as the water heat rose, on came the fan. That fan sounded like a coffee grinder until its blade profile was amended but then came snag number two. The fluid was taken up the frame from pump to motor under pressure and then returned to the supply reservoir and as these were early units some flexible hoses were included in the lines. On Series Two, the hoses were replaced by very workman-like solid pipes all neatly clipped to the frame and then when the fan came in the pipes sung the song of a 'banshee'. Series Three went back to flexibles and as they came in the noise went out, so Series Two had to be modified accordingly.

Then we had retarder troubles as nearly every vehicle seemed to have different braking characteristics which caused your Author to have more than one exploratory

Top: The Dominator engine and transmission assembly. This picture shows how the drive from the Gardner 6LXB engine is taken through the Voith gearbox, and thence into the Dennis-built drop box. This drop box contains an idler wheel to restore clockwise motion to the drive shaft contained in the casing that runs from the foot of the drop box to the angle drive unit, and the propeller shaft mating flange. The pump that had to be fitted as an afterthought is mounted on the outside face of the drop box and has two flexible pipes for input and delivery purposes. Two larger flexible pipes take the heated torque convertor/retarder fluid from the gearbox into the heat exchanger mounted on top of this unit, so that it can be cooled by water in the radiator system, and the two large copper pipes that provide connections to or from the front mounted radiator are also clearly visible. The heat exchanger works very well, and helps to keep the interior of the buses warm in winter something that was never previously easy to achieve if the efficient Gardner engine provided the motive power.

Above: A recent variant of the Dominator double-deck chassis is the air suspension alternative. Here the first such unit to be produced stands in the Abbey Park Road Garage yard of Leicester City Transport that purchased it together with a second similar chassis for evaluation purposes. Leicester also ordered the first single-deck Falcon model that will have many components common to the Dominator, but the motive power will be provided by a horizontal Gardner engine to be mounted behind the rear axle and driving forwards to the Voith gearbox that will be fitted within the wheelbase. This Dominator was to have formed the base of a 1980 Show Bus, but its place was taken by the prototype Falcon chassis also Leicester-bound.

drive. At length, the penny dropped. During construction one computer control module was accidentally damaged on one of the first buses on the line. There was no replacement readily to hand so to ensure the customer was served on time, the box off No 2 was put on to No 1, that from No 3 on to No 2 and so on. Alas, each box is individually matched to its transmission unit at the manufacturer's works just to ensure that all do work in the same way on installation but now that action was nullified so there was a rush of activity whilst box and unit numbers as found on each vehicle so affected were carefully listed and then a big change day ensued.

The retarders also did not always work on receipt and here was a very silly cause for those separate cut out switches were not marked 'on' or 'off'. As they were symmetrical about their centre lines, some worked one way others the reverse, so the position of the 'on' contacts had to be located, the switch tumblers made to point the same way and the necessary wording then applied with a small paint brush so that no one in the garages could ever become confused in the future.

Once all this had been sorted out, the retarder came into its own and it seems from experiences to date that the life of the brake liners on these machines will be about four times as great as those on buses of equivalent weight that lack this feature, whilst the transmission unit itself looks like giving the 200,000 miles life between overhauls that was always sought.

As usual, though, there are some adverse points.

The gear selector push buttons could, perhaps, be more robust but there is an alternative four-button assembly that gives all ratios or cuts out top gear, or cuts out top and second, so retaining the vehicle in fluid drive, or engages reverse, and this is about to be tried by way of experiment.

The transmission system also incorporates a cushion drive assembly to smooth out any oscillation vibrations that might otherwise be carried from the engine into the gearbox. This looks from the outside rather like a fluid flywheel but consists internally of a star shaped inner driving hub which fits into a driven hub which possessed a similar internal configuration.

Between the internal driving and driven vanes are a series of rubber bushes so that those on one side of each take the driving forces whilst those on the other side the braking torques, and these rubbers which have a fairly hard time deteriorate to the point of requiring replacement after about 50,000 miles. The job is, though, a fairly easy one and even if a major failure does occur, the end result is never so expensive as it would be if that other version was incorporated of having a flexible centred metal driving plate.

Those braking torques are, of course, magnified by the retarder, a little matter that in the early days brought a protest from the propellor shaft joints, but these were soon stiffened up and here we were back to Loline days.

We also found that various drive line coupling flange fixings tended to work loose but this could well be due to the use of metric threads as these have given rise to similar lack of tightness – and rather worse, loss of bearing pre-loading in other situations, and so one of the proprietory fixing compounds has to be applied to the threads on initial assembly.

Other annoyances have been a lack of battery charge due to too small a generator drive ratio which gave rise to a Series three redesign to bring in different pulleys and belts, a perpetually leaking filter in the fan drive pressure line cured finally by a campaign change, an electrically-driven fan that passes air through the engine oil cooler that was also insufficiently robust to cope with the work it had to do, and spring bolts whose accessibility was much improved when they were reversed during chassis erection and last, but by no means least, the virtual impossibility of removing a damaged radiator on the version carrying a particular body. Here some captive nuts at the back of the mounting bracket were all that proved to be necessary.

Of the good points overall reliability has been quite high, fuel consumption is very reasonable and thanks to the stiff frame the ride is very good for the frame remains rigid whilst the springs do the flexing, a state of affairs that may well have been sadly reversed on some other buses that I could mention, but even so, an air suspension version is now under development.

These later words, though, also apply to the whole of the chassis, a chassis which can also accommodate single-deck bodies as well as the double-deck versions.

Of the new generation of double-deck chassis that have come on to the market during the last three years, the Dennis Dominator is perhaps the least complex and due no doubt to its relatively conventional nature the company has begun to achieve a commercial success with some 400 examples being either on order or in daily use at the time of writing and some of the customers have never previously been known to favour Guildford products.

It is very pleasing to see such an old established name re-establishing itself in a field from which only a few years ago it seemed to have departed for ever. For Hestair Dennis is now big in buses. As the rear engined Dominator was developed so was a front-engined Jubliant chassis that is now very successful in certain export markets notably Hong Kong where its rugged characteristics are much appreciated.

Further design work in 1980 produced the horizontal rear engined Falcon chassis originally intended for single-deck bodies – the first being ordered by Leicester City Transport – but this chassis and the Vec-engined Falcon II which has a simpler transmission layout can also take double-deck bodies and 1981/82 will see some of these entering service.

Finally Dennis have readopted a very familiar name and so in the Spring of 1981 took the first orders for a new Lancet mid-engined chassis power unit with conventional or fully automatic transmissions and this design of a medium/light weight nature can be built to full size or midi bus dimensions.

May all these enjoy considerable success and no more consequently be heard of that old 'stop-go' policy.

8
The Seddon Saga

As a young transport enthusiast, I was fortunate to be able to become very well-acquainted with the traffic superintendent of our local municipal operator who initially kindly consented to help me with the projected writing of a history of the former tramway system that expired in the summer of 1946, but this acquaintanceship developed to the point where he would frequently take me for a tour of the bus depot and it was during the course of one of these evening excursions that I noticed a most peculiar vehicle standing amongst a number of petrol-engined Leyland single-deckers that were awaiting disposal, but this 'oddity', unlike its neighbours, was spanking brand new and painted in an exotic livery of dark blue, light blue and silver, which had been applied in loops of colour.

The rest of the machine was also by the standards of the day somewhat unusual. It was about 26ft long, had a folding door at the front, small windows, a full width front with two windscreens, and those windscreens had very little rake so that the vehicle was somewhat box like, but below the windscreen protruding through the dash plate, was the cowl of a conventional radiator and on the radiator grill was a round badge with the name 'Seddon Diesel' inscribed thereon, but who or what was Seddon?

Needless to say, I asked my friend who to my astonishment told me that the vehicle had actually been built only a short distance away from that very bus depot and had been brought along so that it could be checked over the following morning by the Ministry of Transport vehicle examiner, presumably for informative purposes only, for this vehicle was intended for export and did, I believe, eventually go to work in the Iberian peninsula.

I went to work, too, opening the cab door and taking my place on the driver's seat when I had a good look not only at the controls and other fittings but also at the brass plate that gave both the name and address of the manufacturers and then I followed up the look with a letter when, as a result of that inquiry, I came to meet Mr Robert Seddon himself and also to know rather more about the firm and its products than I could ever have envisaged.

The Seddon family prior to World War 1 had a butcher's business in Salford but when Herbert Seddon, one of the two sons, was demobilised in 1919, he through a chain of circumstances decided to buy a Commer which could carry a demountable body and use the vehicle for goods work on weekdays, and seaside excursions at the weekends. Here, he was assisted by a friend called Foster who was in the dairy business but the two didn't have sufficient money to complete the purchase so the balance had to be borrowed from Mr Seddon senior when with the loan came the condition that when Robert, his eldest son, was demobilised, he, too, would enter the field of road transport.

Thus was the firm of Foster and Seddon formed, a firm which over the next twenty years slowly developed as the partners reconditioned wagons, ran a bus service from Swinton to Salford until that municipality bought them out, had a Morris agency, and also did the odd haulage job, but Robert Seddon saw that there was a gap in the range of vehicles being manufactured by the established concerns and one morning he proceeded to tell me how he had settled down to design a truck which would meet a demand he was certain existed, when much of the work was undertaken on his kitchen table.

The first Seddon was built in the Ford Lane, Salford premises in about 1937 and proved to be a 6ton forward control two-axled lightweight truck of 13ft 6in wheelbase

Above: The first Seddon psvs were based on the 14ft 6in wheelbase Mark IV chassis which had a Perkins P6 engine. The front end of this Seddon-bodied vehicle of 1948 vintage clearly displays its goods vehicle ancestry. Clyde Valley Coaches of Holytown were the owners of this rear entrance model but purchasers could have a forward passenger door if they wished.

which was powered by the also new Perkins P6 4.73litre diesel engine which was then known as the Panther. This lightweight indirect injection engine was intended originally for petrol engine conversions and Seddons was the first manufacturer to install it in a new chassis, if the word 'manufacturer' can really be used in this connection. The truck, though, was cheap and it worked, so by 1938 the partners were sufficiently encouraged to take a stand at the Glasgow Show and sell it under the catchy slogan – two and a half tons, 30mph and £30 tax, but then came the war and an opportunity for the firm as it was permitted to continue to build the six-tonner under a Ministry of War Transport licence, output going to civilian hauliers until around 1943 when trailer production became the order of the day. It must have been a momentous decision to begin truck assembly in 1938 when the giants such as Leyland or AEC or Foden had such a grip on the market, but there came an even greater decision in 1946 when realising that the world was short of transport, the company moved its plant to a then disused shadow factory in Oldham and proceeded slowly but surely to increase output from one or two a week to double figures. With the increase in output came some new variations on an old theme, namely, 6ton tractor or tipper chassis with wheelbases of 9ft and 10ft respectively, but the long flat was still the most popular and one that was exported to South America came to carry a somewhat locally-built bus body – news of this obviously was relayed back to Oldham, and then came the first true Seddon passenger

chassis which clearly had been derived from the six-tonner.

The 8.5in deep chassis frame was new but everything forwards of the cab arch was a repeat of what had gone before – or almost so – because with the move to Oldham came a new radiator with a polished cast aluminium cowl, a different dash plate and a stronger front end. The P6 engine, though, still provided the horsepower – all 70 of them at 2,200rpm, there was still the 12in diameter clutch, a five-speed constant mesh gearbox and vacuum hydraulic brakes. Behind the cab arch, though, the frame widened out from 33in to 44in and also had the usual psv low loading sweep over the rear axle that was set further back to give a 14ft 11in wheelbase, and, if a customer wanted that axle could be of the two-speed variety – another Seddon first – then a four-speed box was employed, the springs were lengthened to 60in to give a better ride and within the maximum length of 27ft the bodywork could accommodate 32 stage carriage type seats or 28 full luxury ones. Unladen weight was 2ton 12cwt.

This passenger chassis was known as the Mark IV and it soon began to sell well. The Bombay State Railways took an initial batch of 75 and then repeated the order. Other useful export sales were recorded and in Britain the City Coach concern, Dallam Motor Services, Youngs Buses (Paisley) and Ripponden and District among other operators took small numbers of this simple but surprisingly reliable machine although it must be appreciated when one looks back that they were none too comfortable to drive. That P6 engine was noisy, the bonnet was bulky and lacked any sort of sound proofing, the engine was held down on what can only be described as solid mountings and, finally, the control pedals worked in slots cut in the floor plate, these slots giving rise to an assortment of draughts. Chassis price in 1950 was £1,290, or £1,340 with a two-speed rear axle, but add a Seddon 31 seat front or rear entrance body and you paid just £2,540 – and that included painting.

By 1950, though, further development had taken place with the appearance of the 16ft 4in wheelbase Mark IV that was to the same basic specification only now there was a neater dash with recessed headlamps, a chrome plated bumper bar, new gear and clutch pedals passing through holes and much tidier bonnets that took up much less space in the cab (the Mark IV was similarly updated) but as the position of the driver's seat to the gearbox was identical to that of the Mark IV, the gear lever still came up behind the driver and one had to reach backwards whenever a ratio change was necessary as also was the case on every Seddon goods chassis but as most passenger vehicles of the time were of the full forward control layout, a high percentage of drivers found this Seddon feature rather offputting at first.

The company had quickly begun to build its own cabs adopting a most attractive coachbuilt design and then moved on to offer single-deck bus bodies which were based on metal section frames and it was the first such product that I had seen when I first encountered a Seddon. These bodies were somewhat austere but nicely finished and could be had with either front or rear entrances when the passenger compartment was usually separated from the cab by a full width bulkhead that helped both the stiffness of the structure and noise reduction at least as far as the passenger was concerned. Again most of the bodied buses were exported but one day when I visited the bodyworks, by now moved to a separate set of buildings known as Moss Lane works only a stone's throw from the Woodstock factory, I noticed that two were under construction for that erstwhile large independent Bullock and Sons of Featherstone, Yorkshire, and these went to work in 1949 in the Selby area as fleet numbers 334 and 335. They were based on the Mark IV chassis and had 31 seats but at the same time someone had made a bid for the high life and so two full luxury coaches were in build, one with a driver's bulkhead and one without, but as Mr Robert said somewhat ruefully later 'There weren't going to be any

more' and so it transpired. Bullocks, though, must have been pleased with their Seddons for they ordered another two but this time elected for the longer and newer Mark VI but by the time they had been delivered in 1950 as fleet numbers 707 and 708, Bullocks were no more having sold out to the West Riding Automobile concern, and so these vehicles came out of the bodyshops in the green paint style that was so wellknown in the Wakefield area until very recent times.

By 1950 Seddon Motors Ltd, or Seddon Diesel Vehicles as it soon became, had another bus chassis in embryo but before we touch on this, let me mention the unusual Mark VIs that came to possess Reo Gold Star petrol engines instead of the inevitable Perkins P6 that was now rated to produce 79bhp at 2,400rpm. I always thought they were intended for a Middle East oil company but a friend more knowledgeable than I said Finland was the true destination but wherever they went one thing is sure, there was a tremendous panic when it was suddenly discovered that these petrol engines were being installed in goods chassis instead of passenger frames and this at a time when they were almost ready for road test, but here thanks to the almost identical front end layouts, rectification was speedily accomplished with next to no material being scrapped in the process but these were not the only Seddon machines to run on petrol, there was at least one other that gave me a tremendous fright.

It came in for a rebore one morning and in the course of the next two or three days off came the head and sump, out came the pistons and a boring bar then did its stuff. A careful clean up followed, the engine was rebuilt and restarting time drew nigh. The rebuilding gang included a newish apprentice who was told to take the engine oil bath air cleaner away, wash out the element in petrol, refill the cleaner and then secure it in place on top of the induction manifold. He subsequently reappeared to say the job was complete when he was asked was he sure that the cleaner had been properly refilled. The reply was in the affirmative so as Friday finishing time was drawing nigh, a restart was attempted. Now the new pistons were a little on the tight side and the starter chugged a little as it began to slowly turn the engine but the accent here is on the word 'little'. After about a quarter of a turn, the engine took a goodly sniff of the neat petrol that formed the contents of that oil cleaner and took off with a roar that could put a Concorde to shame. The pneumatic governor couldn't do a thing as it hit peak revs – and more, and neither could the rebuilders except, of course, to pray that the engine wouldn't disintegrate. Flames shot out of the exhaust and the ears of the foreman but by some miracle nothing blew up and instead we had virtually instant running in – in fact, the driver who took the vehicle away was later heard to declare 'It's a flyer'. Only this was certainly the politest of all the pronouncements that little incident inspired.

Trying to change road springs on low passenger vehicles without the aid of a pit was another exercise that provided food for thought but at least on the next Seddon they were not unduly heavy for this was based on the Mark VIII 3ton goods chassis that also was introduced in 1950, an assembly that featured a Perkins P4 3.15litre engine and flexible engine mountings which with four pot power were certainly wanted. The passenger version thereof known as the Mark 7P had an 11ft 8in wheelbase and 28 seats could be accommodated within the 21ft 6in x 6ft 7in box dimensions of the standard Seddon bodywork. The presence of the 52bhp P4 meant that the vehicle could never be described as being overpowered, but quite a large number were sold abroad for a chassis only cost of about £700 with some going to Bermuda Public Transport Board, a market which had taken a steady stream of Mark IV and Mark VI buses, that left Oldham sporting a tropical version of the standard bus body that contained little or no timber and an insulated roof.

Up to this time every Seddon had been of straight forward design but at the 1952 Commercial Show the company leapt into the unorthodox with a vengeance.

By that time underfloor engined chassis were well on the way to completely eclipsing their front-engined ancestors but not every fleet engineer was impressed by the idea of having a horizontal oil engine which can and then certainly did possess some problems of its own, so out of the Woodstock factory came an underfloor chassis with a VERTICAL engine, a somewhat remarkable combination.

There were two versions, the Mark 10 with the old and tried Perkins P6 engine, and the Mark 11 with the new and larger R6 engine. The Mark 11 had a 16ft 6in wheelbase against the 13ft 11in of the Mark 10 and was intended to carry full size 30ft x 8ft bodywork. The frame flat in the horizontal frame was set quite high at 34in from the road in the unladen condition and the top of the power unit only projected a very small distance above the upper flange. Little alteration was necessary to the manifolds to achieve this result and despite the then very unusual position, access for servicing was quite good, which certainly in the early days was just as well for the high revving R6 (108bhp at 2,700rpm) was far from trouble free. Eventually the faults were cured and the chassis in consequence became very reliable but only about 100 were produced in an eight-year production run going up to 1960 slightly over half of which took the larger form.

Most of the home market examples were fitted with coach bodies but our old friend West Riding Automobile that has so often figured in these pages took two versions and here was a very unusual purchasing process. The first vehicle fleet number 738 entered service on 11 September, 1952 and consisted of a 10P chassis and Seddon 32-seat front entrance body. Carrying the registration number EHL 500 it continued to operate until 21 June 1954 when it was sold back to the builder in a part exchange deal. As a result, a Mark II fleet number 751, registration number FHL 987, entered the West Riding fleet but now the chassis (Mark II/R/8590) sported a 44-seat Duple coach body and survived until 16 September, 1963 when it was sold to the nearby Cudworth operator, A. Rowe & Sons Ltd. Seddons

Right: By the time DHL 549 was produced, the Seddon Mark IV and the larger 16ft 4in wheel base Mark VI alternative had been given flush mounted headlamps and a plated front bumper as standard. There were also new and much neater bonnets. This Seddon Mark IV was one of four ordered by the erstwhile J. Bullock & Sons concern of Featherstone. Two of these were finished in the red, brown and cream livery as CHL 275 and CHL 742 going into service in 1948 and 1950. The other pair which consisted of DHL 549 and DHL 550 came after the West Riding takeover when the four became their new owner's fleet numbers 334, 335, 707 and 708. All had Seddon 31-seat front entrance bodies.

Left: This reproduction taken from a catalogue of the day shows the layout of the Pennine Mark 10 and Mark 11 of the 79bhp Perkins P6 or 108bhp R6 type which were mounted low down and centrally in the frames.

The radiator was on the nearside towards the front with the batteries and spare wheel behind the rear axle. The chassis design predated that of the similar Bedford YRT or YRQ but being ahead of its time only sold in very small numbers.

Below: The West Riding Automobile Company took this Pennine Mark 10 into stock in 1952, Seddon building the 32-seat body. The vehicle was later returned to the builder in part exchange for a Mark 11 that became West Riding fleet number 751 and had a Duple 44-seat coach body. No 738 spent the rest of its life still in its West Riding green livery on the Salford Oldham staff service.

having received EHL 500 kept it using it morning and night on the Salford staff shuttle service introduced when the Woodstock Factory was first opened and it performed on that job for years still in its old green West Riding livery which became more and more faded as time went by.

The unfortunate thing here is that some fifteen years later, Bedfords introduced the basically YRQ or YMT passenger chassis which followed the same basic line of approach and made a significant penetration into the coach market, and one can but wonder why Seddond did not have a similar success for the rides I had from time to time on these West Riding buses were quite enjoyable and I am sure that the modern YRQ or YMT series Bedfords we now operate are very little quieter or give a much better ride than those now almost forgotten Seddon machines.

In 1956, however, certain Mark II components,

namely, the frames, axles and steering gear, were used in the Mark 18 but now the engine, a vertical P6 not an R6, was mounted transversely at the rear. The fifty or so buses produced to this design were all exported mainly to Australia where they were reputed to have performed surprisingly well. Little is known, however, about the 36ft long Mark 20 model which consisted of just one single heavyweight with a Meadows 550 horizontal oil engine, and a 350 gearbox that was exported to Greece where it was fitted with locally built bodywork.

At this stage it is pertinent to mention the activities of the bodybuilding department that had as its main task the production of goods vehicle cabs but a range of commercial bodies was also produced and special designs were undertaken as a matter of course. Amongst

THE NEW Seddon PENNINE IV 33ft P.S.V CHASSIS

WITH 120 B.H.P. — 354 ENGINE

WHEELBASE OPTIONS PERMIT 24-36ft OVERALL BODY LENGTHS 170 B.H.P.—V8-ENGINE OPTIONAL

Seddon Diesel

Right: The much more successful Pennine IV was a very orthodox forward-engine machine that could be obtained in a variety of lengths and wheel bases. This reproduction of the descriptive sales leaflet issued by the manufacturers shows its simple layout. Motive power in this case was provided by the 120bhp Perkins 354 engine but a V8 engine was also offered.

Below: The prototype Pennine 4 complete with Seddon/Pennine body work at Elmwood Garage, Halifax when brand new. It ran there from 29 March 1969 to 12 April. Forming a very good basis for a rural/interurban bus it was not, thanks to the constant mesh gearbox incorporated, ideal for use on busy one-man operated town routes even though this had five ratios.

these were a series of parcel vans for Manchester Corporation Transport and from this introduction came an order for six bus bodies which were to be mounted on Albion Aberdonian chassis and these incorporated Seddon as opposed to Metal Section framing. It was then decided that more business still could be obtained if the Seddon connection was loosened and so a new subsidiary was set up under the style of Pennine Coachworks Ltd and this embarked on the building of passenger or commercial bodies for any customer irrespective of the make of chassis involved.

The first home market Pennine bodies were another batch of six ordered by Great Yarmouth Corporation to 27ft by 7ft 6in box dimensions fitted with 37 seats and mounted on shortened AEC Reliance chassis which were produced in 1964, and one of these appeared on the Pennine stand at the Commercial Show of that year. Further orders followed and soon Pennine was building single-deckers for Reading, Rochdale and Halifax corporations, the Gosport and Fareham and Jersey Motor Transport companies, when some quite elaborate buses resulted – those for Reading in particular coming into this category.

The Seddon company was still expanding and in 1967 a much more significant onslaught was launched on the passenger market which was spearheaded by the new Pennine 4 chassis which followed the old Mark IV formula of utter simplicity. A straight frame parallel throughout its length in plan view and running at a height of 34in carried a Perkins 6.354 engine at the front which drove through a 14in diameter clutch into a five-speed constant mesh gearbox. The specification also included a 50gal fuel tank, a spiral bevel rear axle and dual circuit air brakes with diaphragms in the wheel brake assemblies. Normal braking was obtained through the medium of the usual foot operated brake valve but in addition a hand lever was fitted under the steering wheel which brought in an auxiliary braking system. The engine was set low in the frame and the front axle of the 16ft 6in wheelbase chassis was set well back so as to permit a front passenger door to be incorporated. Here, the entrance was somewhat restricted but as only a relatively small bonnet cowl (in fibre glass) was necessary, a Pennine 4 could be used as the basis for a one-man operated bus.

The standard model was intended for 33ft long bodies but a range of alternatives was available so anything from 24ft to 36ft was possible. The manufacturers produced a demonstrator and we borrowed this for a time when I essayed a drive. The vehicle had commendably light steering and good brakes although these were somewhat sensitive and the pedal had to be treated lightly. The standard of ride, too, was praiseworthy but in some respects its handling took one back to the days of the Mark IV for it was necessary to double declutch whenever a gear change was made and the gear lever was still located behind the driver's seat so one had to reach backwards for it.

As we were running fairly heavy services in a very hilly area, we concluded that it wasn't the machine for us and here the size of the engine was a material factor in arriving at this decision but then we were loaned a second Pennine 4 which came complete with the alternative Perkins Vee 8 of 8.36litre capacity and 170bhp output at

Left: The following Pennine RU of 1969 was a very different machine with its semi-automatic gearbox and 6HLX horizontal Gardner engine. TBU 598G was the initial Seddon-bodied prototype that also began its career as a demonstrator in Halifax and it is here seen in a narrow part of Hepstonfall Village. Halifax JOC later took three Plaxton bodied 33ft long RUs completed to a semi-luxury standard as Nos 318, 319 and 320. TBU 598G was later sold to the Green Bus Company of Rugeley, passed then to Midland Red when the company was taken over and was then sold in 1947 to Lancaster City Transport, an undertaking that kept it for a further three years. Seating capacity for 43 was provided but 20 standing passengers could also be carried.

2,800rpm and this gave what can only be described as a 'cracking' performance when the ability to 'hang on' in, say, third gear on the more ferocious gradients had to be experienced to be believed. It still, though, wasn't an ideal local bus service vehicle although a synchromesh box could be fitted (with a forwards mounted gear lever too) as the entrance steps were on the high side, and because of the location of the power unit the front end layout was not really suitable for intensive one-man operation use even if the engine cover was lower than before but the Pennine 4 became very popular and a very large number was bodied for coach type work. Indeed, for one or two seasons this Seddon topped the sales stakes in that particular field.

This encouraged the Seddon/Pennine organisation to turn a former electrical factory which had begun life originally as the Rhos cotton mill into the base of a new and enlarged bus division and thoughts turned then to a more sophisticated heavyweight chassis, the design and original construction work being undertaken in 1969 or early 1970 and this proceeded to provide the establishment with a few shocks particularly as the initial selling price of a complete bodied vehicle was in the order of £6,200.

The newcomer, known as the Seddon Pennine RU, had a completely straight frame devoid of all kinks and sweeps but which sloped gently upwards towards the rear, the side members being 8in deep. The frame height at the centre of the front axle was only 27in so that a low entrance platform could be provided and it must be remembered here that this was the first new design to come out after the introduction of the bus grant scheme with its emphasis on one-man operation suitability. The front axle was of Seddon manufacture and derived from truck components, having a 6ton rating. The rear axle of Eaton origin incorporated a spiral bevel unit and three alternative gear ratios were available. In exceedingly close proximity to that rear axle was the output flange of a four-speed self-change Wilson type semi-automatic epicyclic gearbox which was coupled to a fluid flywheel which was connected in turn to a Gardner 6HLW 112bhp engine but here again another set of alternatives was listed, namely, a five-speed gearbox and/or a Gardner 6HLX engine which would provide 150 horses. The engine flywheel and gearbox were bolted together to form a single power pack and this pack was carried underneath the rear of the frame, the offside member being taken the full length of the chassis but the nearside main member finished at the engine end of the gearbox when a short rear piece was brought out almost to the outside edge of the bus so as to allow access to the fuel pump and alternator which were mounted on the upper side of the cylinder block and reached through floor traps of very acceptable dimensions.

It will be gathered from the foregoing that the power pack was carried longitudinally and as I have said on a 33ft chassis there was very little distance between the gearbox and rear axle driving flanges and not over much more on the 36ft long version that cost another £150 when the respective wheelbases were 16ft 6in and 18ft

6in respectively: so on the original productions a very unusual propellor shaft was provided when two large doughnut-shaped rubber couplings were fitted to each flange and connected by a short and very solid coupling with four star-like arms at each end, each of which carried a bolt securing it to the doughnut, four more interspaced bolts fastened that component to the flanges.

Conventional springs 3.5in wide were fitted front and rear but the spring and shackle bushes were formed from polyurethane in an attempt to eliminate the need for lubrication. Air brakes were fitted with an air-operated spring parking brake – another Seddon passenger chassis first – and if you wanted a power-assisted steering system could be incorporated. The brakes themselves were of Girling manufacture of the wedge form and both front and rear assemblies were 15.5in diameter and 7in wide.

Another innovation was the intention to employ a combined engine cooling saloon heating system and so a large heat exchanger/radiator was mounted just in front of the offside rear wheels when some internal body ductings were to feed warm air into the saloon, the same ducting was also intended to provide a ventilation outlet when up to twenty changes of air per hour should have been possible.

Because this bus had a flat frame, Seddons modified the body that had been designed for the Pennine 4. This was almost entirely framed in aluminium alloy whereas previous Seddon or Pennine bodies had been steel framed. The welded side and roof frames were jig built and these frames were then bolted to the outriggers provided there being no body underframe as such and it was said that the method of construction would allow up to around a ton in weight to be saved. Seddons again went on to produce a demonstrator and this duly went into service with us for a week or so when it performed quite well so a trial order was placed for three 33ft long RUs but as we had a requirement for something better than a standard stage carriage body, a like number of dual purpose 45-seater bodies was ordered from another source and when in due course the vehicles were completed, we had a few test runs before placing these new toys in service. Here, I was assailed by a most peculiar feeling. I have driven scores of single or double-deck buses, and invariably you put your foot down on the gas pedal and obtain movement, but with the Seddons there was a most weird sensation. It always felt to me as if there was a big hand at the back of the bus pushing and pushing, and one could sense the force involved coming through the back of the driver's seat. It wasn't really unpleasant and certainly when it came to tractive effort our 6HLX engined series could accelerate or climb hills as well as if not better than anything else in the fleet so I could only conclude that the layout of the frame was in some way responsible. I often wondered if drivers in other places had experienced this sort of reaction. I also wondered if our engineering compatriots experienced the same sort of maintenance feelings for the RU was not exactly trouble-free.

The first trouble was a front trouble for the steering

Above: In sharp contrast to the Pennine RU was the Seddon minibus. Designed specifically as a low capacity psv that would be capable of hard work, nicely finished Pennine bodywork was invariably included in the completed vehicle. XVU 336M chassis number 54674 entered service with Greater Manchester Transport in August 1973 but was sold to Tayside Transport in May 1977 to become fleet number 311. One of six such secondhand acquisitions it came to Dundee with an Eaton synchromesh gearbox but was subsequently fitted with an Allison automatic transmission unit. The body accommodates 20 seated passengers.

bushes wore, as did the axle thrust pads, and additionally the king pins came loose in the front axle beam and so what should have been nice neat round holes in that forging assumed an elongated appearance when a new beam or two had to be acquired. From this mini list steering faults developed. The steering was a trifle to light due to the lack of front axle loading and it was rather too easy for an RU to enter into a front wheel skid, and in this type of antic any road vehicle loses all directional control and just heads straight ahead which can be more than a little disconcerting. This lack of front end weight seemed to promote sundry steering wobbles which were also alarming but balancing the front wheels or even taking more tyre fitting care than average could dispose of this annoyance but it wasn't so easy to cope with the suspension defects that had some steering repercussions. The standard of ride was quite good but those 3.5in wide springs were not really sufficiently robust and a good deal of bother could have been avoided if they had been made from 4in plates. Then those polyurethane bushes did wear alarmingly, even though they should not have done when slackness in and around the front shackles quickly affects road wheel geometry and quickly becomes multiplied at the steering wheel rim which is, of course, where the system and the driver come into intimate contact so that in the end a combination of chromium plated pins, brass bushes and grease nipples had to be employed. There was also some chassis movement around the steering box support member but a little stiffening effected a cure.

Some stiffening was also required in the region of the radiator brackets. The cooling/heating idea wasn't sufficiently developed to put into production by the time

the first customer orders were in hand so a more conventional arrangement was provided with the radiator still fitted hard behind the offside front wheel. The brackets would fracture and if they were not promptly found a series of loose water connections very quickly ensued. No engine likes losing its cool and neither does it appreciate a clogged air filter. The ones on the RU were very efficient but they, too, were located in proximity to the splash set up by a road wheel so there was a servicing area that could never be neglected. Also on the offside of the chassis was the main battery isolation switch and here was another component that was badly affected during prolonged periods of bad weather when the switches would corrode or in extreme cases shorting across the terminals would occur and a wiring fire follow. In truth, some of the chassis wiring was suspect but an extra insulation sleeve or a spot of rerouting was all that was needed if you wanted to run an RU successfully through the Manchester and district monsoon periods.

Above: Without any doubt, the underfloor engined Pennine produced initially for the Scottish Bus Group should be the most acceptable psv chassis of all to come out of Woodstock factory. This high level view shows how the offside frame member is splayed outwards to clear the fuel pump and other auxiliaries. This chassis has a conventional gearbox, the striking/selector shaft being clearly visible as it runs diagonally over the front axle. Semi-automatic transmission is also available.

Of power there was usually more than sufficient but if a bus was booked for pulling poor the hydraulic throttle arrangement was usually the culprit. Air could bleed into the fluid to be compressed when the driver put his hoof on the gas pedal and so the amount of travel coming out at the engine end would fall short of the desirable, and here one was back to the pressure charging business mentioned in an earlier chapter.

This brings us to the point where we have three remaining grumbles to air but number one is rather nebulous for it concerns the brakes. These were as has been noted of proprietory manufacture and reasonably efficient but most bus engineers are weaned on cam type operation and so always have grave doubts about anything that employs wedges or other unfamiliar devices so let's pass that one, but number two simply could not be ignored, it was in fact the Achilles heel of the whole bus, and I refer to that too short propellor shaft. If the springs had been stronger – which would have worsened the ride characteristics, it might(?) just have survived but as a design it didn't. A whole series of different sorts of shafts and/or universal joints was tried but none really proved to be 100% successful and in the end the drastic step was taken on the 36ft chassis of moving the whole power pack back to the extreme edge of the chassis when the odd inches so gained could be used to lengthen the universal joint spider centre distances. This remedy could not, though, be applied to the 33ft version and guess what we had?

Grumble three was a body matter for those Seddon bodies were rather too light and because there was no supporting underframe, bearers broke or more significant cracking appeared above the floor line. It did seem as if the two-door versions were more susceptible than were bodies only having a single front entrance but as having a centre door means of necessity that the near side truss panels cannot be continuous along the whole length of the framing, any weakness must be emphasised.

All the foregoing can, though, again be ascribed to insufficient initial development for the RU was surprisingly successful in its early days. There were no Seddons in municipal or pte service in 1968 but by late-1970 there were eight Pennine IV coaches with what was then SELNEC PTE and 26 Pennine RUs working in three corporation transport departments, the 14 then owned by Doncaster representing the first production order that was completed early in 1970. A further 51 were simultaneously recorded as being on order but the biggest RU order of all was that placed by the Crosville Company for no less than 100 complete buses, half of which were to have two passenger doors, the other half a single front entrance/exit.

By 1974, the list was much more impressive for Blackburn then had 6, Burnley Colne & Nelson Joint Committee 20, Darlington 8, Fylde 6, Hyndburn 5, Lancaster 6 and Southampton 5 whilst the South Yorkshire PTE had 36 that had originated either with Doncaster or Rotherham and the corresponding West Yorkshire undertaking had 26, all but three of which had been ordered by the former Huddersfield municipality and, due no doubt to the very competitive price, several had been acquired by various private concerns when Pennine bodies were invariably specified.

As we have seen, the RU chassis had certain inherent faults but Woodstock factory had put a great deal of time and energy into eliminating the more detailed ones and without doubt a cure could have been found for the 33ft long propellor shaft problems but as happens all too often in the passenger transport chassis industry, someone took the decision to suspend all further production and so the last of the 283 examples of this model to be completed went to Doncaster as chassis numbers 56041 and 56042 being delivered on 19 March 1974 just a few days before the South Yorkshire PTE came into being.

112

There was in the series, however, one very unusual RU for it was powered not by a horizontal Gardner engine but by several tons of batteries and a sizeable electric motor. The complete vehicle was sponsored for experimental purposes by the Chloride Electric Group of Companies and was given the catchy and most appropriate name of the 'Silent Rider'. With a range on the average type of city service of around 100 miles, it provided an alternative to diesel oil and there was a suggestion made to the effect that a batch of about 30 might be built for extended trials when a whole group of routes could be converted and in so doing the requisite recharging equipment could be economically provided but as fuel oil did not increase as dramatically in price as had been expected, nothing further was done. One must, though, not write this experiment off as a great deal was learned through it and we may yet see a more widespread use of battery buses in the days to come.

After the official demise of the RU, several undertakings tried to obtain further supplies but without success even though Seddons, or Seddon/Atkinson as the firm had now become, had not completely opted out of the passenger field there being other proposals afoot.

The first of these materialised as a 1972 Show surprise in the form of a 9ft 6in wheelbase 'long life midibus'. It was felt that there was a need for such a machine that would be purpose built and not based on some commercial lightweight chassis adapted for psv purposes.

The Pennine 236 was the result. Basically a very shortened version of the Pennine IV, it had a four- instead of a six-cylindered Perkins engine and to make it suitable for city use, an Allison fully automatic transmission system was employed. Other interesting features were the 7ft 6in overall width, the fitting of single as opposed to twin rear tyres and the very attractive Pennine 25-seat body work with its flat one piece front windscreen. The show vehicle was finished in the colours of SELNEC PTE which by 1974 had no less than 37 in stock.

Again, a battery experimental vehicle was produced but for reasons already outlined, no series production was undertaken. Production of the Perkins-powered vehicles also came to be rather restricted but perhaps here we are back to the state of affairs mentioned in the paragraphs devoted to the Albion Nimbus for, alas, the operating costs of a bus do not decrease in direct proportion to a reduction in seating capacity and if one does have fewer seats then overload problems can and do occur as I discovered one night. We had borrowed a midibus for evaluation and put this to work on a route where takings were to say the least almost conspicuous by their absence. On the Saturday night, I decided to try the vehicle for myself and so commenced to drive it on one return run in passenger service between roughly 19.15 and 20.30hrs. We set off very quietly but there was a church on the line of route that was having some form of social that night and so an unusual number of passengers presented themselves and were somwhat 'unchristian' in their comments when they found the

usual 45/49 seater had been replaced by a pigmy which didn't have over much standing room. Well, not officially, that was. That midibus certainly had a full load test as did the transmission system which thanks to the hills on the route and the load on board, wasn't quite sure which ratio was the best one in the circumstances and so that experience sealed my mind against any further small capacity purchases irrespective of the company that made them, for the next 10 years.

One must here recognise, though, that there are places where circumstances necessitate special remedies and it is interesting to watch the Seddon midibuses of Greater Manchester Transport as they run to and from the Piccadilly Station terminal point after several years usage on what are certainly well patronised workings so, in this instance, at least the 'long life' title is apparently well deserved.

After this essay into the realms of small buses, Seddons then returned to the big time following approaches made to Oldham by the Scottish Bus Group. SBG was looking in the early years of the 1970s for a robust and simple underfloor engined chassis powered by a Gardner engine that would employ orthodox transmission and so act as a replacement to the Bristol and Guy models of similar mien that could no longer be obtained and so did the Pennine VII come into being. Predictably, SBG took the first which as chassis number 55241 was fitted with Alexander Y type 49-seat coachwork and placed in service as ZS 661 (Reg no OFS 661M) with its Eastern Scottish subsidiary in October, 1973.

With a 6LXB 184bhp engine, four or six-speed ZF synchromesh gearbox, full air braking, long centre leaf springs and power assisted steering, the vehicle was obviously going to be a very satisfactory performer a possibility firmly endorsed by the *Commercial Motor's* road test of July 1976 when the author of the test report praised the standard of ride, ease of handling, power to weight ratio and excellent fuel economy. The only adverse comments made concerned the heaviness of the hydraulically-operated accelerator pedal and the positioning of the trafficator switch but one cannot say that either of these truly involve vehicle fundamentals.

Here was a chassis that should surely have appealed to a whole host of coach, bus and dual purpose vehicle operators, particularly as the asking price was very reasonable and delivery reasonably quick but unless one crosses the Scottish border, one does not see many of these Seddon vehicles unless, of course, you encounter a convoy of SBG machines working on the long distance Anglo/Scottish services.

Around Edinburgh or Glasgow, however, the picture is very different as Eastern Scottish now has 215 in use, the pioneer ZS 661 having clocked up something over 157,000 miles at the time of writing (December 1979). It, like its later sisters, has been very reliable with only a degree of clutch trouble being recorded on the service sheets and so another 71 are currently on order. I was, in fact, watching the building of some of this batch within the Seddon shops very recently and could not help

Above: Western SMT Seddon No 2649 (RCS 704R) carries an Alexander T type 490-seat body.

Based on chassis No 61026 it first entered service on 1 June 1977 and is here seen near Kilmarnock. There are 15 vehicles in this particular batch in the series 2645-2659.

thinking how very different they were to those Mark IVs of 30 years ago particularly as the synchromesh gearbox has now been discarded in favour of the fluid flywheel/semi-automatic epicyclic gear alternative.

That other large bus group subsidiary Western SMT is also a confirmed Pennine VII user with 186 in stock commencing with No 2543 of December 1975 and ending with 2961 of November 1979 with another 27 still to come – at the date quoted.

It could be this will become more popular in 1980 for the AEC Reliance is now no longer with us and the updated Leyland Leopard has still to appear and so it forms the only British underfloor alternative although the independent company that was concerned in its inception is no more for Seddon/Atkinson sold out to the American-based International Harvester Group in 1974 and this transaction might have been responsible for the non-appearance of yet another Seddon chassis.

It was an open secret in the industry at that time when it seemed there was going to be a complete absence of competition in the field that the Oldham designers were working on the draughting out of a double-deck chassis but in the end this project was abandoned. Commercially this decision could well have been of advantage to Seddon/Atkinson for the vacuum was speedily filled by Fodens, Hestair Dennis and MCW but from a industry point of view, one must regret the non-emergence of a vehicle that could well have been technically rather different to its competitors.

At this stage, I wonder what it would have been called if it had come to be marketed.

A name such as the Pennine XX would not have been very imaginative and, personally, I would never have fancied the 'Oldhamer' even if I am one but more by adoption than birth. No, my choice would rest on the word 'Salfordian' as a tribute to Mr Robert Seddon, a gentleman whom I remember over the years with a great deal of admiration and not a little affection. Even if he was not able in his life span to see Woodstock factory increase in size from its original 'shadow factory' form to the present extensive range of buildings or be involved in the production of what are very much more complex vehicles than those of, say, 1950, he did lay the foundations of what is now a major manufacturing unit and I hope, therefore, that his family name continues to adorn the radiator grilles of a whole range of highly acceptable passenger vehicles for very many years to come for it is almost certain that if it had not been for his kindness to me about 30 years ago, *Looking at Buses* could never have been written.

9

'T'Main Man'

I began *Looking at Buses* with a light-hearted commentary on the way in which a fleet engineer might well pass his day, so what better way to end this second offering than to concentrate similarly on the activities of that seemingly more exalted personage – the general manager – if the phrase 'light-hearted' can be applied to such an official's daily routine. If, though, there is a doubt on that score, there is none in the label attached to the job for from those two words involved came the source of the title but not I hasten to add the inspiration for that arose from a momentous encounter.

Now I have commented previously on that supply of prewar copies of the monthly magazine *Passenger Transport* that were handed over to me usually quite unopened by our local tobacconist which made the task of going for my father's smoking requisites rather more pleasurable than would otherwise have been the case. The tobacconist by the way received them because he, as an alderman of the borough council was also chairman of the local passenger transport committee, but the significance of that office was quite unapparent to me for years to come. What was much more important was the chance the issues gave to find out something about the doings of the industry and the men that ran it. Now, it is one thing as an enthusiast to know that Mr So and So is boss of your local transport concern but how often do you know what he looks like? Well, in those prewar days there was a plethora of meetings and conferences at which all the notables of the day foregathered and it did not seem to matter whether their attendance was sponsored by one of the combine companies, or the municipal concerns, or their own private businesses, all that mattered was that they participated in these events

when their photographs would come to adorn numerous glossy pages.

Now I never met one of these heroes in the flesh until around 1946 but my only transport-orientated relative, to whit my bus-driving uncle, had had the honour some years earlier, for he had been involved in some incident and although not in any way blameworthy, he found himself required to give a personal account of the circumstances to 'Sir'. He had been employed by that same municipal undertaking for around twenty years at the time and was a company man through and through even though discipline was fierce and the pay and conditions by today's standards abysmal but he had never in that time even spoken to his gm let alone seen the inside of his office. The interview truly was the high spot of his transport career and he later retailed in the fullest detail all that a very retentive memory could recall of the way he was ushered into the sanctum and of the questions and answers that followed but his most awestruck comments related to the room in which all this took place. Here I still recall his telling of the obvious quality of the sizeable carpet that graced the floor, the vast size of the desk complete with two telephones, the oak panelling, the carved stone fireplace and, wonder of wonders, the living fire that glowed in the grate. Now it so happened that my tobacco-consuming parent also had command of a fair sized staff and also had a private office that I often visited but this possessed the construction and furnishings of an antique henhouse so no wonder I was impressed by all that I came to hear. No wonder, too, various third form school books came to bear within their covers a variety of carefully pencilled inscriptions that all bore a single legend, namely, 'G.G. Hilditch,

Right: As mentioned in the text, the writer still has distinct recollections of the Guy vehicles owned, in what are now long gone days, by Oldham Corporation. This illustration shows the interior of one of the later three-axled double-deckers depicted in Chapter 5. The ceiling cove panels finished in a very low clerestory which accommodated a forced draught (forced by the progress of the vehicle) ventilation system that was never really necessary in that part of Lancashire. Much less desirable though to one small passenger was the high front waist line that prevented that same person enjoying the forward facing view from the front seat that he expected of right.

General Manager', exercises on reflection that did far more for morale and ambition than they ever did for my current education.

In such a manner, however, did I come to learn of such men as R. Stuart Pilcher of wavy mane, bow tie and commanding presence, or W.J. Womar, or Owen C. Silvers, or W. Vane Morland or Majors Hickmott or Chapple. Almost to a man they were characters who stamped their personalities upon their undertakings and staffs and who could perhaps also in the main be described as martinets. Here followed an odd fact for although they administered that fierce discipline that they too must doubtlessly have known in their younger days, they were also so very often looked up to with a mixture of awe, respect and affection by the men they commanded, men who tended to view their more unusual foibles with rather more than a little fondness. I can best illustrate what I mean here by retailing a tale told me around twenty-five years ago by two survivors of the 'good old days' whose fire-spitting chief had an almost household name. They described in graphic terms how if the great man felt liverish in the morning he would sally forth on a tour of the tramway track, find a place where it was under repair then find fault with everything and finally sack on the spot the whole of the permanent way gang but then they evaporated this tale of management sadism by adding that he was really a kindly soul at heart so one could be sure that if the gang wasn't reinstated by lunch they would certainly be back at work next morning.

One must wonder, though, what effect all this had on the speed with which major relays were completed.

Times, though, change and no longer are staffs or passengers mesmorised, hypnotised or reduced to shivering speechlessness by the managerial effect or presence. I know as you will now learn, and here we come to the matter of that missing inspiration.

I was sat comfortably in my Halifax office one morning some years ago waiting for something to turn up when up from the area of the reception desk floated the sounds of a considerable commotion. We were at the time in the process of 'recepting' a male complainant who hailed from one of the remotest parts of the joint committee area (and you cannot get more remote than that) whose grumble was urgent, imperative and downright earth-shattering – but then most of them are – and this particular individual just would not be satisfied until he aired his problem at – to is quite the wrong word in this context – someone in authority and as usual when as gm you want him, the traffic superintendent has gone on long distance safari to plant a few flowering bus stop seeds so I received the full force for our visitor was as a last desperate resource ushered into my office (small, no fireplace and no oak panelling) when the conversation went as follows:

Him: 'Who are tha?'
Me: (with dignity) 'The name is Hilditch and I am the general manager.'
Him: 'Sithee ah don't care a (the word was of a basic nature) whether thart manager or whatever tha sed or none, what ah want ta know is (wait for it) are tha t' main man?'
Me: (and please remember that after around ten years in Yorkshire I was almost as fluent as a JOC native) 'I am that lad.'

It worked like a charm. There came forth a satisfied 'Nathenthen' and in a surprisingly short time thereafter one satisfied customer was returning whence he came when I silently reaffirmed to myself that if you want any success as a transport manager, you need just four essential attributes, namely:

1 A thick skin.
2 A sense of humour.
3 The ability to read or interpret either a crystal ball or *Old Moore's Almanack*.
4 A generous helping of pure good luck.

The latter factor is by the way the essential one in that prolonged period when as a junior one is seeking a way to the top, so let us just digress for a paragraph or two and investigate the promotion progression and perhaps surprisingly for those who have never as wise readers wished to join the bus industry the biggest hurdle of all that anyone who wants to pursue a career in transport has to overcome is that of obtaining his (or her) very first job in the industry for suitable openings are surprisingly few in number and here it seems to matter not if you are wanting to begin in traffic, administration or engineering, but if you are lucky and find your name on the payroll then if you aren't decidedly and very, very definitely enthusiastic about passenger transport and all attached thereto, don't both going any further because you aren't going to enjoy what will inevitably follow.

There isn't any use at all expecting that advancement is going to be handed out on a plate as it were, for one wants interest and some ability, factors that must become obvious to one's superiors, the determination to earn the necessary technical qualifications and a very decided 'the job comes first attitude' – and that, alas, is something that seems to be sadly lacking in Great Britain today in virtually every sphere, for if the newspapers are correct then far too many people are only interested in what they can get out of a job rather than in what they can also offer to it. You also need determination to offset

Below: Most bus enthusiasts will usually admit to having a favourite vehicle. As a schoolboy, this scribe had a definite leaning towards those three Leyland-bodied Leylands of 1935 vintage even if they were directly responsible for the disappearance of certain much-appreciated tramcars. Unfortunately, he does not have a photograph of his prime favourite No 103, but the Leyland Truck and Bus Division kindly extracted this picture of 104 from the archives. The other member of the trio was 102.

Left: The arrival of 103 and partners resulted in the ending of one of those two tramway services that terminated at Shaw Wrens Nest. This view of that very same location in about 1933 should be compared to the view of the same location reproduced in Chapter III. The tram number 54 was originally an open topper of 1902 that was rebuilt by Oldham Corporation in about 1922 being vestibuled in the process to become one of the first two totally enclosed cars. It lasted until December 1939.

the discouragement you are bound to experience when the early days of a career aren't going too well and also in a few later ones as well, and here transport being what it is, any aspiring junior will find that the day will come when he will have to move elsewhere to obtain promotion when living in digs in a strange city with, say, three nights at night school and a whole host of strange transport tribal customs to contend with during the working day isn't everyone's ideal of heaven but from promotion comes experience and that is something that no training course can ever really provide. You simply cannot tell what pressures a job places upon the occupant of a post until you have held it for yourself, so when in doubt DON'T criticise.

During this promotion period, you will find that you will meet up time and time again with a series of contemporaries who will feature on the same short lists until one by one they drop off the merry-go-round as successes are recorded, contemporaries who will all too often reappear at a later stage as competitors for a still higher position and so by the time one has managed to achieve the dizzy height of chief accountant, traffic manager or chief engineer, you know a great many other people, you know all about the activities of several different undertakings, you have lived in a series of different houses and doubtlessly by this time being married have curtains joined up at the bottoms, the sides, and diagonally to prove the point, but now that gm's job is within striking range and so you keep an ear open for the industry's gossip that comes via an amazing grapevine and an eye on the vacancy columns of the successors to those one time glossy transport magazines only they now, rather like the industry they serve, aren't just as glossy as they once were.

Then you will see 'IT'. An advertisement for a job – perhaps it will be with a smaller undertaking but a 'main

man' is wanted so off goes a letter of application and if you are lucky (note the reappearance of the word) an invitation to an interview follows.

Here, as all my road passenger transport career has been followed in municipal undertakings, I cannot comment on what may or may not happen in the company scene but I doubt if the processes are all that much different as the end result is the same – someone new is going to have his name ensconced on the notepaper and, rather more to the point, on the flanks of numerous buses only first that person has to go through the selection process that must follow that invitation to interview.

First, though, having gained the short list, you pluck on the nearest tendril of the aforementioned grapevine and sense the resulting vibrations for in half a hundred offices all over the land sundry characters will be talent spotting and more than ready to make a book on possible starters, the final field and last, but not least, who will be first past the post, only sometimes here the tipsters lose out because as in the case of all other forms of contest, the favourites don't always win for so much depends upon the day, the questions and the questioners.

Municipal interviews usually take place in civic buildings and there is nothing like an acre or two of best Victorian Gothic to give a serious atmosphere to a serious occasion when our aspiring general manager nervous and knowing sadly all that he doesn't know will be ushered – in strict alphabetical order – into the torture chamber, there to face the inquisition that can vary from all 60 members or so of a full council to a select band of half a dozen highly experienced characters who have seen and heard it all before and know all the tricks of the interviewing trade. The transport committee chairman will then ask a series of set questions and his colleagues will widen the discussion as fancy and the time permit.

Oft times a seemingly innocent query is well laden with hidden hazards and so if at all possible previous research is to be recommended. It does one's case no good at all to reply to the question 'How would you buy new buses' with a blithe 'Oh, by loans, of course' if the finance committee member who asked it in the first place is a cash-on-the-nail fanatic and particularly as you only have around half an hour in which to try to convince the assembly that they just cannot do without you, and in any event, your services at the price preferred are an absolute bargain, but it goes without saying that someone, somewhere, will also have done a bit of research when you and all your fellow short list victims were the subject of the operation. So it doesn't do to overelaborate.

What, of course, those public guardians are looking for is someone who has the professional background, quick wits, ability, stamina and interest to head an undertaking and also has that very important ability to get on with people for again those pre-1939 methods are now as dead as the proverbial dodo.

There are, of course, very odd occasions when general managers are conscripted rather than selected and here I would illustrate the case of Mr William Rogerson. He was originally engineer and manager of a certain borough's electrical department but around 1908 there was trouble at the tramshed and the tramways manager of the day suddenly resigned following some sad events for which he was in no way to blame. When he had left, a municipal sub-committee was set up to decide what should be done and a few weeks later the chairman of that body reported to his council colleagues in the following terms:

'We have as instructed looked into the situation and have decided that the borough electrical engineer (who has ample time to devote to his new duties) shall also become general manager of the tramways department. We have here interviewed Mr Rogerson and told him that the question of an increase in salary cannot yet arise as he must first prove his worth.'

I always thought that that paragraph was a gem although sometimes my resulting chuckle must have been a wry one but perhaps Mr Rogerson, too, was consoled when his name came to appear a very few days later on the flanks of the trams but if he didn't know before, he would find out then that if his salary was limited so would be his limits of authority whereas no such boundaries would constrain his day-to-day problems but those problems would be very different to the ones his successors must face in 1980.

Our own managerial race winner will now find just what these are when he has had about half an hour in his new office, an office where the coal fire will have gone out in the last round of economy cuts, and the carpet, still the old one, will be rather more threadbare than it was in the days of yore, but if he has any doubts as to where to start, all he need do is turn out the last set of accounts when gloom and despondence could well strike for from those accounts stem the balance factor and it is not just a case of red or blue ink.

A municipal undertaking will be operated by a district council singly usually but sometimes in combination through a transport committee whose members are invariably members of a political party when they will obviously have some allegiance to the aims and aspirations of that party. Politics do, though, tend to be secondary to the main purpose of representing the members of their ward electorate and to follow up any points that the electorate might raise. It follows from this that bus services – or the lack of them – being rather

Right: Despite daily journeys into the town, opportunities to ride on number 103 were few and far between because local routes P or 13 and 14 were in prewar days always worked by single-deckers although a single double-deck trip was worked each morning and night at rush hours on route P. From around 1936 onwards, North Western Road Car Company worked its third share of the mileage with a Bristol single-decker with unusually luxurious Eastern Coach Works bodies of the type shown in this evocative shot taken in Cheadle on one of the company's 'snob' routes. Sadly in postwar days, 854 instead of being rebodied was broken up when according to legend its 5LW engine was used to power a works generator.

contentious subjects, are often given an airing but there is another sort of erring and that is to err on the side of overprovision for the electorate being human wants the best possible service but now comes the nasty bit for that same electorate has a personal interest in paying the lowest possible fare either by way of ticket price or ticket price plus rate fund contribution in combination but again high rates are never popularly received and have a way of promoting nasty electoral consequences when Polling Day next comes around so here we are back with politics even if we would rather avoid the subject which can be classed as factor number one.

The second factor in the balance equation is represented by the staff who are also human and so not unnaturally want the best possible wages and conditions for the least possible amount of effort and would certainly not tolerate the sort of things that their predecessors had to endure in, say, Mr Rogerson's day. Additionally, to a man and woman they will in turn be represented by various trade unions who have a shot or two in their respective lockers and there is nothing quite like a day spent in deep negotiation with the odd half dozen or so of these bodies to make you realise as a gm that the buck really does cease to pass when it reaches your desk but the art of negotiation is something else that no training course is ever going to teach one for here you are firmly back with practical experience.

The third factor is represented by all the firms that supply all the things a transport undertaking has to purchase to continue its operations from the humble ticket to a brand new garage. Those firms are in business to make a profit out of your purchases and so you cannot afford not to keep a weather eye fixed firmly on material acquisitions and costs and here one cannot do better than to remember the words put into the mouth of one Mr Micawber by a certain Charles Dickens.

Factor number four is the restricting factor. A bus undertaking has to comply with a myriad of conditions, licensing, operating and administrative, and here it is for obvious reasons and example very necessary to ensure that you never fail to follow the standing orders of one's own local authority, and thus come to pass orders for a fleet of new buses without the necessary approvals but even if the system does seem to be unduly bound up in red tape, one has to appreciate that one is spending public money and it is only right and proper that every single halfpenny can be properly accounted for if the need should arise, so you have to make full allowance for possible delays in turning proposed intention into accomplished fact.

Here, therefore, is a brief explanation of this balance factor, or to sum up, the need to balance resource with requirement so that as far as is practically possible management meets the policy requirements laid down by the council and the committee so at this stage reader you will have some indication as to why I listed that fortune telling ability in my earlier catalogue of desirable attributes but the day hasn't yet begun. In any event, though, I wouldn't recommend a start in that office before nine of the clock because the secretariat won't have had the time otherwise to open, stamp, sort and present a very voluminous postbag and no wise management ever upsets the secretariat and particularly so if the content thereof is purely female, so if insomnia is rife, follow the lead of that other general manager and take a dawn tour of inspection but as you leave the house make sure you haven't forgotten anything. Why so do you ask? Nathenenthen!

One general manager arose one morn and drove to the rear of the central bus station in his own car. He then left his highly recognisable old motor and insinuated himself into premises that were totally devoid of life – well not totally for from the canteen came a buzz of conversation and the mighty rattle of crockery. His staff were obviously taking very early refreshment. Unseen he slipped on to a bus that was scheduled to depart at 6.25am precisely for foreign parts or a town about 18 miles away but at 6.25am precisely nothing happened. The clock struck the half hour and wasn't far off the next quarter when out of the canteen strolled a driver and conductor who leisurely boarded the vehicle which then burst into life and burst out of the station at a breathtaking rate. Our secret rider waited in vain on his upstairs seat for the conductor to come aloft but that worthy stayed below smoking for some eight miles during which time a certain Head of State was working out the contents of a very interesting list of disciplinary charges when dilatory fare collection, wrong destination blinds, over exuberant driving and various other sub-headings were heading for the charge sheet or rather two charge sheets.

Eventually, though, the conductor who was a new starter and didn't know who the gm was, finished his third cigarette and reached the top deck when yet another conversation ensued. It went like this.

Conductor: 'Where to?'
GM: (with dignity and succinctness) 'Pass.'
Conductor: 'I'll see it then.'

At this stage slight consternation for our gm had changed his suit that morning and didn't have his pass with him so he (briefly) acknowledged the omission and asked for a ticket to the terminus.

Below: In many respects, the years from 1935 to 1940 were the most interesting of all to passenger transport enthusiasts of the author's generation. The business was still expanding and in virtually every city one could see a fascinating mixture of old and new as the trams slowly disappeared and new buses or trolleybuses took their place. This photograph was taken in the centre of Leicester in January 1939 and accurately portrays the atmosphere of the day. Additionally, as there were no readily accessible enthusiast magazines, one never knew what one might see around the next corner.

Right: The old and new mix did, though, continue for some years after 1945 as operators made the very best use of such transport assets as they had. One interesting exercise that involved a certain staff member was to discover if a batch of wartime Daimler chassis that were sound but had decrepit bodies could accept prewar Roe bodywork mounted on vintage AEC chassis that came into a somewhat similar category. The answer was that they could and as a result Leeds City Transport came to acquire some quite unusual vehicles. Incidentally, on this type of Roe body the teak main pillars ran in a single piece from the bottom panel rail to the upper saloon roof line.

Conductor:	'Two and six, please.'
GM:	(Now there was greater consternation for he didn't have 2s6d). 'Sorry, I forgot I'm only going to Odspot Top (this was the half way point) today.'
Conductor:	(making it qute plain in basic English as he took back the string of 2s6d Ultimate tickets and ripped off 1s4d worth instead that someone should know just what he wanted). 'That will be 1s4d.'

Our gm produced just sufficient coinage and here we come to the nub of the story for even if the conductor was a new starter and hadn't recognised his boss, that boss appreciated all too well that if this story got out, the garage would collapse with laughter and there was no way in which an unpaid fares voucher could have been requested.

He alighted ensuring as he did so that the driver did not spot him as the bus now about three minutes early reached that half way stage and then as he waited for the first bus out of the morning to make its appearance as it worked homewards on the half-hourly frequency service, the light dawned. As the AEC Mark V Regent working the track came to a halt, the driver who was an old hand gave a start of surprise and a smart salute as he saw who was propping up the bus stop pole but he was even more surprised when the propper galloped around the radiator, slid back the cab door and suggested that the occupant might care to have a smoke whilst he had a test ride for as he truthfully explained it was quite some time since he last handled a synchromesh Regent. Our anonymous general manager really enjoyed that trip back to the home port for as he chortled to himself all the way – whoever heard of an inspector asking for the ticket or pass of a service bus driver, but so was the biter nearly

bitten. Were there any repercussions? Well, as our general manager friend murmured darkly a little later, there is more than one way of killing a pig but the moral of the story is this – never forget that seemingly quite innocuous actions can have unforeseen repercussions.

After such an early morning outing our new gm will initially be very pleased to see the inside of his office but immediately on entry he will ascertain just why the desk borders on the outsize and the reason simply is to accommodate the morning's mail, mail which falls into three categories, namely, the part that can be passed out to the Departments which will act thereon without further managerial action being called for, the part that will be going to the various senior officers when the cryptic message 'Speak' could well be endorsed on the top of numerous letters and, finally, the part (often the largest one) that will be retained on the desk for home consumption. If at all possible, a start will promptly be made on dictating as many replies as possible to the latter so that the secretary can be assured of spending some part of her day gainfully, but serious literary composition is all too often disturbed by the ringing of the telephone because no matter how early you arrive you will find usually placed on the chair where they just cannot be ignored bright yellow telephone message sheets that will say for example – 'Please ring Mr Smith at such and such a number urgent'.

Now it wouldn't be so bad if you only had to cope with outgoing calls but incoming ones also become manifest when one either fends off the various inquiries or begins to act as an instant information bureau. The contents of those queries can best be summed up by the heart-rending words an old friend uttered not all that long ago. A delegate at one of those now not quite so numerous annual conferences, he was stood by the lifts in the foyer of the rather smart headquarters hotel waiting vertical

Above: Many enthusiasts no doubt wonder what it might be like to be a general manager and on such occasions ponder as to what type of bus they would purchase if they were able to effect policy. Fortunately for us all, different people have very different ideas on the subject but when one person came to find that he had come into that very fortunate category these five Daimler/Roe double-deckers resulted. For the record, bus number 9 which had a Gardner 6LW engine and Diamatic two-pedal transmission, was new in May 1961 and cost £6,091 15s.

Left: Rather similar in general layout to Great Yarmouth Corporation Daimler number 9 was the demonstration Guy Arab of the early sixties that comprised a Gardner 6LX powered Mark V chassis and an interesting Strachans body. The front profile was swept back to a peak at the dome whilst the rear corners were quite square so that the rear windows were rather wider than usual. The vehicle was finished in a livery of ivory with two dark green bands.

transport when three such conveyances arrived simultaneously. As three pairs of doors slid slowly back as if by magic he unable to make a choice sadly shook his head and murmured 'Decisions, decisions, its always decisions'.

What has to be decided at this stage, though, is just which of the pieces of paper before you deserve or demand personal attention, and here you simply cannot let the pile grow too big for if you do then something important might come to be buried at the bottom. It's not possible to provide a priority rating here but staffing/industrial relations matters, inquiries from other transport concerns, or operator associations, passenger complaints, letters from other local authorities or Government departments, and the minutes of your own council or its committees or sub-committees would perhaps be most likely to be given priority as might that indispensable publication 'Notices & Proceedings' for

that is the vehicle by which you come to learn about any acts of audacious piracy that your competitors might be planning.

One's day is made, though, if you come across a 'funny' and if you wonder what I have in mind here, well we did have a letter from a lady asking if her dog could be granted permission to ride in the lower saloons of double-deckers as Fido was very allergic to tobacco smoke. We did have a communication that explained that the reason why a certain wooden bus shelter was disappearing piece by piece was because a local pensioner was making children's toys from the timber and there was an inquiry from a householder asking when the bus that was spoiling the view was going to be removed. This caused a bit of head scratching until a check revealed that fleet number XYZ that should have been resting in the garage was several miles away having been driven off the premises by persons quite unknown – and so they remained.

Much, much more numerous than these, though, are the various daily returns that provide an almost instant picture of the state of the nation. The engineer's list will show how many buses were wanted for service the previous day, how many were provided, and just how long those currently sick in the garages have actually been indisposed. The traffic return will show over the same 24 hours how much mileage was lost and why, how many of the traffic staffs are away from work and why, how many rest days were worked, what the holiday/sickness state is, and how many new recruits are in training. A staff statement will then compare how many bodies are being employed in each category this year as opposed to last with comment thereon, and last but by no means least, the accountancy section will submit its offerings that cover the takings for the day for this year and last year and how much is being spent in materials and labour or, additionally, in the latter case, by way of overtime, and it is from all this that one begins to appreciate that it's not the buses that cause the difficulties despite what you have read in *Looking at Buses* but other human beings and matters financial.

For 20 years now passenger carrying figures have been in slow decline thanks to competition from the private car, the closure of cinemas, the reduction in the working week and the ever increasing fares. On the other hand, how can fare increases be avoided if a bus which cost £7,000 in 1968 now comes out at £55,000 or wages leap by 20% at a stroke, or the price of fuel suddenly goes through the roof. Obviously they cannot unless you cut back expenditure-wise or some fairy godmother provides the necessary cash subsidy, but again as we now have a disappearing bus grant, and some county council transport subsidy belt tightening, one has to try to reshuffle all the cards in the pack and trust that fate will deal out a few possible alternative solutions.

I well remember here the huge fuss that involved every single member of the staff when my then undertaking made application for what was I think only the second time in its history to raise its fares. We produced volumes of evidence, the Council debated the issue at length, suggested fare scales were evolved and discarded, the opposition some responsible, some not flexed its muscles and the general manager of the day and his senior assistants went around looking ever more worried until the public hearing was over, a hearing that went on over two or three days and attracted newspaper headlines. Now, though, fare increase applications whilst never appreciated by anyone are simply a matter of pure routine even if you do have to spent time beforehand pointing out yet again that an undertaking is not going to be better off at the end of the day by reducing fares as to offer a 50% cut means doubling the number of bodies carried just to stay as you were or that you aren't such an imbecile as to know that another fares rise is almost certainly going to cost you another percentage or two of

your passengers who will be lost by virtue of 'resistance' let alone ongoing recession.

This paper/administrative diet is, though, larded as the day proceeds by callers and meetings. Most of the former have prearranged appointments and want to sell you something from new buses to a different ticket machine system and it must follow here that most undertaking executives can only afford time to see the more important visitors and here I personally include complainants but all others have to be left to the departmental heads. Callers have always been a feature of the transport scene or at least in my time, meetings though are now in quite another league.

I am certain that the only meetings some of my previous chiefs ever went to were their monthly committee and council gatherings and the odd special event such as an establishment committee to seek permission to make some staffing or salary change, so perhaps they took in up to four such occurrences in the month but that was in the good old days. Now, thanks to ever pressing financial problems, a lot of well meaning but not very practical legislation and local government reorganisation one goes from gathering to gathering and agenda to agenda and what they contribute to the welfare of the job at the end of the day is dubious in the extreme. Here, the gm who becomes caught up in the corporate management scenario, or the steering group/working party syndrome is to be pitied for most of the time so spent could well prove to be highly unprofitable.

I could go on at length here but have neither the space nor time but you will note that the chances of actually looking at buses between 09.00 and 16.00 are about nil and when a few such days have rolled by you come to realise that unlike the chief engineer and traffic manager you are no longer involved with the detailed aspects of hardware or operations but instead have to grapple with much more intangible problems. You also come to appreciate that operations and engineering cannot do without each other being wholly complementary, and neither can exist without an administration/accountancy back up, but unless all the departmental heads have also got the same message, there can be hiccups in the system when a little of the wisdom of a certain Solomon would not come amiss.

Our new gm having had a day full of such mundane matters, or a romp with those more modern innovations as, for example, health and safety at work requirements, the workings of an industrial relations tribunal or things relating to equal opportunities or race relations, etc will suddenly find that he doesn't seem to have done what he set out to accomplish and yet the afternoon's post is flowing back over that desk with the urgency of a spring tide. He may not sign all the letters but he will try to read them so as to keep in touch but he will pause in the task when the local evening paper arrives just to make sure that he hasn't been 'mentioned in despatches'.

Here one can run up against those members of the populace who like to write letters of complaint when the need for that thick skin becomes very apparent for one should now replace the title of general manager by the alternative description 'sitting duck'. He cannot ever win but at least he can try. One gm found himself described in interesting terms in a rather vitriolic letter that came out in print one night but the writer did at least have some courage of conviction and provided a name and address in marked contrast to those that hide themselves under a pen name. Now the basic facts were wrong so the lady involved was invited to the transport department and then provided both with a cup of high octane tea and some explanations – not excuses – as to why the things she wanted just could not be offered. At the end of the afternoon, she apologised in a most charming way and offered to make amends but was told that this was quite unnecessary, her conversion was more than sufficient reward for the trouble so taken. Those involved thought they had reached a very successful conclusion only they hadn't for two nights later came a second letter when the complainant illustrated to all and sundry in most generous terms just how wrong she had been and if anything the praise was embarrassing in its fulsomeness. Now this letter was published about two hours before a certain transport committee was due to meet and sad to say the general manager was indulging in a little feather preening as he entered the local town hall which, incidentally, was both Victorian and Gothic. His pleasure, though, was of somewhat short duration for immediately he opened the committee room door, one elderly alderman – of liberal persuasion – looked up and said somewhat sardonically 'I really must congratulate you mister manager, doesn't your mother-in-law write a "bxxxxy" good letter!'

There just wasn't any answer to that sally, and what response can anyone make to those most hurtful letters of all when it is suggested in unfortunate phraseology that a transport executive is deliberately cutting back on service provision and has no feeling whatsoever for the needs of his customers. I do wonder if people will ever come to realise that professionals do have a dedication to their jobs and would much rather run a thousand miles than nine hundred and ninety nine, or have their names on more bus sides instead of less.

Mention of that transport committee, though, automatically leads me back to matters municipal for the committee acts as a form of board of directors and will sanction when it is so empowered, or recommend to full council when it is not, such things as capital expenditure programmes, annual estimates of expenditure or income, fares increases, major alterations to routes or the introduction of new ones, major alterations to plant or buildings and virtually every matter of policy that has to be implemented. The committee will also receive reports on operations generally and pass comment thereon and here we must spare a line or two for that most important person the committee chairman. He is the political head of the undertaking having been nominated for the office by his fellow party members and during his term will be the spokesman for the transport concern within the council. He can and does have a considerable influence on the way in which the sort of things mentioned above come to be cleared and so it is

very necessary that there should at all times be the very best possible relationship between the chairman, his committee, and the general manager.

A transport committee will, though, only meet on one night of the month and there are at least 27 others. Here again our new gm will find that he cannot operate in isolation for the finance committee will often be involved in expenditure proposals, a bus or garage alteration scheme will almost certainly involve the planning committee, the provision of new bus shelters or having a road widened for buses the works or highways committees, and a traffic management scheme to traffic committee. It goes almost without saying that in all these matters our gm will find that he will have to work closely with all his fellow chief officers and if they turn out to be as mixed a bag of prima donnas as ever graced a town hall, then things can become decidedly delicate. This is one aspect of that need to be able to get on with people that is seldom appreciated outside the trade.

What is seldom appreciated is just how big a business municipal business is and it really is surprising what it does accomplish but I am sure it would accomplish a great deal more with a great less need for 'superabundant administration' if only we could see a return to the county borough style multi-purpose authority, but that is another matter and methinks I should not preach such sedition within these pages.

What I must do, though, is to make it quite plain that unlike the uninformed might think the need to answer to a body of non-professional/non-technical people is neither irksome nor a source of resentment and if our new gm should harbour any such thoughts then these should be quickly dispelled for that lay committee will provide the best of a good many worlds. For example, service not pure profit will invariably be the keynote of the policy and when it comes to service it must be appreciated that the members as ward councillors are in direct touch with the electorate that provides the passengers so a great many potential problems, thanks to this close relationship, will be resolved before they ever come to fester, to everyone's benefit. The committee too will always be able to ensure that when decisions are made they will seem to be made fairly and last but not least the members will soon let our new man see that he might perhaps just not be God's gift to local transport – in short, they will tell him what he ought to know unlike some members of the staff who could well be tempted to tell him what they think he would like to hear. There is a very subtle and important difference here.

A certain gm went into committee one night to be greeted by a senior member who then said, 'That was a very old car gm that I saw you driving in yesterday, isn't it time it was put down?' Our gm, like most of the race, lived by his wits, had the answer off pat and was quite prepared to get a plug in as he gave it so he replied, 'If alderman you paid me what I am worth I could buy a new one.' Alas, the alderman wasn't an alderman for nothing and after years of verbal warfare was now in a fireproof condition. Without a second's delay, he lowered an eye lid and grunted, 'If we paid thee what thart worth lad,

Above: A brand new product from a brand new manufacturer. Leicester City Transport Metrobus No 37 stands in the Abbey Park Road Garage yard during the afternoon of 6 February 1980 immediately prior to entering service. One of a trial batch of four, it possesses a centre exit that is by no means as popular a feature as it was a few years ago and, of course, the MCW-designed and built chassis/underframe that has turned an old-established bodybuilder into a complete vehicle manufacturer in its own right.

tha'd ruddy well walk' but then, perhaps, he too was a bus passenger, but before we touch again upon their view let me end with what could be the high spot of the month, namely, the council meeting.

If an undertaking has problems, it is here that they will be discussed in open forum and having to attend committees and council where one might have to give an account of one's stewardship is the best discipline that our new gm is ever going to know. He may sometimes be bored by it all, sometimes amused and sometimes frustrated but, at the end of the day, if he studies all that is involved, he will come to realise that it is all the result of about 150 years of local authority development and during that time a lot of very clever men and women have produced the only truly workable democratic system that the world has yet seen.

The democratic electorate sadly doesn't always appreciate this service motive as perhaps it should as one gm found one evening when having no committees to attend he decided to finish the day with a bus ride. The route he chose had been altered earlier that same week and now instead of going from point A to point B via a main road lined with green fields, it was diverted to pass through an area where some new housing could be expected to bring in some new business but this diversion added about five minutes to the overall running time and 500% to passenger complaint level. He took his place in the queue and was thinking about life in general and buses in particular when he heard his name mentioned.

Besides him stood a well dressed rather important looking character carrying a large brief case who, seeing he had aroused his companion's attention, repeated what he had just said, namely, 'That b . . . y fool Jones (that wasn't the gm's name but it will do) he gives you the screaming abjabs. Imagine altering this route after all these years, he couldn't run a chicken farm.' More observations of the same sort then followed.

Now it was true that the bus was a minute or two late but we were in the evening peak period so our gm simply asked if the condition was painful. The passenger looked at him with some disbelief and asked had he heard aright. Our gm repeated the inquiry adding
(a) he was always solicitous about bus riders health, and
(b) hadn't they better introduce each other, when he, as it happened, was Mr Jones. The passenger obviously thought this was hilarious, he quite enjoyed having his leg pulled, but then in rolled the bus and as they gained the platform the driver of that one-man operated vehicle looked up, saw his boss, and said how pleased he was to see his gm having a ride with him that night – in fact, did he want a drive? The effect this had on the passenger had to be seen to be believed, and so yet another gm ended his excursion still shaking with laughter – you really do need that sense of humour, but try to keep it in bounds or it might rebound.

Whilst giving a talk to the Inner Wheel Club, a certain gm flashed a slide on the screen, pointed to a bowler-hatted figure resting against the dash of a tram and told the assembled ladies that there was the first gm who had been attracted to that town when the trams started in around 1900 by the huge salary of about £200 pa. He added gratuitously that we were now in the 1960s and it hadn't gone up all that much in the intervening years. After his talk had ended, a dear old soul came around to thank him for a most interesting discourse but then added to his consternation that she was so concerned about his salary that she would raise the matter with her husband when she returned home that night for was she

not the wife of the chairman of the finance committee – so who was embarrassed now?

Despite all these trials and tribulations, some of which could well be of his own making, our new municipal gm will find that he really has a most fascinating job and if he cannot derive job satisfaction in full from it then he should never have joined the transport industry in the first place, but certainly it isn't a job that gets any easier with the passing of the years. Despite the difficulties, though, his ambition should be to hand it on in due course to his successor when at the very least the undertaking that was placed in his care some years before is in no worse shape than it was when it came – and hopefully rather better, or if he is exceedingly fortunate that it is decidedly better and he has come to be universally recognised as one of the very few innovators that the industry has ever seen.

Perhaps there is scope here for a future piece on those rare and gifted individuals who blazed trails forwards that were later followed by the rest of the industry, but now I must end on a somewhat critical note.

I never had any doubt that I wanted to be the general manager of a transport undertaking and equally I never had any doubt that I wanted that undertaking to be municipally controlled. When in earlier years I sometimes looked backwards, I would wonder why this was so for certainly in that circa 1939 period it was the companies that had the glamour routes, the more glamorous vehicles and, of course, the much more glamorous financial returns for it was a very sad combine subsidiary that could not turn in a dividend of at least 10% but the average was invariably much higher than that. What, therefore, attracted me to the corporation side of the business? It could only have been the solid, dependable and indeed downright comforting sense of tradition and permanence that stemmed from the display of a municipal coat of arms on the sides of the buses, the trams and the trolleybuses, senses that also reflected interesting degrees of individuality and enterprise.

Above: Rather too many years ago, two transport-minded characters would sometimes take a tram ride together and were also known to hop on a bus. If anyone in those Pilcher or Mancunian days had suggested that they would come to spend an afternoon in 1978 driving this lefthand drive articulated monster around the streets of a certain British city, their response could well have been incredulous and impolite. This, perhaps, goes to prove that in transport at least even in this day and age one never knows just what will turn up next. An interesting bus to drive particularly when one gets it stuck on a corner, whilst driving it in reverse gear can only be likened to the act of setting a long goods train back into a siding.

I have now had almost 40 years in the transport business and over 20 of these years have been spent as 'main man' and as a result of all the resulting experience, I wonder no longer. Consequently, I make no apology whatsoever if my enthusiasm for municipal transport shows through in this chapter but here is the immediate source of my grumble for there is so little of it.

Local transport is, as I have indicated previously here, an emotive local issue and if in the future service networks cannot be supported from the farebox then surely it is high time that the local authorities be charged with the task (where it does not so presently appertain) of operating the systems on a direct basis and not via any form of agency for the job of every municipal transport concern is to provide the citizens of the area with the best possible amount of transport at the lowest possible price and here I fully endorse the principles of direct accountability so involved.

Perhaps some day our national transport planners will see the light when we come to be blessed with a wide range of small to large undertakings that will provide those desirable independent operating and vehicle purchasing policies together with the requisite career making facilities for those younger people who, as I did when I was their age, want to enter full-time into the fascinating and quite unique world of road passenger transport.

127

Postscript

This second volume contains yet again a series of references to a variety of public service vehicles that can be roughly classed as being successes, near successes, or sadly failures, and it is interesting to analyse just why a particular machine has to be included in either of the latter categories.

On odd occasions, perhaps, there was a basic design fault but all too often such failure as there was was really of a commercial nature and came about either through an internal change in company marketing policy or a lack of response from the customers in what was, and is still, a very conservative industry.

Even some of the success stories are not, though, entirely without their problems and non-technical readers may additionally be surprised at the way in which successors to what was an acknowledgedly successful vehicle come to figure all too often on garage casualty sheets.

This seems to be due to the fact that buses like fashions tend to follow fashion, only psv fashions are initially based on economic logic and here, by way of example, the thought that one-man operation could lead to a reduced cost of operation was basically responsible for the change to the rear engined configuration, a little matter that has given rise to a deal of head scratching and sighing for the 'good old days' in a variety of bus garages up and down the land.

All this, though, makes life so much more interesting for the transport engineer, even if those transport executives who have a traffic or accountancy background have to be forgiven for wondering as to whether or not the bus busters will ever get it right in the end and so come to produce a virtually infallible psv.

This, though, is only one aspect of the work as the final chapter has endeavoured to show because there are those who think that dealing with buses isn't a difficult business at all but that rather all transport problems – and very many others as well are human problems, and they are surely the most difficult of all to resolve.